The
Psychedelic
Reader

The
Psychedelic
Reader

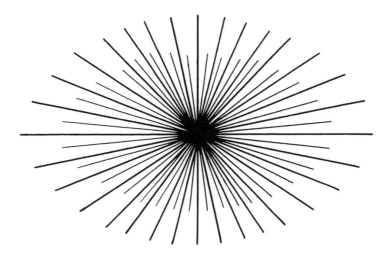

Selected from The Psychedelic Review

Edited by Gunther M. Weil,
Ralph Metzner and Timothy Leary

A Citadel Press Book
Published by Carol Publishing Group

Carol Publishing Group Edition, 1997

A Citadel Press Book
Published by Carol Publishing Group
Citadel Press is a registered trademark of Carol Communications, Inc.

Editorial, sales and distribution, rights and permissions inquiries
should be addressed to Carol Publishing Group, 120 Enterprise Avenue,
Secaucus, N.J. 07094

In Canada: Canadian Manda Group, One Atlantic Avenue, Suite 105,
Toronto, Ontario M6K 3E7

Carol Publishing Group books may be purchased in bulk at special
discounts for sales promotions, fund-raising, or educational purposes.
Special editions can be created to specifications. For details, contact
Special Sales Department, Carol Publishing Group, 120 Enterprise Avenue,
Secaucus, N.J. 07094

Manufactured in the United States of America
ISBN 0-8065-1451-5

10 9 8 7 6 5 4 3 2

CONTENTS

INTRODUCTION

IN JUNE, 1963, the *Psychedelic Review* was inaugurated as a forum
for the exchange of information and ideas in the on-going psychedelic
social dialogue. An editorial in the first issue stated:

> The synthesis of consciousness — expanding substances
> which we regard as one of the most outstanding achievements
> of technological society, has now provided us with a means
> of transcending and overcoming many of the distortions which
> operate in the very society that has brought about such
> substances. It is now possible to affirm the general character
> of our social technocracy without succumbing to its totali-
> tarian demands. The creation and futherance of internal
> freedom for large numbers of people through the intelligent
> use of psychedelic substances are now a practical reality.

Since that time the *Psychedelic Review* has published original
research reports, scholarly essays, pharmacological and therapeutic
reviews, artistic and poetic explorations, and phenomenological accounts of trascendent and visionary experiences. Reader response has
been and continues to be excellent and the score board of growth
indicates an increasingly wider audience for the theory and practice
of consciousness expansion.

Thousands of people have requested back copies of the early
issues of the *Psychedelic Review,* often in pursuit of specific articles,
and it has been the unenviable task of the editors and publisher to
inform them that these early issues are out of print and unavailable.
In response to these requests the Board of Editors has selected the

INTRODUCTION

especially important articles from the first four issues of the journal and offer them here under one cover.

It is our hope that this volume will fill this gap in the availability of information from the *Psychedelic Review* and also serve as a general introduction to the contemporary serious literature of consciousness.

You have before you a book that answers a demand, perhaps your own, for more information, advice and illumination in the scientific-religious foreground of consciousness expansion.

A constructive and productive dialogue needs intelligent and knowledgeable individuals. When the dialogue reaches the level of practical social innovation the wider dissemination of the theory and data becomes an obligation.

Today we are faced with an increasing acceleration of scientific and personal interest in human potential. This interest generates controversy. However, there are no heroes and villains in this controversy, simply, as Alan Watts has suggested, the age-old and universal game of hide and seek now played on the stage of social change. The counter in this game is knowledge. Historically speaking, the game period we are now in is dominated by the "hide" principle. The knowledge needed by the individual "to affirm the general character of our social technocracy without succumbing to its totalitarian demands" is just beyond his sight and reach. Just as we recoil at the power we can unleash externally we are now discovering that equally great magnitudes of creative-destructive power lie within our nervous system. We slowly realize that the external mirrors the internal.

But we are beginning to explore and apply this internal potential. The social and scientific controversy surrounding the psychedelic substances indicates that the game is changing. The polarity of hide and seek is shifting from hide to seek and we are all seeking for a solution to the Sisyphean problem of carrying the external and internal weight of Western "knowledge" and technology.

The information and practical advice we require for this task is now here. You will find some of it in these essays. The scientific

INTRODUCTION

breakthroughs of the post-Einsteinian era are just beginning to be incorporated into the social consciousness. Nevertheless, we still require more information. Some of the information we do have is inaccessible and some of it is misleading. The newspapers, periodicals, and (often) professional opinion fall under the influence of the 19th century social and scientific totems and taboos. We receive incomplete descriptions, threats, and stronger and louder claims to control and authority. The dialogue promises to become more intense. There is the additional eventuality of legislative and judicial control which may prematurely cloud the significant issue of the exploration of consciousness. Hence, only a widespread and accurate understanding of the psychedelics will maintain a socially mature dialogue.

GUNTHER M. WEIL
For the Board of Editors

FROM
PSYCHEDELIC
REVIEW
NUMBER ONE

"Can This Drug Enlarge Man's Mind?"

Narcotics numb it. Alcohol unsettles it.
Now a new chemical called LSD has emerged with phenomenal
powers of intensifying and changing it — whether for good or ill
is a subject of hot debate.

GERALD HEARD

Since earliest times man has felt impulses to rise above his every-day self and achieve either some higher insight or some release from mundane concerns — or both. Western saints and Eastern mystics have subjected themselves to strenuous spiritual exercises; others, less dedicated, have resorted to chemical aids, from the ceremonial wine of the ancients and the opiates of the Orient to the sacramental peyotl plant of Aztec tribes and the social stimulants of our own day.

In our time, moreover, psychologists and other students of human perceptions, from William James to Aldous Huxley, have tried out on themselves certain experimental drugs in an effort to induce states that would lend extraordinary lucidity and light to the mind's unconscious and creative processes — possibly even assistance to these. Today these newer drugs — mescaline, psilocybin, and the latest and most potent of them, Lysergic Acid Diethylamide, or LSD — are spreading so widely on a "research" basis that major questions are arising as to their effects and proper use.

Their enemies call them "mind-distorting" drugs, and warn that their therapeutic values are unproven, that they may upset even a normal person, and that they are already being abused for "kicks." Their proponents prefer to call them "consciousness-changing" agents, and argue that in selected cases, for individuals of strong mental and creative powers, LSD may widen their window on the world and on themselves as well. On the evidence so far, both sides seem agreed that LSD is not habit-forming; numerous takers of it report that the experience is a strenuous and exhausting one, to be repeated only after much thought.

Should man in any case put such a potentially dangerous substance into his system? It is claimed for LSD that it is far less toxic

1

than alcohol, tobacco, or caffeine. At the same time one of its leading students and advocates, Dr. Sidney Cohen remarks: "It is quite possible that LSD attracts certain unstable individuals in their search for some magical intervention." Can trance-like insight produced by chemicals be the source of higher wisdom and creativity, like a kind of Instant Zen? This remains unproven — especially since so many persons coming back from LSD can describe their experience only as indescribable.

One of those who can describe it best is the writer of the following article, the distinguished philosopher Gerald Heard, author of The Eternal Gospel, The Doppelgangers, Is God in History?, *and other books, and a leading student of psychic research.*

What will men of the future consider the greatest achievements of our time? Releasing hydrogen energy? Putting a man on the moon? Extending the average human life to a century or more?

Last year Dr. Glenn T. Seaborg, Chairman of the United States Atomic Energy Commission, gave his forecast of what he thought might be our most revolutionary discoveries or advances in the next generation. Addressing the graduating class of Northern Michigan College in his home state, he asked his listeners to project themselves forward to their thirtieth reunion in 1992, and selected fifteen items on which to speculate. Fourteen of these — ranging from the realizing of space communications to capturing solar energy and the remaking of daily life by electronic computers — dealt with physical advances, and thus with the same objective that Francis Bacon had put before the pristine scientists of ten generations ago: "the relief of man's estate." The fifteenth, however, would not have occurred to Elizabethan England's "wide-browed Verulam," or indeed to any researcher until the last dozen years.

"Pharmaceuticals that change and maintain human personality at any desired level," was Dr. Seaborg's definition of this major new possibility of power — and, he was quick to add, of potential danger too. He was thinking of such recently introduced drugs as mescaline, psilocybin, and no doubt particularly of the phenomenal one known as LSD, about the uses of which much controversy is raging today. Of them he went on to say: "It may . . . become necessary to establish new legal and moral codes to govern those who prescribe use of these materials. Who should prescribe . . . and under what conditions, such a drug to a person in a position of high authority when he is faced with decisions of great consequence?"

"Can This Drug Enlarge Man's Mind?"

Of course man has had mood-changing drugs at his disposal for millennia. First came alcohol, the great relaxant; then opium, the painkiller; then caffeine, the spur of the nervous system; then cocaine, hashish, and a score of other less common vegetable extracts. And in the last few years a wide variety of tranquilizers has been developed.

They all, however, fall into one or the other of two classes. They either weaken the mind's common-sense grasp of things, as does alcohol or opium, or they strengthen that grip, as does coffee or dexedrine. They do not leave the mind unclouded and yet at the same time permit it to view things in quite an uncommonsensical way. They do not raise the mind to high lucidity and yet at the same time make the world it views appear fraught with an intensity of significance that everyday common sense cannot perceive.

In LSD, or Lysergic Acid Diethylamide, however, a drug now exists that can accomplish all these aims. As Dr. Seaborg and several medical authorities cited in these pages emphasize, it is certainly not to be taken lightly, and research has only begun on its possibilities as a therapeutic aid in psychiatry. For many who have taken it under proper, controlled conditions, it has brought about an astonishing enlargement of sensitivity and perceptiveness, and it may thus cast new light on the wellsprings of creativity.

If you ask, Of what possible use is such a drug? or, What is the difference between the effects of taking LSD and, say, hashish in a Tangier dive or opium in Hong Kong? the answer might be given in terms of an early Franciscan, the ex-lawyer Jacoponi da Todi, when asked the same "what's the use" question after he spoke of the exhilarating effect that joining Saint Francis's company had on him. His response was, "a better order in all my living."

Not an opiate or a narcotic, LSD is a chemical able to produce profound changes of consciousness which, in healthily constituted persons, seem to leave no untoward aftereffects. And while it can give an ecstatic experience, at the same time it lends an extraordinary intensity of attention.

You see and hear this world, but as the artist and the musician sees and hears. And, much more important, it may also give far-reaching insights into one's own self and into one's relationship with others. Some takers of it have even felt that they had won an insight into the "nature of the Universe and the purpose of Life." These insights can be remembered and, if the person wishes, can be incorporated into his or her everyday living to bring it a "better order."

So here may be a major breakthrough that meets the problem of letting in a free flow of comprehension beyond the everyday threshold of experience while keeping the mind clear. And this seems to be accomplished by a confronting of one's self, a standing outside one's self, a dissolution of the ego-based apprehensions that cloud the sky of the mind.

The drug was discovered by accident in 1943. Dr. Albert Hofmann of Sandoz Ltd. in Switzerland, while doing research with derivatives of the ergot alkaloids, somehow absorbed synthesized LSD into his system and found it to have surprising effects on consciousness. It was soon recognized as the most potent and reliable of the consciousness-changing drugs. A remarkable fact about it is the extreme minuteness of the effective dose. The optimum dosage — that which produces for the subject the most informative results — lies between 100 and 150 "gamma"; and 100 "gamma" is approximately one ten-thousandth of a gram. (Mescaline, another of the "consciousness-changers," has to be taken in a dosage four thousand times that of LSD to produce similar mental results, and in this amount it does have physical effects on most subjects — sometimes unpleasant ones.)

A good psychiatrist, of course, must be the overseer of all LSD research. He must, as did the physicians who trained the volunteers for the ascent of Mount Everest, have "vetted" the subject. He must know whether this or that particular psyche is likely to function satisfactorily at these rare altitudes. Then, a person intimately acquainted with LSD should be at the side of the subject as he embarks on his journey. It should not be undertaken alone. A companion should be on call to act as an assistant — for instance, to play music, change the lighting, answer any questions, or write down any remarks the subject should wish recorded — and also as a monitor, or night watchman, so to speak, ready to report if possible trouble may be lurking ahead (in which case the voyage can be called off instantly by administering a counteracting chemical).

So, though the subject should not be intruded upon, he should not be left figuratively or literally in the dark. The optimal circumstances are simple, though contrary to present clinical and laboratory protocol. For the ideal setting is not a hospital or research lab, but rather an environment that is neither aggressive nor austere, and in which he may feel at home, perhaps a quiet house surrounded by a garden.

The first stage under LSD is surprising in a paradoxical way.

4

From what he has learned about this research, the subject is of course expecting a surprise. But during the first hour after swallowing the tiny pills, he usually experiences nothing at all. He may feel some relief at finding himself remaining completely normal, and perhaps a secret sense of superiority at the thought that possibly he is too strong to give in to a drug that will take him away from reality. An uncommonly able businessman, the head of a major corporation, who had much wished to take LSD, in fact waited fully three and one-half hours for something to "happen." Although it is uncommon for LSD to be so long in taking effect, the occasions on which this has occurred have led some researchers to speculate that the onset of the experience can be held at bay for an extra hour or two by the subject's unconscious nervousness or his suspicion that he might have been given nothing more than an innocuous placebo.

Yet as the first hour wears away, quite a number of subjects become convinced that they are feeling odd. Some, like the witches of *Macbeth,* feel a pricking in their thumbs. Others — and this, too, is a common reaction to the weird, the uncanny, the "numinous" — feel chill, with that tightening, or horripilation, of the skin as, in the vernacular, "a goose goes over one's grave." They report, "I am trembling" — but, putting out their hands, find them steady.

In the second hour, however, most subjects enter upon a stage which can leave no doubt that a profound change of consciousness is occurring. For one thing, the attending psychiatrist, or "sitter," can see that the pupils of the subject's eyes are now nearly always dilated. This symptom is the first and often the only undeniable and visible physical effect of LSD, and it gives the physiologist almost his only clue as to which area of the brain is now being acted upon. For the center that controls the pupils' reaction to light is known, and it lies deep.

During this second hour we can say that the subject is "gaining altitude." How does he record this heightening of consciousness? By far the most common remark refers to the growing intensification of color. Flowers, leaves, grass, trees, are seen with tremendous vividness — "with the intensity that Van Gogh must have seen them," is an often-used description. They seem to pulse and breathe; in fact, even everyday, fixed objects around the room may take on "flowing," "waving" shapes, as if invested with some life force of their own. Intensification of sounds, too (such as the singing of birds, though far away), is often commented on with fascinated surprise. Music frequently becomes an absorbing delight even to the nonmusical —

5

while to the musical it has on occasion become almost unbearably intense. "Under LSD I asked that my favorite recording of my favorite Beethoven quartet (Opus 135) be played," one musical taker reported; "but after a few minutes I had it turned off. Its emotions had become too searing — and besides, I had suddenly made the discovery that one of the instruments was playing ever so slightly off pitch."

Another effect is stranger and deeper. The subject feels that time itself — time urgent, pressing, hurried, or contrariwise, time slack, lagging, heavy on his hands — is now in "right time." When he discovers what an ample store of unhastened attention he can give to all the rich content brought him by eye and ear, he finds it hard not to believe that somehow time has been stretched. But a glance at his watch tells him it is a new-given power of superattention that is allowing him to make such full use of every moment.

It is, however, in the next couple of hours that for most people the full power of the experience comes over them. Till then, however absorbed, the subject has still been an observer. Now, although sights and sounds, the artistic splendor of the world, and the magic of music may still amaze him, they are, as it were, the décor, the scenery of a drama. Now the whole outside world becomes a composition that embraces and interfuses everything. And yet this composition, though constantly changing, is also (strange paradox) all the while complete and instant in a fathomless peace. At this point one could say that he crosses a watershed. In this all-pervading Energy he feels around him, the subject realizes that he cannot be isolated. It is flowing through him, as it flows through all that surrounds him.

Here his experience with time goes still further. Time appears to have stopped, disappeared. What has now befallen the "voyager" is not merely that he is on the high seas with his ship in a vast calm, but that the ship itself no longer seems distinct from the infinite ocean. He stands outside of and apart from his familiar ego, all its protective barriers having been shed; and this can lead in some to transcendent experience, while in others to a deep panic. To those for whom their ego is their only possible self, the only possible mode of consciousness, its disappearance is a kind of death.

It is here that the subject, however independent-minded, may literally welcome a helping hand. Of all the senses, touch is naturally most firmly anchored in the material world. So it is the least liable to illusions. It has been found that if at the moment of this "trans-

6

valuation of all values," this double change of the view of one's self and one's view of nature, a hand is actually held out to the subject, he will be able to keep his bearings. If the subject uses this simple "sea anchor," he may discover that he is not merely "riding the swell" but has entered a condition of what until then may have been inconceivable. With his consciousness enlarged out of all bounds, he may — if all goes well — find that he no longer feels anxiety about past or future.

It is not that he has gone into amnesia. He can clearly recall past concerns and future appointments; but he recalls them as a wise guardian carries in his mind the affairs of his ward. His personal appetites, meanwhile, generally become suspended. Most people never eat or drink during the experience, though it may last a full day; even constant smokers, while they may start with a cigarette, put it down as soon as they begin to "climb." There is not the slightest repugnance to food and drink. It is simply that the subject feels the appetites are irrelevant. Any sexual sensation, any erotic fantasy or preoccupation, is nearly always reported as absent. So, for all its liberating powers, LSD remains noneuphoric: as the Greeks would say, it is "eudaemonic" — "a possession by the spirit of wholeness."

After these climactic hours, during which he may either have sat still and wordless while contemplating the myriad images borne in on him, or conveyed volubly to his companion or monitor what he has seen and felt, the voyager returns gradually to shore, sometimes dipping back into the tides of the far sea until the lingering powers of the chemical disperse.

In the *Odyssey* Penelope, the first hostess in recorded history, gives what one might call the first psychoanalytic interpretation of a dream. The returning Ulysses, appearing in disguise and keeping his identity concealed from her after his ten years' absence, questions her about a dream she has had concerning the fate of her exigent suitors. She answers:

> *Many and many a dream is mere confusion,*
> *a cobweb of no consequence at all.*
> *Two Gates for ghostly dreams there are: one gateway*
> *of honest horn, and one of ivory.*
> *Issuing by the ivory gate are dreams*
> *of glimmering illusion, fantasies,*
> *but those that come through solid polished horn*
> *may be borne out, if mortals only know them.*

7

I doubt it came by horn, my fearful dream —
too good to be true, that, for my son and me.

What Penelope is saying is that there are two categories, or channels, of subconscious insight: one, coming in through the "Gate of Horn," of things that "may be borne out" (that is, having to do with events, both present and future, in our actual lives) and the other, through the "Gate of Ivory," of apparently the sheerest fantasy. And it is certainly recognized by all students of psychical research that there is a deep current of the mind which brings to the surface (sometimes by way of dreams, but not necessarily always) raw data — an incoherent babbling, irresponsible glossolalia, sufficiently confusing to justify the epithet "glimmering illusion, fantasies." Clues as to this second traffic, when they do appear, are ambiguous; symbols are so fractured that for a long while they are quite unrecognizable.

Here lies one reason why many decades of modern psychical research into this anomalous traffic have produced such baffling and frustrating results. Another is that whereas the flow running through Penelope's "Gate of Horn" is as constant and copious as the daily tides, the springs that feed the "Gate of Ivory" seem sporadic and indeed capricious. No wonder then that psychoanalysis, which confines itself to the masses of sea wrack brought up through the "Gate of Horn" and stranded on the beaches of our waking mind, attracts such an army of deep-sea psychobiologists, while those who wait by the other water gate have but a few minnows to show after nearly three generations of research.

Psychoanalysis is concerned mainly with man's conflicts between his sexual urges and the taboos imposed upon him by society, and with the effects of these conflicts on his everyday living. But the traffic we associate with the "Gate of Ivory" deals with data apparently belonging to those higher registers of the mind which very few researchers outside the psychical field have even noticed. It is true that mystics and saints have reported, time and again, "out-of-this-world," indescribable experiences that did change their lives and bring a "better order" in their living. But these experiences came as the result of many years of severe mental and physical discipline carried out within a doctrinal frame of reference, which often brought them to the brink of insanity. For many the experience was only a brief flash. For some it came two or three times during a lifetime of discipline. For instance Plotinus, so his biographer and disciple Porphyry tells us, only three times in his long life of striving for it attained to "the state." But until now there has been no other way of opening up this other passage of perception, of keeping it open for any length of time, or of doing it at will. How is this free flow of findings to be obtained?

We now recognize that our minds have, as oculists say of our eyes, not one but a number of focal lengths. The aperture of our understanding alters, in the way that we alter the aperture of our telescopes and microscopes to bring objects into clear focus at specific ranges. But, though our minds do shift, though our range of perception will at times change gear, we cannot make that shift deliberately, consciously. Nor when it occurs can we hold on to it. And when the most common, as well as the most profound shift — that from waking to sleeping — takes place, we are not able to observe it as we experience it. This problem has teased psychologists for sixty years, and the greatest of them, William James, saw that if it was to be solved, the experimenter must use psychophysical means on himself. He tried nitrous oxide as a means of enlarging consciousness, only to find that at a certain point communication ceased, and he came back murmuring, "The Universe has no opposite." Then he tried peyotl, the button cactus that grows along the Rio Grande and is used in the religious rites of Indians in the Southwest as a sacrament lending lucidity — only to be daunted by the stumbling block of severe nausea.

Leave chemicals aside for the moment. There is an "other" state of mind, known to and described by poets as well as higher mathematicians and other scientific geniuses, in which a deeply "insightful" process can take place. The current president of India, the philosopher Dr. Sarvepalli Radhakrishnan, has termed this process "integral thought" as against "analytic thought" — the latter being the inductive procedure whereby through the patient gathering, analysis, and arranging of data there would at last emerge a general "law." "Integral thought" is the art of the sudden insight, the brilliant hypothesis, the truly "creative" leap. To have truly original thought the mind must throw off its critical guard, its filtering censor. It must put itself into a state of depersonalization; and from such histories as Jacques Hadamard's *The Psychology of Invention in the Mathematical Field* we know that the best researchers, when confronting problems and riddles that had defied all solution by ordinary methods, did employ their minds in an unusual way, did put themselves into a state of egoless "creativity" which permitted them to have insights so remarkable that by means of these they were able to make their greatest and most original discoveries.

9

Paracelsus found that there was a "ledge of the mind," free of all caution, to which wine could lift him; there, though unable to hold a pen, he could still dictate, until intoxication swept him into speechlessness. Descartes, sleeping on the floor with writing paper beside him, scrawled down the insights that flashed across his mind in a half-waking state, when the creative and critical levels of his brain were both working. Harvey, the discoverer of the circulation of the blood, told his biographer Aubrey that if he stayed in a disused coal shaft in total dark and silence, his uninterrupted mind would reach a span it could not encompass above ground, when trying to "think regardless of consequence" amid the wary, hostile medical world of his day. Henri Poincaré, the great French mathematician, described his subliminal processes of discovery in these words: "It is certain that the combinations which present themselves to the mind in a kind of sudden illumination after a somewhat prolonged period of unconscious work are generally useful and fruitful. . . . This, too, is most mysterious. How can we explain the fact that, of the thousand products of our unconscious activity, some are invited to cross the threshold, while others remain outside?" (In his classic study of poetic creation, *The Road to Xanadu*, John Livingston Lowes cited this passage as bearing on the deep movements of Coleridge's own psyche.)

Can LSD provide any assistance to the creative process? Even when given under the best of conditions, it may do no more (as Aristotle said when appraising and approving the great Greek Mysteries) than "give an experience." Thereafter the subject must himself work with this enlarged frame of reference, this creative *schema*. If he will not, the experience remains a beautiful anomaly, a gradually fading wonder — fading because it has no relevance to "the life of quiet desperation" which Thoreau saw most of us living and which we cannot help but live.

What, then, should be done about it? LSD is certainly one of the least toxic chemicals man has ever put inside his system. Compared with alcohol, nicotine, coffee — our three great stand-bys — it could be called almost a docile mare as against these mettlesome stallions, so far as most people are concerned. Is it of any use with psychotics? Most researchers doubt it. With the extreme neurotic? Again there seems to be considerable question. Although among these categories LSD appears to do no physical harm, cases of severe adverse psychological effects have been reported. It is the unique quality of *attention* which LSD can bestow that will or will not be of benefit. Intensity of attention is what all talented people must obtain or command if they are to exercise their talent. Absolute attention — as we know from, for example, Isaac Newton's and Johann Sebastian Bach's descriptions of the state of mind in which they worked — is the most evident mark of genius functioning. On the other hand, the masterful Sigmund Freud remarked that psychoanalysis, even when exercised by himself, would not work with the extreme neurotic because of the hypertrophied ego-attention which such a patient had sacrificed his life to build up. The psychotic is even more absorbed in his distortive, self-obsessed notion of reality. Give, then, either of these victims of their own egos still greater capacity to attend, and it is highly unlikely that they will do other than dig still more deeply the ditch of their delusion and build more stubbornly the wall of their self-inflicted prison.

But for the truly creative person (and I refer specifically to that person capable of exercising "integral thought") LSD may be of some use. It could help him to exercise integral thought with greater ease and facility, and at will. And for a number of sensitive people willing to present themselves for a serious experiment in depth, LSD has shown itself of some help in permeating the ego, in resolving emotional conflicts, and in reducing those basic fears, the ultimate of which is the fear of death. However, the practical answer to What should be done about it? seems to be that LSD remain for the time being what it is: a "research drug," to be used with greatest care to explore the minds of those who would volunteer to aid competent researchers by offering themselves as voyagers to the "Gate of Ivory."

The Subjective After-Effects

of Psychedelic Experiences:

A Summary of Four Recent Questionnaire Studies

The results presented below were extracted from four recent studies in which LSD or psilocybin was given to volunteer subjects and the after-effects of one experience assessed by means of questionnaires. The studies selected are concerned only with *subjective claims,* not with objective ratings or indices. Studies of specific descriptions of the content of psychedelic experiences are not included; the questionnaires were used to obtain from the subjects *general evaluations* of their experience and its effects.

Subjects, methods and background of each of the four studies will be briefly described. Only a brief discussion is given of the tables (the original papers may be consulted for more extensive evaluation). The purpose of this summary is to present these strikingly similar and in part hitherto unpublished data together in convenient form.

(1) Ditman, K.S., Hayman, M. and Whittlesey, J.R.B. "Nature and Frequency of Claims Following LSD." *J. Nervous & Mental Disease*, 1962, 134, 346-352.

The data are based on 74 questionnaires returned by subjects who had been given 100 micrograms of LSD six months to three and one-half years previously. The LSD was given in "a permissive but non-treatment" setting in order to compare the LSD experience with that of delirium tremens. . . . "Our subjects received no intended psychotherapy during the LSD experience. In general, the atmosphere was relaxed and permissive, with the subjects well-protected from outside disturbances. They underwent the experience in a darkened room, and were allowed various sensory stimuli such as music, paintings, and exposure to sunlight in a garden setting. Usually, the LSD was given to groups of three to five subjects. At least one 'sitter' was constantly present who himself had experienced LSD." Half the subjects were patients, i.e., undergoing some form of psychotherapy. The others were colleagues, psychotherapists, lawyers, writers, etc. This study will be referred to subsequently as the *"Ditman Study."*

(2) Sherwood, J.N., Stolaroff, M.J., and Harman, W.W., "The Psychedelic Experience — A New Concept in Psychotherapy." *J. Neuropsychiat.*, 1962, 3, 370-375. And Savage, C., Harman, W., Fadiman, J. and Savage, E., "A Follow-up Note on the Psychedelic Experience," in Sanford M. Unger (Ed.), *Psychedelic Drug Therapy: A New Approach to Personality Change.* To be published early in 1964.

A questionnaire overlapping much of the questionnaire in the Ditman Study was used, and the results are presented together in Tables (1) and (2). All subjects had undergone the LSD experience 3 to 14 months previously. All 96 subjects were paying patients. Subjects were typically given 100-200 μg of LSD plus 200-400 mg of mescaline, individually, after intensive preparation. This preparation included discussion of aims, of willingness to surrender old concepts and preconceived ideas, and of the necessity for trust. "All of the pre-treatment contacts aid in the development of these key factors within the subject, willingness and trust, which are essential to the movement into and most effective use of the psychedelic experiences." The inhalation of a 30% CO_2 and 70% oxygen mixture B is also used in the preparation, which "gives the subject an opportunity to 'practice' the sort of surrender which will be called for on the day of the LSD session."

"The psychedelic session is held in the congenial surroundings of a tastefully furnished room containing a tape-and-record player console and various carefully chosen works of art. The subject spends a good fraction of the day lying comfortably on a couch listening to music. . . . The therapist will usually initiate rather little conversation during the session. The subject is ordinarily encouraged alternately to explore within, and to respond to stimuli in the outer environment (such as flowers, room furnishings, works of art, photographs of close relations, etc.). . . . The subject is urged to postpone analyzing his experience until after the session and to accept the experience as it occurs without labeling or evaluating." This study will be referred to subsequently as the *"Savage Study."*

(3) A survey of 194 questionnaire returns from the file of Dr. Oscar Janiger was presented by W. M. McGlothlin in *"Long-Lasting Effects of LSD on Certain Attitudes in Normals: An Experimental Proposal,"* a RAND corporation reprint (1962).

The Subjective After-Effects

"Of the 194 subjects 73 were undergoing psychotherapy and took LSD an average of 3.6 times as a therapeutic aid. The remaining 121 subjects were volunteers and averaged 1.9 sessions. The average interval between the administration of LSD and the completion of the questionnaire was 10 months and the average maximum dosage 171 μg." The non-therapy groups contained twenty physicians, seven psychologists, one dentist; artists, writers, musicians, ministers; teachers, engineers, housewives, secretaries, students and others. "The conditions under which LSD was administered varied somewhat. The therapy group was made up of patients under several psychotherapists and the conduct of the session depended on their orientation. It should be mentioned that for some of this group LSD was somewhat incidental to their overall treatment and the results are perhaps not comparable to those of patients for whom drug treatment played a major role. The artists participated in a creativity study in which they were asked to paint specific objects while under the effects of LSD. The other non-therapy subjects were generally left undisturbed, and wrote a subjective report the following day." This study will be referred to subsequently as the *"Janiger Study."*

(4) Timothy Leary, George H. Litwin and Ralph Metzner. "Reactions to Psilocybin Administered in a Supportive Environment." (To be published in *J. Nervous & Mental Disease.*)

The data presented are based on questionnaires returned by 98 subjects, one day to three weeks after they had been given psilocybin. Occupationally, the subjects included graduate students, professional writers and artists, psychologists, musicians, housewives and inmates in a correctional institution. They were given doses of psilocybin ranging from 4 mg to 100 mg, with a medium dose of 16 mg. "The drug was given in comfortable home-like surroundings, with no medical or experimental procedures introduced during the session. Subjects were given all available information on the drug and were allowed to regulate their own dosage, within a maximum set by the experimenter. Subjects were free to explore whatever aspects of an experience they wished." Preliminary discussions and reading were designed to prepare the subjects for a pleasant experience involving insight and expanded awareness. Therapy was not attempted during the session, although the inmate subsample were involved in an experimental behavior-change program and therefore expected change. Music, art, pictures, etc., were available during sessions, which were held in small groups ranging from 3 to 10 participants. A "guide" who had experienced psilocybin previously was always present. This study will be referred to subsequently as the *"Leary Study."* [1]

[1] Grateful acknowledgement is made to the authors of these studies and, in the case of the Ditman Study, to The Williams & Wilkins Company, Baltimore, for permission to reproduce these data.

TABLE (1)

"Looking back on your LSD experience, how does it look to you now?"

Item	Percentage*	
	Ditman Study (N = 74)	Savage Study (N = 96)
A very pleasant experience	72	85
Something I want to try again	66	89
An experience of great beauty	66	81
Greater awareness of reality	64	92
Feel it was of lasting benefit to me	50	85
The greatest thing that ever happened to me	49	78
A religious experience	32	83
A very unpleasant experience	19	33
A disappointing experience	7	1
An experience of insanity	7	18
Did me harm mentally	1	1
Like travelling to a far-off land	39	
Very much like being drunk	32	
Return to feelings of childhood	28	
Physical discomfort and illness	17	

* Percentages are the responses in the first two of the following four categories: "Quite a bit," "Very much," "A little," "Not at all."

TABLE (2)

"How were you, or what were you left with, after your LSD experience?"

Item	Percentage*	
	Ditman Study (N = 74)	Savage Study (N = 96)
A new way of looking at the world	48	85
A greater understanding of the importance and meaning of human relationships	47	86
A new understanding of beauty and art	43	64
A greater awareness of God, or a Higher Power, or an Ultimate Reality	40	90
A sense of greater regard for the welfare and comfort of other human beings	38	78
A realization that I need psychotherapy	17	26
More ability to relax and be myself	40	74
Improvement noted by person closest to me	42	64

Greater tolerance of others	40	75
A sense of futility and emptiness	7	8
A frightening feeling that I might go crazy or lose control of myself	3	8
Sense of relaxation and freedom from anxiety and tension	56	
A better understanding of the cause and source of my troubles	41	
A set of new decisions and new directions for my life	39	
A new sense of fun and enjoyment	39	
A sense of now knowing what life is all about	27	

* Percentages are the totals of the two categories: "Quite a bit" and "Very much."

TABLE (3)

Principal areas of claimed improvement attributed to LSD
(Ditman Study)

Item	Percentage (N = 74)
More ability to relax	40
More comfort with people	37
More initiative since LSD	36
Less anxiety	34
Increased interest in:	
Nature	38
Art	34
Music	33
Changes in "perspective":	
Deeper significance to things	46
Things seem more real	40
Problems less important	39
Colors brighter	39
Changes in "attitude":	
More tolerant	40
More accepting of ideas	38
More broadminded	37
Less irritable	33
Changes in sense of values	47
Problems such as emotional, financial, drinking, legal, etc., improved	33

17

Improvement in income, living quarters and body-weight	15
Increased sex satisfaction	14

TABLE (4)

Changes attributed to LSD
(Janiger Study)

Item	Percentage (N = 194)
Major objective changes (in job, marital status, etc.)	16
Positive change in interpersonal relations:	
with co-workers and employees	43
with acquaintances	41
Increased interest in:	
social reform	18
political and international affairs	22
anthropology	24
morals and ethics	35
Other universal concepts (meaning of life)	48
Positive change noticed by person closest	45
Changes in sense of values (money, status, human relationships, religion, etc.)	48
Looking back on the LSD experience, it was:	
a very pleasant experience	66
a very unpleasant experience	32
something I would want to try again	74
a religious experience	24
an experience giving greater understanding of myself and others	61
an experience of lasting benefit	58
LSD should be used for:	
becoming aware of oneself	75
gaining new meaning to life	58
getting people to understand each other	42

TABLE (5)

Subjective reactions to psilocybin
(Leary Study)

Item	Percentage (N = 98)
1) How supportive (relaxing, warm, accepting) was the total situation?	
Very supportive	56

	Mildly supportive	22
	Neutral	10
	Mildly or very rejecting	11
2)	Was the experience pleasant?	
	Wonderful or ecstatic	32
	Very pleasant	38
	O.K.	23
	Unpleasant or very unpleasant	7
3)	Did you learn a lot about yourself and the world?	
	Tremendous insights	23
	Learned a lot	22
	Learned something of value	43
	Learned nothing	9
	More confused	2
4)	Has the mushroom experience changed you and your life?	
	Dramatically better	12
	Changed for better	50
	No change	37
	Worse	1
5)	How about taking the mushroom again under trustful, secure circumstances?	
	Very eager	56
	Like to	34
	Don't care	6
	Rather not	4

Discussion

Table (1) shows that in both the Ditman and Savage studies, a majority of the subjects claim that the experience was pleasant and gave them increased awareness. 50% in the Ditman study and 85% in the Savage study report lasting benefit. The higher figures in the Savage study are probably attributable to the more intensive preparations and to the conduct of sessions centered around the individual subject. The percentage of experiences reported to be harmful or unpleasant is very small in both studies.

Table (2) reviews some of the descriptions which subjects consider appropriate to their LSD experience. "Greater understanding of interpersonal relationships" and "a new way of looking at the world" are frequent in both samples. In the Savage study, "awareness of God or a Higher Power or an Ultimate Reality" is the most frequent item, and this is significantly correlated ($r = .68$)

19

with reports of lasting benefit. In the Ditman study, "those who had a religious orientation, particularly those with a mystical orientation, claimed the most benefit from the experience and found it the most pleasant." These results suggest that perhaps something akin to a religious conversion experience is taking place in some of the subjects.

Table (3) lists the principal area of improvement attributed to LSD in the Ditman study.

Table (4) gives comparable figures from the Janiger study; most frequently reported changes occurred in interpersonal relations and in values. 75% of all the subjects in this study indicated LSD should be used for increasing self-awareness.

Table (5) gives the results of the Leary study: 70% find the experience pleasant, 88% learn something from it, 62% report that it changed their life, and 90% want to try it again.

On some of the questions it is possible to collate the results from all four studies. Thus the percentages reporting a pleasant experience in the four studies are 72, 85, 66 and 70, or an average of 73%. Percentages reporting lasting benefit or change are 50, 85, 58, and 62, or an average of 64%. Percentages wishing to repeat the experience are 66, 89, 74, and 90, or an average of 80%.

In three of the studies, an attempt was made to evaluate the longevity of these claims, i.e., to what extent they are maintained after longer periods of time. In the Savage study, answers were compared at four time periods: less than three months after the LSD session, three to six months, six to twelve months and over twelve months. The results indicated that "felt benefit tends to become apparent some time after the LSD experience and to be sustained fairly well over at least the first year following." In the Janiger study, results were compared after: 0-100 days, 100-389 days, and more than 389 days. Results indicated that "there is a definite decrease in claimed effect as a function of time, and that the decrement is sharpest during the first six months or so. Of individual questions, "becoming aware of self," changes in values, and claims of "lasting benefit" seem to be fairly resistant to erosion by time. In the Ditman study 16 alcoholic patients returned a second questionnaire, approximately three and one-half years after their original LSD experience. They "made fewer claims than they had on the first questionnaire. About two-thirds still claimed periods of abstinence ranging from one to one and one-half years, as they had on the first questionnaire, and three-fourths of these alcoholics still claimed some lasting benefit (fewer arrests, increased self-understanding and esthetic interest).

None of the Ss, however, had maintained their sobriety to the time of the second questionnaire.

It should be remembered that these four studies are all reports of *subjective* claims and need to be supplemented by studies of changes in objective behavioral indices. Furthermore, in general, these positive results do not agree with the majority of studies of psychedelic drugs in the psychiatric literature. There are two kinds of studies of drug-effects: those in which observations and evaluations are made by the researcher-psychiatrist, and those in which the subject records his own impressions and observations. The first kind of study tends on the whole to lead to negative evaluation — the substances are seen as "psychotomimetic," producing "depersonalization," space-time "distortions," etc. When subjects describe their own experiences, they use phrases such as "awareness of higher reality," "transcendence of time and space," of what may be essentially similar subjective effects. It is important to keep this relativity of observations and labels in mind, in evaluating these results.

The Editors

The Hallucinogenic Fungi Of Mexico:

An Inquiry Into The Origins of The Religious Idea Among Primitive Peoples

R. GORDON WASSON

This paper was first given as the *Annual Lecture* of the Mycological Society of America, Stillwater, Oklahoma, 1960. It is reprinted here, with the author's permission, from the *Botanical Museum Leaflets*, Harvard University, 1961, 19(7).

WHEN I RECEIVED in Mexico your President's invitation to speak here today, I knew that your Committee had made an unorthodox choice, for I am not a professional mycologist. As the appointed hour approached my trepidation kept mounting, for I saw myself an amateur about to be thrown to a pack of professionals. But your President's gracious introductory remarks, however unmerited, have put me at my ease and lead me to hope that we shall all enjoy together a mushroom foray of a rather unusual nature.

Those of you who do not know the story will be interested in learning how it came about that my wife, who was a pediatrician, and I, who am a banker, took up the study of mushrooms. She was a Great Russian and, like all of her fellow-countrymen, learned at her mother's knee a solid body of empirical knowledge about the common species and a love of them that are astonishing to us Americans. Like us, the Russians are fond of nature — the forests and birds and wild flowers. But their love of mushrooms is of a different order, a visceral urge, a passion that passeth understanding. The worthless kinds, the poisonous mushrooms — the Russians are fond, in a way, even of them. They call these "worthless ones" *paganki*, the "little pagans," and my wife would make of them colorful centerpieces for the dining-room table, against a background of moss and stones and wood picked up in the woods. On the other hand, I, of Anglo-Saxon origin, had known nothing of mushrooms. By inheritance, I ignored them all; I rejected those repugnant fungal growths, expressions of parasitism and decay. Before my marriage, I had not once fixed my gaze on a mushroom; not once looked at a

23

mushroom with a discriminating eye. Indeed, each of us, she and I, regarded the other as abnormal, or rather subnormal, in our contrasting responses to mushrooms.

A little thing, some of you will say, this difference in emotional attitude toward wild mushrooms. Yet my wife and I did not think so, and we devoted a part of our leisure hours for more than thirty years to dissecting it, defining it, and tracing it to its origin. Such discoveries as we have made, including the rediscovery of the religious role of the hallucinogenic mushrooms of Mexico, can be laid to our preoccupation with that cultural rift between my wife and me, between our respective peoples, between the mycophilia and mycophobia (words that we devised for the two attitudes) that divide the Indo-European peoples into two camps. If this hypothesis of ours be wrong, then it must have been a singular false hypothesis to have produced the results that it has. But I think it is not wrong. Thanks to the immense strides made in the study of the human psyche in this century, we are now all aware that deep-seated emotional attitudes acquired in early life are of profound importance. I suggest that when such traits betoken the attitudes of whole tribes or peoples, and when those traits have remained unaltered throughout recorded history, and especially when they differ from one people to another neighboring people, then you are face to face with a phenomenon of profound cultural importance, whose primal cause is to be discovered only in the well-springs of cultural history.

Many have observed the difference in attitude toward mushrooms of the European peoples. Some mycologists in the English-speaking world have inveighed against this universal prejudice of our race, hoping thereby to weaken its grip. What a vain hope! One does not treat a constitutional disorder by applying a band-aid. We ourselves have had no desire to change the Anglo-Saxon's attitude toward mushrooms. We view this anthropological trait with amused detachment, confident that it will long remain unchanged for future students to examine at their leisure.

Our method of approach was to look everywhere for references to mushrooms. We gathered the words for "mushroom" and the various species in every accessible language. We studied their etymologies. Sometimes we rejected the accepted derivations and worked out new ones, as in the case of "mushroom" itself and also of 'chanterelle." We were quick to discern the latent metaphors in such words, metaphors that had lain dead in some cases for thousands of years. We searched for the meaning of those figures of speech. We sought for mushrooms in the proverbs of Europe, in myths and mythology, in legends and fairy tales, in epics and ballads, in historical episodes, in the obscene and scabrous vocabularies that usually escape the lexicographer; in the writings of poets and novelists. We were alert to the positive or negative value that the mushroom vocabularies carried, their mycophilic and mycophobic content. Mushrooms are widely linked with the fly, the toad, the cock, and the thunderbolt; and so we studied these to see what associations they conveyed to our remote forebears. Wherever we traveled we tried to enter into contact with untutored peasants and arrive at their knowledge of the fungi — the kinds of mushrooms that they distinguished, their names, the uses to which they put them, and their emotional attitude toward them. We made trips to the Basque country, to Lapland, to Friesland, to the Provence, to Japan. We scoured the picture galleries and museums of the world for mushrooms and we pored over books on archeology and anthropology.

I would not have you think that we ventured into all these learned paths without guidance. We drew heavily on our betters in the special fields that we were exploring. When we were delving into questions of vocabulary, when we worked out an original etymology for a mushroomic word, we were always within reach of a philologist who had made of that tongue his province. And so in all branches of knowledge. Sometimes it seems to me that our entire work has been composed by others, with us merely serving as rapporteur. Since we began to publish in 1956, persons in all walks of life have come to us in increasing numbers to contribute information, and ofttimes the contributions of even the lowliest informants are of highest value, filling a lacuna in our argument. We were amateurs unencumbered by academic inhibitions, and therefore we felt free to range far and wide, disregarding the frontiers that ordinarily segregate the learned disciplines. What we produced was a pioneering work. We know, we have always known better than the critics, the flaws in ours, but our main theme, which we adumbrated rather diffidently in *Mushrooms Russia and History* in 1957, seems to have stood up under criticism. If I live and retain my vitality, you may see published over the coming years a series of volumes, to be called perhaps *Ethnomycological Papers,* and, at the end of the road, there may be a new edition of our original work, reshaped, simplified, with new evidence added and the argument strengthened.

It would give me pleasure to enumerate the names of those to whom we are indebted, but how tedious the roll call would be for you who are obliged to listen! There is one name, however, that in this audience I must cite. For more than ten years, we have been collaborating closely with Professor Roger Heim, Membre de l'Institut, and on all matters mycological he has been our guide and teacher. For these many years, he has been the director in Paris of the Laboratoire de Cryptogamie and, even longer, editor of the *Revue de Mycologie*. More recently, he has also borne the burden of directing the Muséum National d'Histoire Naturelle, that renowned center for advanced teaching and research in the biological studies, one of the glories of French culture. But these titles to academic distinction, though themselves of the highest order, do not tell you the story. Vast as is his learning and his experience in field and laboratory, sound as is his judgment in the vexed problems that you mycologists face every day, formidable as he is in polemic, it is as a rare human being that I commend him to you. Patient with the beginner, inspiring as a teacher, model of generosity toward others, prodigious worker in field and laboratory, and classical stylist in the French language, who could be more delightful whether in his published writings, or as correspondent, or as companion in the field? In the presence of Roger Heim, the time-worn conflict between science and the humanities fades away. One senses that the field of science for him is merely the New World that civilized man, the exponent of the humanities, is exploring and assimilating. What guardian angel had me in his keeping when, after the Second World War, I ascended the steps of his laboratory in Paris to meet him for the first time, a stranger, an American, an ignoramus in the complex, the vast, the exacting discipline that you and he share together? At once he made me feel at home and it was not long before he was developing enthusiasm for our ethnomycological inquiries. Later he became our indispensable and beloved partner in our Middle American forays.

I do not recall which of us, my wife or I, first dared to put into words, back in the '40's, the surmise that our own remote ancestors, perhaps 4,000 years ago, worshipped a divine mushroom. It seemed to us that this might explain the phenomenon of mycophilia vs. mycophobia, for which we found an abundance of supporting evidence in philology and folklore. Nor am I sure whether our conjecture was before or after we had learned of the role of *Amanita muscaria* in the religion of several remote tribes of Siberia. Our bold surmise seems less bold now than it did then. I remember distinctly how it came about that we embarked on our Middle American explorations. In the fall of 1952 we learned that the 16th century writers, describing the Indian cultures of Mexico, had recorded that certain mushrooms played a divinatory role in the religion of the natives. Simultaneously we learned that certain pre-Columbian stone artifacts resembling mushrooms, most of them roughly a foot high, had been turning up, usually in the highlands of Guatemala, in increasing numbers. For want of a better name, the archeologists called them "mushroom stones," but not one archeologist had linked them with mushrooms or with the rites described by the 16th century writers in neighboring Mexico. They were an enigma, and "mushroom stone" was merely a term of convenience. Some of these stone carvings carried an effigy on the stipe, either a human face or an animal, and all of them were very like mushrooms. Like the child in the Emperor's New Clothes, we spoke up, declaring that the so-called "mushroom stones" really represented mushrooms, and that they were the symbol of a religion, like the Cross in the Christian religion, or the Star of Judea, or the Crescent of the Moslems. If we are right — and little by little the accumulating evidence seems to be in our favor — then this Middle American cult of a divine mushroom, this cult of "God's flesh" as the Indians in pre-Columbian times called it, can be traced back to about B.C. 1500, in what we call the Early Pre-classic period, the earliest period in which man was in sufficient command of his technique to be able to carve stone. Thus we find a mushroom in the center of the cult with perhaps the oldest continuous history in the world. These oldest mushroom stones are technically and stylistically among the finest that we have, evidence of a flourishing rite at the time they were made. Earlier still, it is tempting to imagine countless generations of wooden effigies, mushroomic symbols of the cult, that have long since turned to dust. Is not mycology, which someone has called the step-child of the sciences, acquiring a wholly new and unexpected dimension? Religion has always been at the core of man's highest faculties and cultural achievements, and therefore I ask you now to contemplate our lowly mushroom — what patents of ancient lineage and nobility are coming its way!

It remained for us to find out what kinds of mushrooms had been worshipped in Middle America, and why. Fortunately, we could build on the experience of a few predecessors in the field: Blas Pablo Reko, Robert J. Weitlaner, Jean Bassett Johnson, Richard Evans Schultes, and Eunice V. Pike. They all reported that the cult still existed in the Sierra Mazateca in Oaxaca. And so we went there, in 1953. In books and articles we have described time and time again our later adventures, and some of you, surely, are familiar with them. So far as we know, we were the first outsiders to eat the mushrooms, the first to be invited to partake in the agapé of the sacred mushroom.* I propose here this evening a new approach, and will give you the distinctive traits of this cult of a divine mushroom, which we have found a revelation, in the true meaning of that abused word, but which for the Indians is an every-day feature, albeit a Holy Mystery, of their lives.

Here let me say a word parenthetically about the nature of the psychic disturbance that the eating of the mushroom causes. This disturbance is wholly different from the effects of alcohol, as different as night from day. We are entering upon a discussion where the vocabulary of the English language, of any European language, is seriously deficient. There are no apt words in them to characterize your state when you are, shall we say, "bemushroomed." For hundreds, even thousands, of years we have thought about these things in terms of alcohol, and we now have to break the bonds imposed on us by the alcoholic association. We are all, willy nilly, confined within the prison walls of our every-day vocabulary. With skill in our choice of words we may stretch accepted meanings to cover slightly new feelings and thoughts, but when a state of mind is utterly distinct, wholly novel, then all our old words fail. How do you tell a man born blind what seeing is like? In the present case, this is especially true because superficially the bemushroomed man shows a few of the objective symptoms of one intoxicated, drunk. Now virtually all the words describing the state of drunkenness, from "intoxicated" (which, as you know, means "poisoned") through the scores of current vulgarisms, are contemptuous, belittling, pejorative. How curious it is that modern civilized man finds surcease from care in a drug for which he seems to have no respect! If we use by analogy the terms suitable for alcohol, we prejudice the mushroom, and since there are few among us who have been bemushroomed, there is danger that the experience will not be fairly judged. What we need is a vocabulary to describe all the modalities of a Divine Inebriant.

These difficulties in communicating have played their part in certain amusing situations. Two psychiatrists who have taken the mushroom and known the experience in its full dimensions have been criticised in professional circles as being no longer "objective." Thus it comes about that we are all divided into two classes: those who

* This was on the night of June 29-30, 1955.

have taken the mushroom and are disqualified by our subjective experience, and those who have not taken the mushroom and are disqualified by their total ignorance of the subject! As for me, a simple layman, I am profoundly grateful to my Indian friends for having initiated me into the tremendous Mystery of the mushroom. In describing what happens, I shall be using familiar phrases that may seem to give you some idea of the bemushroomed state. Let me hasten to warn you that I am painfully aware of the inadequacy of my words, any words, to conjure up for you an image of that state.

I shall take you now to the monolingual villages in the uplands of southern Mexico. Only a handful of the inhabitants have learned Spanish. The men are appallingly given to the abuse of alcohol, but in their minds the mushrooms are utterly different, not in degree, but in kind. Of alcohol they speak with the same jocular vulgarity that we do. But about mushrooms they prefer not to speak at all, at least when they are in company and especially when strangers, white strangers, are present. If you are wise, you will talk about something, anything, else. Then, when evening and darkness come and you are alone with a wise old man or woman whose confidence you have won, by the light of a candle held in the hand and talking in a whisper, you may bring up the subject. Now you will learn how the mushrooms are gathered, perhaps before sunrise, when the mountain side is caressed by the pre-dawn breeze, at the time of the New Moon, in certain regions only by a virgin. The mushrooms are wrapped in a leaf, perhaps a banana leaf, sheltered thus from irreverent eyes, and in some villages they are taken first to the church, where they remain for some time on the altar, in a *jícara* or gourd bowl. They are never exposed in the market-place but pass from hand to hand by pre-arrangement. I could talk to you a long time about the words used to designate these sacred mushrooms in the languages of the various peoples that know them. The Aztecs before the Spaniards arrived called them *teo-nanácatl,* God's flesh. I need hardly remind you of a disquieting parallel, the designation of the Elements in our Eucharist: "Take, eat, this is my Body. . . ."; and again, "Grant us therefore, gracious Lord, so to eat the flesh of thy dear son. . . ." But there is one difference. The orthodox Christian must accept by faith the miracle of the conversion of the bread into God's flesh: that is what is meant by the Doctrine of Transubstantiation. By contrast, the mushroom of the Aztecs carries its own conviction; every communicant will testify to the miracle that he has experienced. In the language of the Mazatecs, the sacred mushrooms are called '*nti*[1]

$\check{s}i^3tho^3$. The first word, 'nti^1, is a particle expressing reverence and endearment.* The second element means "that which springs forth." In 1953 our muleteer had travelled the mountain trails all his life and knew Spanish, though he could neither read nor write, nor even tell time by a clock's face. We asked him why the mushrooms were called "that which springs forth." His answer, breathtaking in its sincerity and feeling, was filled with the poetry of religion, and I quote it word for word as he gave it:

> El honguillo viene por sí mismo, no se sabe de dónde,
> como el viento que viene sin saber de dónde ni porqué.
> The little mushroom comes of itself, no one knows whence,
> like the wind that comes we know not whence nor why.

When we first went down to Mexico, we felt certain, my wife and I, that we were on the trail of an ancient and holy mystery, and we went as pilgrims seeking the Grail. To this attitude of ours I attribute such success as we have had. It has not been easy. For four and a half centuries the rulers of Mexico, men of Spanish blood or at least of Spanish culture, have never entered sympathetically into the ways of the Indians, and the Church regarded the sacred mushroom as an idolatry. The Protestant missionaries of today are naturally intent on teaching the Gospel, not on absorbing the religion of the Indians. Nor are most anthropologists good at this sort of thing. . . . For more than four centuries the Indians have kept the divine mushroom close to their hearts, sheltered from desecration by white men, a precious secret. We know that today there are many *curanderos* who carry on the cult, each according to his lights, some of them consummate artists, performing the ancient liturgy in remote huts before minuscule congregations. With the passing years they will die off, and, as the country opens up, the cult is destined to disappear. They are hard to reach, these *curanderos*. Almost invariably they speak no Spanish. To them, performing before strangers seems a profanation. They will refuse even to meet with you, much less discuss the beliefs that go with the mushrooms and perform for you. Do not think that it is a question of money: *'no hicimos esto por dinero,* "We did not this for money," said Guadalupe, after we had spent the night with her family and the *curandera* María Sabina. Perhaps you will learn the names of a number of renowned *curanderos,* and your emissaries will even promise to deliver them to you, but then you wait and wait and they never come. You will brush

* The superscript digits indicate the pitch of the syllable, 1 being the highest of four. The initial apostrophe indicates a glottal stop.

past them in the market-place, and they will know you, but you will not know them. The judge in the town-hall may be the very man you are seeking; and you may pass the time of day with him, yet never learn that he is your *curandero*.

After all, would you have it any different? What priest of the Catholic Church will perform Mass to satisfy an unbeliever's curiosity? The *curandero* who today, for a big fee, will perform the mushroom rite for any stranger is a prostitute and a faker, and his insincere performance has the validity of a rite put on by an unfrocked priest. In the modern world religion is often an etiolated thing, a social activity with mild ethical rules. Religion in primitive society was an awesome reality, "terrible" in the original meaning of that abused word, pervading all life and culminating in ceremonies that were forbidden to the profane. This is what the mushroom ceremony is in the remote parts of Mexico.

We often think of the mysteries of antiquity as a manifestation of primitive religion. Let me now draw your attention to certain parallels between our Mexican rite and the Mystery performed at Eleusis. The timing seems significant. In the Mazatec country the preferred season for "consulting the mushroom" is during the rains, when the mushrooms grow, from June through August. The Eleusinian Mystery was celebrated in September or early October, the season of the mushrooms in the Mediterranean basin. At the heart of the Mystery of Eleusis lay a secret. In the surviving texts there are numerous references to the secret, but in none is it revealed. Yet Mysteries such as this one at Eleusis played a major role in Greek civilization, and thousands must have possessed the key. From the writings of the Greeks, from a fresco in Pompeii, we know that the initiate drank a potion. Then, in the depths of the night, he beheld a great vision, and the next day he was still so awestruck that he felt he would never be the same man as before. What the initiate experienced was "new, astonishing, inaccessible to rational cognition." * One writer in the 2nd century A.D., by name Aristides, pulled the curtain aside for an instant, with this fragmentary description of the Eleusinian Mystery:

> Eleusis is a shrine common to the whole earth, and of all the divine
> things that exist among men, it is both the most awesome and the most

---

* For this and the following quotations see Walter F. Otto: The Meaning of the Eleusinian Mysteries, published in *The Mysteries,* 1955, ed. by Joseph Campbell, Pantheon Books, Bollingen Series XXX, 2; pp. 20 et seq Italics are mine.

luminous. At what place in the world have more miraculous tidings been sung, where have the dromena called forth greater emotion, *where has there been greater rivalry between seeing and hearing?*

And then he went on to speak of the "ineffable visions" that it had been the privilege of many generations of fortunate men and women to behold.

Just dwell for a moment on that description. How striking that the Mystery of antiquity and our mushroom rite in Mexico are accompanied in the two societies by veils of reticence that, so far as we can tell, match each other point for point! Our ancient writers' words are as applicable to contemporary Mexico as they were to classic Greece! May it not be significant that the Greeks were wont to refer to mushrooms as "the food of the gods," *brōma theon,* and that Porphyrius is quoted as having called them "nurslings of the gods," *theotróphos**? The Greeks of the classic period were mycophobes. Was this because their ancestors had felt that the whole fungal tribe was infected "by attraction" with the holiness of some mushrooms and that they were not for mortal men to eat, at least not every day? Are we dealing with what was in origin a religious tabu?

In earliest times the Greeks confined the common European word for mushroom, which in their language was *sp(h)óngos* or *sp(h)óngê,* to the meaning "sponge," and replaced it by a special word, *múkês,* for the designation of mushrooms.‡ Now it happens that the root of this word *múkês* in Greek is a homonym of the root of the Greek word for "Mystery," *mu.* A bold speculation flashes through the mind. The word for "Mystery" comes from a root that means the closing of the apertures of the body, the closing of the eyes and ears. If the mushroom played a vital and secret role in primitive Greek religion, what could be more natural than that the standard word for "mushroom" would fall into disuse through a religious tabu (as in Hebrew "Yahweh" gave way to "Adonai") and that the Greeks substituted an alternative fungal term that was a homonym of "mystery"? You can hear the pun, see the gesture, "Mum's the word," with the index finger over the mouth. . . . We must remember, in considering this problem, that in antiquity the

* Giambattista della Porta: *Villa,* 1592, Frankfort, p. 764.

‡ Holger Pedersen in an early paper contended that the basic fungal words of Europe were identical: Old High German *swamb,* Slavic *gomba,* Lithuanian *gumbas,* Latin *fungus,* Greek *sp(h)óngos, sp(h)óngé,* and Armenian *sung, sunk.* (Published in Polish: 'Przyczynki do gramatyki porównawczej

ecology of Greece and the Greek isles was different from now. Deforestation and the goats had not wrought the havoc of the intervening centuries. They had not left the mountains naked to the sun. On the wooded isles and in the forests of the mainland, there must have been a wealth of mushrooms.

Let us consider possibilities other than the mushroom. In the Mazatec country the Indians, when there are no mushrooms, have recourse to alternatives. Thanks to the brilliant work of Dr. Albert Hofmann of Sandoz, the Swiss pharmaceutical firm, we are now sorting out and identifying a whole series of indoles that have remarkable psychotropic properties. As you all know, he has isolated the active agents in some of our Mexican mushrooms, psilocybin and psilocin, two tryptamine derivatives and members of the indole family of substances. He has defined their molecular structure. The magic indoles are present in other plants used widely among the Indians of Mexico. He has isolated and identified three of the active agents in *ololiuqui,* the famous seeds, subject of many studies, that have long been used in Mexico for their psychotropic properties.* In the Mazatec country the seeds of *ololiuqui* are one of the alternatives used when the sacred mushrooms are not available. Imagine our surprise, when we began looking for these seeds in quantity last year, to discover that the Zapotec Indians employ two seeds: in some villages one, in others the other, and in some both. There is no question which seed was the *ololiuqui* of the Aztecs. It is a climbing morning-glory known to science as *Rivea corymbosa* (L.) Hallier filius.** The seeds

jezyków slowianskich,' in *Materyaly i Prace Komisyi Jezykowej Akademii Umicietnosci w Krakowie,* Cracow, 1(1) : 167-176.) Since then some philologists have declined to accept this thesis as more than a possibility, especially as to the Slavic term, but Professor Roman Jakobson in a recent personal communication to me says: 'The etymology of Holger Pedersen, the great Danish specialist in the comparative study of Indo-European languages, seems to me and to many other linguists, e.g., the distinguished Czech etymologist V. Machek, as the only convincing attempt to interpret the fungal name of the European languages. Not one single serious argument has been brought against Pedersen's "attractive" explanation, as Berneker defines it, and not one single defensible hypothesis has been brought to replace this one.'

* The Chemistry of Natural Products, paper read by Dr. Hofmann, Aug. 18, 1960, in the I.U.P.A.C. Symposium, Melbourne.

** The best summary of the *ololiuqui* literature and problem is Richard Evans Schultes' A Contribution to Our Knowledge of *Rivea corymbosa,* the Narcotic Ololiuqui of the Aztecs, Botanical Museum, Harvard University, 1941. Also see Humphrey Osmond's Ololiuqui: The Ancient Aztec Narcotic, *Journal of Mental Science,* July 1955, 101(424) : 526-537. Dr. Osmond reports on the effects of the seeds on himself.

are brown and almost round. The second plant was identified at the National Herbarium in Washington as *Ipomoea violacea* L.,‡ also a climbing morning-glory but easily distinguished in the field from *Rivea corymbosa*. The seeds are long, black, and angular, and so far as we now know, they are used only in some parts of the Zapotec country. Both are called in Zapotec *badoh*, but the black seeds are *badoh negro*, black *badoh*, to distinguish them from the true *ololiuqui* seeds.°

Dr. Hofmann found that the alkaloidal components of the two seeds were identical, and they yielded d-lysergic acid amide and d-isolysergic acid amide, in the LSD 25 family of substances and known heretofore only as derivatives of ergot. Is it not surprising to find in higher plants such as the Convolvulaceae the same lysergic acid derivatives as in the lower fungi? The third substance found

‡ **Ipomoea violacea** Linnaeus Pl. Sp. (1953) 161.

Convolvulus indicus Miller Gard. Dict. (1768) No. 5.

Ipomoea tricolor Cavanilles Icon. Pl. Rar. 3 (1794) 5.

Convolvulus violaceus Sprengel Syst. 1 (1825) 399.

Convolvulus venustus Sprengel Syst. 1 (1825) 399.

Ipomoea rubrocoerulea Hooker Bot. Mag. (1834) t. 3297.

Pharbitis violacea (L.) Bojer Hort. Maurit. (1837) 227.

Tereietra violacea (L.) Rafinesque Fl. Tellur. 4 (1839) 124.

Ipomoea Hookeri G. Don Gen. Syst. 4 (1838) 274.

Pharbitis rubrocoeruleus (Hook.) Planchon Fl. des Serres 9 (1854) 281.

Convolvulus rubrocoeruleus (Hook.) D. Dietrich Syn. Pl. 1 (1839) 670.

Ipomoea puncticulata Bentham Bot. Voy. Sulph. (1945) 136.

° Credit for the discovery of the ceremonial use of *Ipomoea violacea* seeds goes to Thomas MacDougall and Francisco Ortega ("Chico"), famous Zapotec guide and itinerant trader. They have not yet delimited the area of diffusion, but they have found *badoh negro* seeds in use in the following Zapotec towns and villages in the uplands of southern Oaxaca: San Bartolo Yautepec, San Carlos Yautepec and Santa Catarina Quieri, all in the district of Yautepec; Santa Cruz Ozolotepec and San Andrés Lovene, District of Miahuatlan; and finally a settlement called Roalo, between Zaachila and Zimatlan, just south of the city of Oaxaca. In San Bartolo *I. violacea* is used to the exclusion of *Rivea corymbosa*, but in the other towns both are used. These data are based on personal correspondence and also Thomas MacDougall: *Ipomoea tricolor*: A Hallucinogenic Plant of the Zapotecs, in *Boletín* of the Centro de Investigaciones Antropológicas de México, No. 6, March 1, 1960. Reports from Juquila, to the west of the Zapotec towns mentioned above, indicate that *I. violacea* seeds may also be used among the Chatino Indians.

in these seeds was *chanoclavine,* also isolated by Dr. Hofmann et al. some years ago from a culture of *Claviceps* species.*

Thus it comes about that, thanks to the achievements of our biological chemists, we may be on the brink of rediscovering what was common knowledge among the ancient Greeks. I predict that the secret of the Mysteries will be found in the indoles, whether derived from mushrooms or from higher plants or, as in Mexico, from both.

I would not be understood as contending that only these substances (wherever found in nature) bring about visions and ecstasy. Clearly some poets and prophets and many mystics and ascetics seem to have enjoyed ecstatic visions that answer the requirements of the ancient Mysteries and that duplicate the mushroom agapé of Mexico. I do not suggest that St. John of Patmos ate mushrooms in order to write the Book of the Revelation. Yet the succession of images in his Vision, so clearly seen and yet such a phantasmagoria, means for me that he was in the same state as one bemushroomed. Nor do I suggest for a moment that William Blake knew the mushroom when he wrote this telling account of the clarity of "vision":

> The Prophets describe what they saw in Vision as real and existing men, whom they saw with their imaginative and immortal organs; the Apostles the same; the clearer the organ the more distinct the object. A Spirit and a Vision are not, as the modern philosophy supposes, a cloudy vapour, or a nothing: they are organized and minutely articulated beyond all that the mortal and perishing nature can produce. *He who does not imagine in stronger and better lineaments, and in stronger and better light than his perishing eye can see, does not imagine at all.* [Italics mine. From *The Writings of William Blake,* ed. by Geoffrey Keynes, vol. III, p. 108]

This must sound cryptic to one who does not share Blake's vision or who has not taken the mushroom. The advantage of the mushroom is that it puts many (if not everyone) within reach of this state without having to suffer the mortifications of Blake and St. John. It permits you to see, more clearly than our perishing mortal eye can see, vistas beyond the horizons of this life, to travel backwards and forwards in time, to enter other planes of existence, even (as the Indians say) to know God. It is hardly surprising that your emotions are profoundly affected, and you feel that an indissoluble bond unites you with the others who have shared with you in the sacred agapé. All that you see during this night has a pristine quality: the land-

* A. Hofmann with R. Brunner, H. Kokel, and A. Brack, *Helv. Chem. Acta,* 1957, 40:1358.

scape, the edifices, the carvings, the animals — they look as though they had come straight from the Maker's workshop. This newness of everything — it is as though the world had just dawned — overwhelms you and melts you with its beauty. Not unnaturally, what is happening to you seems to you freighted with significance, beside which the humdrum events of everyday are trivial. All these things you see with an immediacy of vision that leads you to say to yourself, "Now I am seeing for the first time, seeing direct, without the intervention of mortal eyes." (Plato tells us that beyond this ephemeral and imperfect existence here below, there is another Ideal world of Archetypes, where the original, the true, the beautiful Pattern of things exists for evermore. Poets and philosophers for millennia have pondered and discussed his conception. It is clear to me where Plato found his Ideas; it was clear to his contemporaries too. Plato had drunk of the potion in the Temple of Eleusis and had spent the night seeing the great Vision.)

And all the time that you are seeing these things, the priestess sings, not loud, but with authority. The Indians are notoriously not given to displays of inner feelings — except on these occasions. The singing is good, but under the influence of the mushroom you think it is infinitely tender and sweet. It is as though you were hearing it with your mind's ear, purged of all dross. You are lying on a *petate* or mat; perhaps, if you have been wise, on an air mattress and in a sleeping bag. It is dark, for all lights have been extinguished save a few embers among the stones on the floor and the incense in a sherd. It is still, for the thatched hut is apt to be some distance away from the village. In the darkness and stillness, that voice hovers through the hut, coming now from beyond your feet, now at your very ear, now distant, now actually underneath you, with strange ventriloquistic effect. The mushrooms produce this illusion also. Everyone experiences it, just as do the tribesmen of Siberia who have eaten of *Amanita muscaria* and lie under the spell of their shamans, displaying as these do their astonishing dexterity with ventriloquistic drum-beats. Likewise, in Mexico, I have heard a shaman engage in a most complicated percussive beat: with her hands she hits her chest, her thighs, her forehead, her arms, each giving a different resonance, keeping a complicated rhythm and modulating, even syncopating, the strokes. Your body lies in the darkness, heavy as lead, but your spirit seems to soar and leave the hut, and with the speed of thought to travel where it listeth, in time and space, accompanied by the shaman's singing and by the ejaculations of her percussive chant. What you are seeing and what you are hearing appear as one: the music assumes harmonious shapes, giving visual form to its harmonies, and what you are seeing takes on the modalities of music — the music of the spheres. "Where has there been greater rivalry between seeing and hearing?" How apposite to the Mexican experience was the ancient Greek's rhetorical question! All your senses are similarly affected: the cigarette with which you occasionally break the tension of the night smells as no cigarette before had ever smelled; the glass of simple water is infinitely better than champagne. Elsewhere I once wrote that the bemushroomed person is poised in space, a disembodied eye, invisible, incorporeal, seeing but not seen. In truth, he is the five senses disembodied, all of them keyed to the height of sensitivity and awareness, all of them blending into one another most strangely, until the person, utterly passive, becomes a pure receptor, infinitely delicate, of sensations. (You, being a stranger, are perforce only a receptor. But the Mazatec communicants are also participants with the *curandera* in an extempore religious colloquy. Her utterances elicit spontaneous responses from them, responses that maintain a perfect harmony with her and with each other, building up to a quiet, swaying, antiphonal chant. In a successful ceremony this is an essential element, and one cannot experience the full effect of the role of the mushroom in the Indian community unless one attends such a gathering, either alone or with one or at most two other strangers.) As your body lies there in its sleeping bag, your soul is free, loses all sense of time, alert as it never was before, living an eternity in a night, seeing infinity in a grain of sand. What you have seen and heard is cut as with a burin in your memory, never to be effaced. At last you know what the ineffable is, and what ecstasy means. Ecstasy! The mind harks back to the origin of that word. For the Greeks *ekstasis* meant the flight of the soul from the body. Can you find a better word than that to describe the bemushroomed state? In common parlance, among the many who have not experienced ecstasy, ecstasy is fun, and I am frequently asked why I do not reach for mushrooms every night. But ecstasy is not fun. Your very soul is seized and shaken until it tingles. After all, who will choose to feel undiluted awe, or to float through that door yonder into the Divine Presence? The unknowing vulgar abuse the word, and we must recapture its full and terrifying sense. . . . A few hours later, the next morning, you are fit to go to work. But how unimportant work seems to you, by comparison with the portentous happenings of that night! If you can, you prefer to

37

stay close to the house, and, with those who lived through that night, compare notes, and utter ejaculations of amazement.

As man emerged from his brutish past, thousands of years ago, there was a stage in the evolution of his awareness when the discovery of a mushroom (or was it a higher plant?) with miraculous properties was a revelation to him, a veritable detonator to his soul, arousing in him sentiments of awe and reverence, and gentleness and love, to the highest pitch of which mankind is capable, all those sentiments and virtues that mankind has ever since regarded as the highest attribute of his kind. It made him see what this perishing mortal eye cannot see. How right the Greeks were to hedge about this Mystery, this imbibing of the potion, with secrecy and surveillance! What today is resolved into a mere drug, a tryptamine or lysergic acid derivative, was for him a prodigious miracle, inspiring in him poetry and philosophy and religion. Perhaps with all our modern knowledge we do not need the divine mushrooms any more. Or do we need them more than ever? Some are shocked that the key even to religion might be reduced to a mere drug. On the other hand, the drug is as mysterious as it ever was: "like the wind it cometh we know not whence, nor why." Out of a mere drug comes the ineffable, comes ecstasy. It is not the only instance in the history of humankind where the lowly has given birth to the divine. Altering a sacred text, we would say that this paradox is a hard saying, yet one worthy of all men to be believed.

If our classical schloars were given the opportunity to attend the rite at Eleusis, to talk with the priestess, what would they not exchange for that chance? They would approach the precincts, enter the hallowed chamber, with the reverence born of the texts venerated by scholars for millennia. How propitious would their frame of mind be, if they were invited to partake of the potion! Well, those rites take place now, unbeknownst to the classical scholars, in scattered dwellings, humble, thatched, without windows, far from the beaten track, high in the mountains of Mexico, in the stillness of the night, broken only by the distant barking of a dog or the braying of an ass. Or, since we are in the rainy season, perhaps the Mystery is accompanied by torrential rains and punctuated by terrifying thunderbolts. Then, indeed, as you lie there bemushroomed, listening to the music and seeing the visions, you know a soul shattering experience, recalling as you do the belief of some primitive peoples that mushrooms, the sacred mushrooms, are divinely engendered by Jupiter Fulminans, the God of the Lightning-bolt, in the Soft Mother Earth.

Provoked Life:

An Essay On The Anthropology Of The Ego

GOTTFRIED BENN

Gottfried Benn (1886-1956) was one of the leading German lyric poets of this century and the major spokesman of the writers of the expressionist period in Germany. A physician by profession (he practiced medicine throughout his life) he did a considerable amount of original research in his field. In poetry he stood for the exploration of novel and often extreme experiences for the expression of which he created a new language combining divergent elements from the medical, vernacular and refined poetic vocabularies, coining new expressions, using daring images, and revolutionary ideas.

A trenchant social critic, Benn exposed the dangers of our technological era and the trend toward overemphasis of the rational and intellectual. He was anything but conservative in his writings and supported unlimited creative expansion and expression. He strove for a reconciliation between the natural, instinctual basis of man and his intellect; he worked for the resolution of dichotomies characterizing our lives, inner and outer, real and unreal, natural and artificial. Benn advocated the realization of our "antinaturalistic" nature, the creation of a "cerebral reality," a "provoked Life out of the materials of dream and stimulation."

The essay *"Provoziertes Leben"* (Provoked Life) was written in the early 1940's and appeared in the volume: "Ausdruckswelt, Essays und Aphorismen," 1949, Limes Verlag, Wiesbaden, Germany. We gratefully acknowledge the permission of the Limes Verlag, Wiesbaden, Germany, to translate and reprint this essay.

I

Several years ago a film was shown in Berlin, a film about Negroes called "Hosiannah," in which one saw Negroes getting intoxicated through communal singing. The disposition to do this lies in their nature, the process itself was sensual and conscious. Similar phenomena are reported about the North American Indians: The "Great Nightsong" is one of their principal ceremonies, where the men hold one another, move rhythmically and go into a trance. Closeness to intoxication is evidently a primitive quality as is the transition to a collectively heightened sense of being. The assembly provokes the transition through rites, movements, and certain ancient chants. It is a call of the race. Its nature is religious and mythical, an exciting communion with the totality which expands individual existence.

THE PSYCHEDELIC READER

Over against the trances induced by ritual movements and rhythm, are those induced by plant extracts, whose distribution is far more universal. Several million of the earth's inhabitants smoke or drink Indian hemp, as countless generations have done so through two thousand years. Three hundred million people chew betel; the great rice-eating population would sooner give up rice than the areca-nut; not to chew means to die. The three largest continents stimulate themselves through caffein; in Tibet, time is measured using a cup of tea and its effects; tea was found among the remains of prehistoric people. Chemicals which affect the brain, means of altering consciousness — these were primitive man's first approaches to his nervous system. How the effects were discovered is a mystery. A primal urge and a secret. Among a thousand roots, shrubs, trees, mushrooms, flowers — this one! Countless individuals probably died of poisoning before the race had reached its goal: enhancement, expansion — provoked life. Caravans with opium travel through the desert. Sykone is renamed Mekone, i.e. poppy-ville. On the tomb of Ariadne, a bearded god bends over her sleeping form, the god of sleep, carrying poppy-heads and the poppy-horn. The queen of the Incas was named after the miraculous plant Erythroxolon Coca; Mama Cuca; the stone idols have one cheek filled with coca leaves as a sign of divinity; everywhere there are bottle-shaped pumpkins, in which the leaf is kept, mixed with chalk and plant ashes, ready to be taken; the long needle with which you take it out is moistened by mouth. The effects of a mouthful of coca last forty minutes, equivalent to three kilometers on flat terrain, two kilometers in the hills — this is the dosage measure.

The ingestion takes place in the rancho of dreamers in Ecuador, in tents, while the medicine man beats the drums, or in empty cellars lined with stone projections used as seats by the guests, sometimes with the women, sometimes without: the "black drink," the "white water," the "happiness pills," or the "weed of graves," which brings unity with the spirits. Stages of excitement, stages of dream — you are beside yourself, but you feel, you learn from twitches and breathing disturbances, you get apathy or mobility as desired. From hidden centres, from the depths it emerges: to rest, to move no more: withdrawal, regression, aphasia. Hours are filled with the satisfaction of the desire to drift along as formless life. To call this animalistic is to be mistaken: this process is far below the animals, below the reflexes, it is near roots, chalk and stone. This is not the apathy of a dying race, not degeneration, these are youthful people; it is something more primary: defense against the beginnings of consciousness, its senseless imperative projects — thus, change space, obliterate time, blow away the grim passage of hours.

As long as memory traces, and civilizations, have existed in the brain, this organ of classification: forget them! In front of the Bistro drawn figures, home-owner idealists, worn out child-bearers, curves without deflections, normalized garbage — ah — garcon — another cocain-pulque, or in the restroom a pinch of snuff applied to the mucous membrane of the anus; or plug a soaked filling into a specially cultivated decayed tooth — ah — already the perspectives are beginning, ceaselessly spilling out of crosslines, winding and flickering; — Helena gave the heroes Nepenthes with their food, certainly an opiate preparation, when the mood was low or just before the battle, — ah, my battle too begins — first fields, colored like jewels, then red birds, — a *purely cortical reality* — lattice patterns are particularly frequent — "jewelers and artists should see this, they could take patterns from it," the colors become finer, strings are hanging from the surfaces, marvels are looking out of things.

The ego disintegrates, the places of disintegration are the planes of attachment. There is a kind of cosmic coldness, sublime and icy, in the structure, but fire in the medial axis; feelings of limbs lengthening and shortening, feelings of swelling and joining; simultaneously more sensitive thresholds: a storm of impressions, suggestibility to external influences, directed toward something universal, a feeling of totality: "Noon feeling." The senses exchange functions: "at the stroke of the clock purple color emerges"; alternating experiences of merging and distanciating; cutting through ego-feeling, smiling without affect, crying without object. Feelings of capacity: "the solution of dimly sensed problems seems immanent," — "everywhere the unheard of rejoicing of powerful harmony" — "Lord, let me bloom," — (Bucke's "cosmic emotion").

Another: "A great tension came over me. Great things had to be revealed to me. I would see the nature of all things, all the problems of the world would dissolve. I was out of my senses." Promenade of a god on the banks of the Po. "Golden late afternoon light." Then: "Only beauty in the eternal transformation of forms and colors. An increasing feeling of liberation came over me. Here everything would be resolved, *in the end everything was rhythm.*" (Klages came to the same conclusion, not so suddenly, but at the

41

end of a long life and with the aid of many books. Quantum theory says the same thing.)

Strange penetration of depth, cosmic osmosis (Magnaosmose): "I need time to finish my world view, which in skeleton form already is grounded on one sentence: *God is a substance.*" God is a substance, a drug! An intoxicating substance with affinity for the human brain. Certainly possible, at any rate more probable than that he is an electroshock machine or a Spemann Tritonlarva, formed by stuffing tadpole tissue in the mouth area. . . .

Complex structures become brittle, one can see through the rifts: "I had a peculiar muscle sensation. I *could have removed every single muscle separately from my body.*" (Long, long ago! The "muscle soul" arises, its contribution to the development of consciousness.) The cortex loses its recently acquired property of specific sensory quality (seeing, hearing, smelling, tasting) and answers in forms of general resonance. The "external" is not yet there; grounds yes, but hunting and fishing grounds: — the prehistory of "reality."

II

With the formation of the concept of "reality" the crisis began, the premorbid stage, its depth, its nihilistic existence. Indian-Javanese art (the socle of Borobudur) was in the other stage as late as 800 A.D. In its almost obscene luxuriance and exuberance of limbs and shapes, in the endless relief of animals, plants, human growths, bears, flowers, Bahadurs, hermits, tortoises, jackals, monkey-princes, all represented without pointedness, undifferentiated, inexhaustible, — the human beings all with the same roundish, smooth, full bodies with relatively small heads, all the same shape, all naked: in all this you can read the "Tat-tvam-asi," the "you are this also" of the Hindu doctrine, you can see ethical and physiological promiscuity, the original monosexuality of the primitive organism, which performed seed-formation, copulation and impregnation within itself, but you can also see the inner world still accessible to everyone, serene, mild and joined in dance, a world that knows a binding principle which in constant renewal surrounds the spiritual core of being. From this core emerges the great Night-or-Day chant, the great chant of the socle, of prelogical worlds still capable of giving fulfillment.

1300 years before this socle, in the southern part of our continent, the concept of reality began to be formed. The Hellenistic-European agonistic principle of victory through effort, cunning, malice, talent, force, and the later European Darwinism and "superman," was instrumental in its formation. The ego emerged, dominated, fought; for this it needed instruments, material, power. It had a different relationship to matter, more removed sensually, but closer formally. It analysed matter, tested, sorted: weapons, object of exchange, ransom money. It clarified matter through isolation, reduced it to formulas, took pieces out of it, divided it up. Compared to the soft Javanese wave-feeling, this attitude appears brutal and low. Its price was the separation of ego and world, the schizoid catastrophe, the inevitable western neurosis: reality. A tortuous concept and all were tortured by it, the intelligence of countless generations was divided over it. A concept which hung like a punishment over the West, with which the West fought, without grasping it, to which it sacrificed enormous quantities of blood and happiness; a concept whose inner tension and fragmentations it was impossible to dissolve through a natural viewing or methodical insight into the inherent unity and peace of prelogical forms of being. At a certain critical juncture Kant attempted to insert formal protections, but succeeded only in driving the development still further, so that it ("reality") now contained only causal-analytical results, including those of biological experiments, everything else was dream, animism, psychogenic arabesque. Goethe alone succeeded in overcoming the split, in a process lasting several decades, publicly recorded; his was a permanent solution but it was of a purely personal nature. Except for him no one else overcame the concept, no one else could; instead the cataclysmic character of this idea became clearer and clearer, as for example with Nietzsche. The latter took the idea of "reality" so much at its face value that (in extremely bold fashion) he attempted to "penetrate" it with ideas and thoughts of breeding, sending out Zarathustra "to create the creator." Nothing would have been further removed from the mind of this ancient Ormudh-Ahriman dualist; he would presumably, after taking one look at the impenetrable sun, have contemplated the poppies growing between the rose fields of Schiras and then lightly touched the ground with his forehead: you gave the Schire-Teriak and I take it! Finally, a state, a social organization, a public morality, for which life is economically usable life and which does not recognize the world of provoked life, cannot accept its destructive force. A society, whose hygiene and race cultivation as a modern ritual is founded solely on hollow biological statistics, can only represent the external viewpoint of the mass; for this point of view it can wage war, incessantly, for reality is simply raw material, but the metaphysical background remains forever obscured. The preceding, however, deals with this background and relates it to the problem of sublimation, to the "émotions sublimes" of Janet, i.e. to enhancement phenomena and expressive values.

III

The issue concerns the mythical collectivity as a foundation for life, as an unreflective sense of being, and its remnants in our nature and ways of realizing it. Compared to the tribal life of primitives which arises naturally from their inner properties, compared to the image-soaked faith of the Asistic peoples, what life-content the denatured European brains can realize in terms of occupational activities, clubs, family gatherings, summer excursions and so-called feasts can only be regarded as flat, conventional and shopworn; the few primal crimes which may occur in one decade are not sufficient to maintain the belief in a moral tradition of the race. Above all what is lacking is any systematic educational effort in the direction of conscious enhancement of vitality, since the epoch as a whole has no fundamental principles at all. If it were not so, one could, by increasing visionary states, say with mescaline or hashish, supply the race with a stream of spiritual insights, which could lead to a new creative period. Or they might hit on the idea of using hypnosis — at present exclusively in the hands of causal-analytical, norm-oriented physicians — not to increase potential in terms of economic utility, but for the liberation of the unconscious, i.e. suppressed, organic functions and archaic mechanisms — surprising experiences would be the result. Pervitin, instead of giving it to bomber pilots and explorers, could be purposefully used in the high schools and colleges for the induction of cerebral oscillations. This may sound extreme to some, but is merely the natural continuation of an old human idea. Whether through rhythm, drugs or autogenic training — we have the ancient human urge to overcome intolerable tensions between outer and inner, between god and not-god, between ego and reality — and we have the old and recent experience of having access to the means of overcoming them. The Buddha's systematic "prayer breathing," the ritual prayer postures of the early Christian hesychasts, Loyola's breathing with every verse of the Lord's Prayer, the dervishes, yogis, Dionysian rites, Mysteries, — all one family, which one could call the physiology of religion. German mysticism, according to Jakob Böhme "the unification of the natural self with the nothing" (note: with *nothing*, not with God), this mysticism, which one scholar has called "an almost experimental psychology of religion of the most ruthless sort," is the same thing — in other words, provoked religion.

All these are historical facts, widespread experiences; even from a biological point of view they are psychological truths. In spite of this such a conception is totally alien to the modern state. On the contrary, the government recently instituted an anti-narcotics program, and its biologists think of themselves as progressive. It would be difficult to make it clear to them that their program has the same relation to the problem of humanity as the mailman does to world government. Moreover, the possibility of helping mountaineers at high altitudes through drugs is actively studied by official physiologists, but the possibility of enhancing formal-aesthetic functions is not studied at all. We now have the establishment of centers for the collection of human milk; for example, a recent report showed that in Frankfort 1200 mothers gave 10,000 litres in two years, one mother gave 753 litres alone, another provided 460 litres when her sixth child was born. *However, potent brains are not strengthened through milk but through alkaloids.* An organ of such small size and great vulnerability, which not only approached the pyramids and gamma-rays, lions and icebergs, but created and invented them, cannot be watered like a forget-me-not, it will find its own supplies. *Existence means nervous existence,* i.e. stimulability, discipline, enormous factual knowledge, art. To suffer is to suffer in one's consciousness, not over deaths. To work is to expand spiritual capacities. In one word: *life is provoked life.*

Of course, someone will immediately mention the notion of *damage,* individual and racial. Drugs, intoxications, ecstasies, spiritual exhibitionism — all this sounds infernal to most people. But the concept of damage belongs in the reference-frame of "causal analysis" and "biology" and has the limited applicability of these systems. But even within these systems, a state which wages wars in which three million men are killed within three years is hardly in a position to talk about damage; this is damage of individual and communal interests which far exceeds the damage of experiments on the expanding ability of drugs. The issue is not damage, but principles, and what kind you want to adopt. If you consider this idea of damage on a more general level, it becomes an interesting observation, that impairments suffered by an entire race have usually brought their compensation which far exceed the value of what was lost. So for example, the loss of skin pigment was initially for the white race an extremely dangerous disability exposing them to unheard of intensities of radiation; but eventually it was compensated by another descendant of the same common primary seed, or ectoderm, namely the extremely powerful nervous system which was capable of dealing with danger. (The human brain was born as a result of or at least after, this impairment.) In other words, in talking of damage the context has to be considered. Whether the degenerating central European brain *can* be damaged is in any case an open question.

One will not reach any insights in this area who does not meditate at length on the nature of the brain. The brain is the perfect example for the pigmy-character of causal theories, it has travelled a most acausal path, all biological hypotheses fail to explain it. It seems clear, since the work of Vershuys, Poetzl and Lorenz, that the brain developed through doubling the number of neurones and simultaneously rearranging the outer (cortical) layers. "There are no intermediary forms." There is no trace of adaptation, summation of minute stimuli, gradual growth and decay until some purposive reorganization takes place — *there were always creative crises.* The brain is the mutative, revolutionary organ par excellence. Its nature was always form, not content, its means expansion, its needs—stimuli. This store-house of rudiments and catacombs brought everything with it from the beginning, it was not dependent on impressions, it produced itself when called for. It was by no means favorably predisposed towards "life," but was equally available for lethal activities, hunger, fasting, walking on nails, charming snakes, magic, bionegatives, death.

"Mens sana in corpore sano" was a proverb of the Roman warrior caste, which has had a modern resurrection in the gymnastics of Jahn and in the Bavarian health cults. Using inner criteria the extravagant body has accomplished more than the normal body; its bionegative characteristics created and carry the human world. By these criteria there is no reality, no history, just some brains which realize at certain time-intervals their dreams, images of the ancient original dreams, made in retrospective insight. This realization may take place in "stone, verse or flute-song" — then we have art; sometimes it takes place only in thoughts or ecstasies. A marvelous sentence from a novel by Thornton Wilder describes the situation: "We come from a world in which we have known unbelievable standards of perfection and we remember faintly the beauty, which we were unable to retain, and we return to this world." Clearly Plato is at hand; endogenous images are the last remaining vestigial forms of our happiness.

(Translated by Ralph Metzner)

The Individual As Man/World

ALAN W. WATTS

(*Prefatory Note*: The following was originally delivered as an impromptu lecture for the Social Relations Colloquium at Harvard University on April 12th, 1963. Although the subject was not discussed in the lecture itself, its theme is closely related to the expansion of consciousness achieved through psychedelic substances. With proper "set and setting," the psychedelics are very frequently successful in giving the individual a vivid sensation of the mutual interdependence of his own behavior and the behavior of his environment, so that the two seem to become one — the behavior of a unified field. Those who uphold the impoverished sense of reality sanctioned by official psychiatry describe this type of awareness as "depersonalization," "loss of ego-boundary," or "regression to the oceanic feeling," all of which, in their usual contexts, are derogatory terms suggesting that the state is hallucinatory. Yet it accords astonishingly well with the description of the individual which is given in the behavioral sciences, in biology and in ecology.

Theoretically, many scientists know that the individual is not a skin-encapsulated ego but an organism-environment field. The organism itself is a point at which the field is "focused," so that each individual is a unique expression of the behavior of the whole field, which is ultimately the universe itself. But to know this theoretically is not to *feel* it to be so. It was possible to calculate that the world was round before making the voyage that proved it to be so. The psychedelics are, perhaps, the ship, the experimental instrument by which the theory can be verified in common experience.)

There is a colossal disparity between the way in which most individuals experience their own existence, and the way in which the individual is described in such sciences as biology, ecology, and physiology. The nub of the difference is this: the way the individual is described in these sciences is not as a freely moving entity within an environment, but as a process of behavior which *is* the environment also. If you will accurately describe what any individual organism is doing, you will take but a few steps before you are also describing what the environment is doing. To put it more simply, we can do without such expressions as "what the individual is doing" or "what the environment is doing," as if the individual was one thing and the doing another, the environment one thing and its doing another. If we reduce the whole business simply to the process of doing, then the doing, which was called the behavior of the individual, is found to be *at the same time* the doing which was called the behavior of the environment. In other words, it is quite impossible to describe the movement of my arm except in relation to the rest of my body and to the background against which you perceive it. The relations in which you perceive this movement are the absolutely necessary condition for your perceiving at all. More and more, a "field theory" of man's behavior becomes necessary for the sciences.

Yet this is at complete variance with the way in which we are trained *by our culture* to experience our own existence. We do not, generally speaking, experience ourselves as the behavior of the field, but rather as a center of energy and consciousness which sometimes manages to control its environment, but at other times feels completely dominated by the environment. Thus there is a somewhat hostile relationship between the human organism and its social and natural environment, which is expressed in such phrases as "man's conquest of nature," or "man's conquest of space," and other such antagonistic figures of speech.

It would obviously be to the advantage of mankind if the way in which we feel our existence could correspond to the way in which existence is scientifically described. For what we feel has far more influence upon our actions than what we think. Scientists of all kinds are warning us most urgently that we are using our technology disastrously, eating up all the natural resources of the earth, creating incredibly beautiful but wholly non-nutritious vegetables by altering the biochemical balances of the soil, spawning unbelievable amounts of detergent froth which will eventually engulf cities, overpopulating ourselves because of the success of medicine, and thus winning our war against nature in such a way as to defeat ourselves completely. All this advice falls on deaf ears, because it falls on the ears of organisms convinced that war against nature is their proper way of life. They have to be unconvinced, and can be, to some extent, by intellectual propaganda, scientific description, and clear thought. But this moves relatively few people to action. Most are moved only if their feelings are profoundly affected. We need to *feel* this view of our individual identity as including its environment, and this must obviously concern scientists who are trying to find ways of controlling human feelings.

This problem has an important historical background. It is curious how the ancient philosophical debates of the Western world keep coming up again and again in new forms. Any question of the definition of the individual always becomes involved with the old argument between nominalism and realism. I do not wish to insult the intelligence of this learned audience, but, just to refresh your memories, the realistic philosophy of the Middle Ages and of the Greeks was not what today we call realism. It was the belief that behind all specific manifestations of life such as men, trees, dogs, there lies an archetypal, or ideal, form of Man, of Tree, of Dog, so that every particular man is an instance of that archetypal form, and that behind all men is something which can be called Man with a capital M, or the "substance" of man, of "human nature."

The nominalists argued that this was a mere abstraction, and that to regard Man (capital M) as possessing any effective existence was to be deluded by concepts. There are only specific, individual men. This idea is carried on in one of the most remarkable forms of modern nominalism, General Semantics, which argues that such abstractions as "The United States," "Britain," or "Russia," are so much journalistic gobbledygook.

Most people working in the sciences tend to be nominalists. But if you carry nominalism to its logical conclusion, you are involved in awkward problems. Not only would there be no such thing as Man, Mankind, or Human Nature, but it would also follow that there are no individual men, because the individual man is an abstraction, and what really exists is only an enormous amalgamation of particular molecules. If you pursue this further and inquire about the individual entities composing the molecules, there is an interminable array of nuclear and sub-nuclear realities, and if *these* in turn are to be regarded as the only realities, then the reality which we call a man is simply the association of discontinuous particles. This is the *reductio ad absurdum* of nominalism carried too far. The nominalist and realist viewpoints are actually *limits* — to borrow a term from mathematics. I have often thought that all philosophical debates are ultimately between the partisans of structure and the partisans of "goo." The academic world puts a heavy emphasis on structure: "Let's be definite, let's have rigor and precision, even though we are studying poetry." But the poets will reply: "We are for goo, and you people are all dry bones, rattling in the wind. What you need is essential juices, and therefore more goo is necessary to liven you up." But when we want to know what goo is, and examine it carefully, we eventually turn up with a structure, the molecular or atomic composition of goo! On the other hand, when we try to examine the structure itself to study the substance of its bones, we inevitably come up with something gooey. When the microscope focus is clear, you have structure. But when you reach beyond the focus and what confronts you is vague and amorphous, you have goo because you cannot attain clarity. Structure and goo are essential limits of human thought; similarly, the nominalist-structural and the realist-gooey will always be essential limits in our thinking. We must be aware that today, the particular academic and scientific fashion leans heavily in the direction of structure and nominalism.

To take a specific example, we all know that in modern medicine nominalism and structuralism hold the field. When you go to a hospital, you are liable to go through a process of examination by specialists working upon you from different points of view. They will treat you as a non-person, from the very moment you enter. You are immediately put in a wheelchair — a symbol of the fact that you are now an object. You will be looked at piecemeal, X-rays will be taken of various organs, and special tests will be made of their functioning. If anything is wrong, you will be taken to a medical mechanic, i.e., a surgeon, who will use his equivalents of wrenches, screwdrivers and blowtorches to make certain mechanical alterations in your organism, and it is hoped you will get along fairly well with these repairs!

But the opposite, minority school of medicine will say: "This is all very well, and the services of the surgeon are sometimes greatly welcomed, but man must be considered as a whole. He has complicated metabolic and endocrine balances, and if you interfere with him seriously at one point, you will affect him unpredictably at many others, for man is an organic whole." Such are accused of being woolly-minded, old-fashioned doctors, mostly from Europe, with a kind of nature-cure background, who will use diet, complicated fasts, and massage. The poor layman doesn't know whether to deliver himself over to these old-fashioned naturalistic doctors or to Mr. Sawbones with his very up-to-date qualifications.

Fortunately, precise science is coming to the rescue of our man-as-a-whole. More recent studies are showing just how diseases formerly regarded as specific entities, or afflictions of a particular organ or area, are actually brought about by responses of the central nervous system, acting as an integrated whole. We are beginning to see how man, as a complex of organs, is not an *addition* of parts, like an automobile. His various organs are not to be treated as if they were assembled together, but by seeing the physical body as a unified or integrated pattern of behavior — which is just what we mean when we talk about an entity or thing. What happens when we have the feeling that we understand something, when we say, "Oh, I see"? If a child asks, "Why are the leaves green?" and you answer, "Because of the chlorophyll," and the child says, "Oh!," that is *pseudo-*understanding. But when the child has a jigsaw puzzle and sees how it all fits together, then the "Oh!" has a different meaning from the "Oh!" following the chlorophyll explanation. To understand anything is to be able to fit various parts into a system which is an integrated whole, so that they "make sense."

As organic diseases are fitted into a whole, and problems of crime or phychosis in individual behavior are fitted in with a pattern of social behavior that makes sense, that is consistent with those kinds of behaviors, we say "Aha! — *now* I see!"

Fascinating work is being done in studying the ways in which the individual as a system of behavior is related to his biological and social environments, showing how his behavior may be explained in terms of those environments. One of the people who has done very important work in this sphere is our distinguished colleague, B. F. Skinner. I cite his work because it brings out these ideas in a marvellously clear, crucial, and provocative way, and because it is evidence for conclusions which he himself does not seem to have realized. One of his most important statements is in his book,
Science and Human Behavior :[1]

> The hypothesis that man is not free is essential to the application of scientific method to the study of human behavior. The free inner man who is held responsible for the behavior of the external biological organism is only a prescientific substitute for the kinds of causes which are discovered in the course of a scientific analysis.

He is talking, of course, about the chauffeur inside the body, or what Wittgenstein called the little man inside the head: this is for him a prescientific substitute for the kinds of causes for behavior which are discovered in the course of scientific analysis. He continues:

> All these alternative causes lie *outside* the individual. The biological substratum itself is determined by prior events in a genetic process. Other important events are found in the nonsocial environment and in the culture of the individual in the broadest possible sense. These are the things which *make** the individual behave as he does. For them he is not responsible and for them it is useless to praise or blame him. It does not matter that the individual may take it upon himself to control the variables of which his own behavior is a function or, in a broader sense, to engage in the design of his own culture. He

[1] New York: Macmillan, 1953, pp. 447-448.

does this only because he is the product of a culture which *generates**
self-control or cultural design as a mode of behavior. The environment determines the individual even when he alters the environment.[1]
[*Emphasis mine—A.W.W.]

I am not going to quarrel with this finding. I am not a clinical
or experimental psychologist and am therefore unqualified to criticize
Skinner's evidence. Let's take it for Gospel, simply for the sake
of argument.

But there is a rather heavy emphasis upon the individual being
the puppet. "All these alternative causes," i.e., the kinds of causes
discovered in the course of scientific behavior, "lie outside the individual," i.e., outside this wall of flesh and bag of skin. The individual
is therefore passive. This is psychology in terms of Newtonian
physics. The individual is a billiard ball upon which other balls
impinge, and his seemingly active behavior is only a passive response.
Skinner admits the individual does and can alter the environment,
but when he does so, he is *being made* to do so. This is put forth
in such a way as to make the individual appear passive and the things
really controlling his behavior outside him.

But the reciprocal relationship between the knower and the
known, common to all the sciences, is set aside here although he
mentions it elsewhere.

A laboratory for the study of behavior contains many devices for
controlling the environment and for recording and analyzing the behavior of organisms. With the help of these devices and their associated techniques, we change the behavior of an organism in various
ways, with considerable precision. But note that the organism changes
our behavior in quite as precise a fashion. Our apparatus was designed
by the organism we study, for it was the organism which led us to
choose a particular manipulandum, particular categories of stimulation, particular modes of reinforcement, and so on, and to record
particular aspects of its behavior. Measures which were successful
were for that reason reinforcing and have been retained, while others
have been, as we say, extinguished. The verbal behavior with which
we analyze our data has been shaped in a similar way: order and consistency emerged to reinforce certain practices which were adopted,
while other practices suffered extinction and were abandoned. (All
scientific techniques, as well as scientific knowledge itself, are generated in this way. A cyclotron is "designed" by the particles it is to
control, and a theory is written by the particles it is to explain, as
the behavior of these particles shapes the nonverbal and verbal behavior of the scientist.)[2]

[2] "The Design of Cultures," *Daedalus,* Summer 1961, p. 543.

In one of his essays, he has a cartoon of one mouse saying to another, "Boy, have I got that guy up there fixed! Every time I press this bar, he gives me some food!"

Although Skinner seems in general to be stressing heavily the point of view that the individual is the puppet in the field in which he is involved, he is nevertheless stating here the opposite point, that the individual organism, mouse, or guinea pig, in the experiment is nevertheless determining the environment even when, as in a laboratory, the environment is designed to control the specific organism. The environment of a rat running in a barn is not designed to control the rat, but the more it is so designed, the more the rat is involved in and shaping its environment. He writes elsewhere that what he has been saying

> does not mean that anyone in possession of the methods and results of science can step outside the stream of history and take the evolution of government into his own hands. Science is not free, either. It cannot interfere with the course of events; it is simply part of that course. It would be quite inconsistent if we were to exempt the scientist from the account which science gives of human behavior in general.[3]

Now we might well object: "Look, Professor Skinner, you say we are completely conditioned behavior-systems. We cannot change anything. At the same time, you are calling upon us to embark upon the most radical program of controlling human behavior. How can you write *Walden II*, a utopia? Are you not a monstrosity of inconsistency by calling for responsible human action and at the same time saying that we have no freedom?" But is this actually a contradiction? He is saying two things, both of which can be valid, but he does not provide a framework in which the opposed points of view can make sense. Similarly, the physicist says light can be considered as a wave or as a particle system. These sound mutually exclusive to the non-physicist. In the same way, the advocacy of a planned development of human resources and potentials, coupled with the idea that the individual is not a self-controlling, skin-encapsulated ego, needs some further concept to help it along. The following passage clinches the problem.

> Just as biographers and critics look for external influences to account for the traits and achievements of the men they study, so science ultimately explains behavior in terms of "causes" or conditions which lie beyond the individual himself. As more and more causal relations are demonstrated, a practical corollary becomes difficult to resist: it

[3] *Science and Human Behavior,* p. 446.

should be possible to *produce* behavior according to plan simply by arranging the proper conditions.[4]

There is the contradiction which necessarily arises in a psychology with a language system which incorporates into present scientific knowledge an outmoded conception of the individual — the individual as something bounded by skin, and which is pushed around by an environment which is not the individual. Skinner is naturally aware that his emphasis on our passive relationship to conditioning causes is rather unpalatable.

> The conception of the individual which emerges from a scientific analysis is distasteful to most of those who have been strongly affected by democratic philosophies . . . it has always been the unfortunate task of science to dispossess cherished beliefs regarding the place of man in the universe. It is easy to understand why men so frequently flatter themselves — why they characterize the world in ways which reinforce them by providing escape from the consequences of criticism or other forms of punishment. But although flattery temporarily strengthens behavior, it is questionable whether it has any ultimate survival value. If science does not confirm the assumptions of freedom, initiative, and responsibility in the behavior of the individual, these assumptons will not ultimately be effectve either as motivating devices or as goals in the design of culture. We may not give them up easily, and we may, in fact, find it difficult to control ourselves or others until alternative principles have been developed.[5]

There the book ends, and there is no suggestion as to what those principles might be, even though they are implied in his conclusions.

> When an individual conspicuously manipulates the variables of which the behavior of *another** individual is a function, we say that the first individual controls the second, but we do not ask who or what controls the first. When a government conspicuously controls its citizens, we consider this fact without identifying the events which control the government. When the individual is strengthened as a measure of counter-control, we may, as in democratic philosophies, think of him as a starting point. [* My emphasis—A.W.W.]

Isn't this political nominalism?

> Actually, however, we are not justified in assigning *to anyone or anything* the role of prime mover. Although it is necessary that science confine itself to selected segments in a continuous series of events, it is *to the whole series* that any interpretation must eventually apply.[6] [My emphases—A.W.W.]

[4] "Freedom and the Control of Men," *The American Scholar*, Vol. 25, No. 1, Winter, 1955-56, p. 47.

[5] *Science and Human Behavior*, p. 449.

[6] *Ibid.*, pp. 448-449.

The Individual As Man/World

We are now listening to a man who represents himself as a behavioristically oriented, non-mystical, on-the-whole materialistic, hard-headed scientist. Yet this passage is the purest mysticism, which might have come straight from Mahayana Buddhism: "We are not justified in assigning to anyone or anything the role of prime mover." No segment, no particular pattern of integrated behavior within whatever universe we are discussing can be called the prime mover. Now this is the *Dharmadhatu* doctrine of Mahayana Buddhism, that the universe is a harmonious system which has no governor, that it is an integrated organism but nobody is in charge of it. Its corollary is that everyone and everything is the prime mover.

In Skinner's language, the popular conception of the inner self, the little man inside the head who is controlling everything, must be replaced by the whole system of *external* causes operating upon the individual, the whole network of causal relationships. But this language obscures a very simple thing: when there is a certain cause in the external environment whose effect is always a particular individual behavior, you are using very cumbersome language for something you can describe more simply. For when you find these two things going together, you are actually talking about one thing. To say that Event A causes Event B is a laborious way of saying that it is one Event C. If I lift up this book by a corner, all the corners are lifted up at the same time. If I lift up an accordion, there is an interval between cause and effect. Similarly when we study the individual's behavior, we are studying a system of relationships, but we are looking at it too close up. All we see is the atomic events, and we don't see the integrated system which would make them make sense if we could see it. Our scientific methods of description suffer from a defective conception of the individual. The individual is not by any means what is contained inside a given envelope of skin. The individual organism is the particular and unique focal point of a network of relations which is ultimately a "whole series" — I suppose that means the whole cosmos. And the whole cosmos so focused is one's actual self. This is, whether you like it or not, pure mysticism. Skinner is saying that although science is a method of observation which, by reason of the blinkers of the head, is limited to our one-thing-at-a-time method of thought, science can only look at the world area by area. But science also becomes the method of understanding its own limitations. When you conduct any experiment, you must be careful to exclude variables you cannot measure. When you want to keep something at a constant temperature, you must put it into some kind of heat-and-cold-proof or shock-proof, or cosmic-ray-proof system. So by excluding variables and by having to do it rigorously, you begin to understand how really impossible it is to do except in very special cases. In this way, the scientist, by attempting to isolate events and by looking as rigorously as he can at one segment of the world at a time, becomes aware of the fact that this looking at things simply in segments, although it is a form of very bright, clear, conscious knowledge, is also a form of ignorance. For it is a form of "ignore-ance," ignoring everything that is not in that segment. Therefore he becomes aware of the fact that just this is *ultimately* what you can't do. You *can* do it only to discover you *cannot* do it.

I commend these observations to you simply to show how a scientific thinker whose whole stance is in the direction of mechanism, of regarding the human being as a kind of biological puppet, must be forced by the logic of his own thinking to conclusions of a rather different kind. He states these questions in veiled language, so that neither he nor his colleagues will see their disastrously unrespectable implications!

Suppose, then, it becomes possible for us to have a new sense of the individual, that we all become conscious of ourselves as organism-environment fields, vividly aware of the fact that when we move, it is not simply my self moving inside my skin, exercising energy upon my limbs, but also that in some marvelous way the physical continuum in which I move is also moving me. The very fact that I am here in this room at all is because you are here. It was a common concurrence, a whole concatenation of circumstances which go together, each reciprocally related to all. Would such an awareness be significant? Would it add to our knowledge? Would it change anything, make any difference? Seriously, I think it would; because it makes an enormous difference whenever what had seemed to be partial and distintegrated fits into a larger integrated pattern. It will of course be impossible finally to answer the question, "Why does that satisfy us?,"because to answer this question exhaustively I would have to be able to chew my own teeth to pieces. In the pursuit of scientific knowledge, always watch out for that snag. You will never get to the irreducible explanation of anything because you will never be able to explain why you want to explain, and so on. The system will gobble itself up. The Gödel theory has roughly to do with the idea that you cannot have any system which will define its own axioms. An axiom in one system of logic must be defined in terms of another system, etc., etc. You never get to something which is completely self-explanatory. That of course is the limit of control, and the reason why all systems of control have ultimately to be based on an act of faith.

The problem confronting all sciences of human behavior is that we have the evidence (we are *staring* at it) to give us an entirely different conception of the individual than that which we ordinarily feel and which influences our common sense: a conception of the individual not, on the one hand, as an ego locked in the skin, nor, on the other, as a mere passive part of the machine, but as a reciprocal interaction between everything inside the skin and everything outside it, neither one being prior to the other, but equals, like the front and back of a coin.

Annihilating Illumination

GEORGE ANDREWS

While being struck by lightning in slow motion
the fire sears away layer after layer
sizzles me down to my ultimate ash
I quiver shrieks of laughing crystals
the radiant frenzy of the storm's soul dwells in the guts of the dragon
the bomb in my belly blasts my body to bits
a million suns burst into being
naked free no rings around me but my own desire
I hold the lightning in embryo in my arms
the blood of the cactus is the blood of a snake and the blood of a star
magnetic dragon throbbing in each corpuscle
shining snake of the light wave our beings are based on
glyph of the nucleus of the cosmos
original flash of let there be light
the boat of the sun navigates through the underworld of my intestines
perpetual pilgrim doomed to wander through the chromatic repercus-
     sions
the intimate structure of the transparent signs
flower of light flowing through the blood of the universe
I wander through the mazes of the glory and the horror of the life
     slime
vital jelly swarming in all possible creatures
I see the dead and the living merge
the dead call to us the living may we recognise them at last
the dead are in our blood each corpuscle an ancestor
the day all the living die the dead shall live
herald of the apocalypse sound the doomsday horn
man stop the wheel of creation and look inside
the stars are all contained within our organs
galactic music spins inside the bones
coruscating symphonies coalesce iridescent vibrations
coupled poles of attraction combust the salt of a fantastic caprice
philosopher's stone cooking in the cauldron of my skull
drain the bitter cup to its last drop
potent is the sorcerer's broth
mighty as the giant bird who swoops down and carries me away

59

to the motionless point around which all motion spins
I see touch and count the seeds of destiny
I see how fate weaves its webs
dreaming worlds into being from the ooze of my own brain
God born of the goo of my membranes
and has suffered ever since the intricate combinations of the opposites
afloat forever abubble on the surface of reality
O to make one perfect thing at last of all the worlds of wandering
a ransom for the soul's pain
drink liquid lightning from the sacred river while it is before you
don't miss a drop no one sees it twice
fire swims and pulses through each cell of my being
the seed of strong delight stirs
myriad joys feel at home in an angel's nest
revolving wheels of splendor palpitate potent beauty
clear colors cascade undulating reflections
of the diamond in the brain the pituitary gland decalcified
the mirror in the mind
the heavenly heart awakens the first beat tells the worlds
germ in the guts of God or God in the guts of a germ
I am that I am the same dance is everywhere
the one law of cyclic change
that constantly accelerating fugue of incandescent experience
flaming sequences of rhythm patterns
I am alive within the living God
I throb unique among the infinite variations
and so what if all the evolution of consciousness only leads to the
        knowledge
that I am a germ in the guts of a greater being
I am older than creation older than all beings
the stars revolve within me
I voyage through the inner space between my atoms
I take space ships to the different parts of my body
each organ becomes a constellation as I spread across the sky
wheeling through the zodiac weaving the fate of future races
conceive a cosmos where life does not need to kill to live
create a system free from pain
in the spawn and seethe of the primeval ocean
out of chaos I pass the current
immortal diamonds shimmering on the foam of the instant now
scintillating images of the flux that never fixes

Annihilating Illumination

explode into extreme intensities
constantly generating golden brilliance
face to face with the annihilating illumination
how much revelation can an organism sustain and stay alive
mortals beware the rays of the absolute
Nerval: "They consider me insane but I know
that I am a hero living under the eyes of the gods."
glistening tender stars in the organs of all forms of life
trembling jewels flicker as they crawl like snakes
hidden energy roots of the soul body contact
subtle link between the sun and our life metabolism
invisible fiery wheel inside me
one spark that transforms everything
I've been to paradise and out the other side
zoomed through it like the midnight express through a whistle stop
I have been torn apart by the fingers of the flash
flayed alive on my electric skeleton
pulverized by the power of the spasm
I am the bridge between the living and the dead
I am the spirit in the shaman's drum
I quiver to the rhythm of the Sphinx
I visit my own body as a stranger
incredible paroxysms of the luminous protoplasm
kindle multiple modulations of rare royal reality
to know that at each moment the crown jewels of the absolute
are dancing in the slime of my tissue
the play of the light in the growing cell
pours through the pulse of my perception
phoenix singing in my flesh
bird that breathes lightning as we breathe air and fishes water
intricate egg of fire fluctuating
in the magnetic field of my affinities and repulsions
where myriads of globules circulate crosswires hum
most amplified fantasy of the diamond body harvest
I free my nucleus gathering ecstasy for the ages
my psyche digests the apocalyptic wisdom
interplanetary nausea
perfection signals tremor on the skin
O frail fine blue star
your faint fragile tonalities swoon triumphant rainbows
as the berserk fury of the thunder's roar fades into words on paper.

FROM
PSYCHEDELIC
REVIEW
NUMBER TWO

PSYCHOSIS:
"Experimental" and Real

—Now is there something wrong with this entire circus.
CARL GIESE

—Consistency, thou art a jewel.
Origin unknown

JOE K. ADAMS [1]

I SHALL ATTEMPT to present a theory of psychosis centered around the topics of cognitive structure, emotion, role, cultural norms, and communication, and to relate my theory to the cultural revolution through which we are now passing, with comparative references to past revolutions. The contribution of the psychedelic drugs in understanding both "psychotic" and "normal" behavior will be described according to this author's convictions, which have much in common with those focused on "transcendental" experiences, but also with those which have placed drug experiences and behavior in the "model psychosis" context. The presentation is necessarily sketchy, because psychosis involves many problems interlocked in such a way that they must be solved simultaneously rather than piecemeal, in any reasonably adequate theory. Many readers, however, have doubtless been thinking along similar lines and will have little difficulty in filling in most of the gaps.

It is assumed that the reader is familiar with the idea that the processes of socialization result in the individual's perception of some objects and events as they in fact are, and of some objects and events as they in fact are not.[2] No animal can survive without some validity in his perceptions, but no animal has only valid perceptions; man is no exception to either of these assertions, but, unlike other animals, his culture (e.g., northern U.S.A.), sub-culture (e.g., proper Presbyterian, midwestern large city), and immediate groups-of-reference (e.g., his nuclear family, family of origin, clubs, professional affiliations) determine to a considerable extent not only what

65

cognitions will occur, but also the degree of validity of a given class of cognitions. As we move from basic cognitive processes such as figure-ground formation and color perception to more complex organization of the cognitive field and to perception of objects as members of a class and as thus possessing certain properties attributed by the perceiver to members of that class, cultural determinants usually play a greater and greater role, and differences between groups become concomitantly greater. Within groups the situation is more complex, as group norms tend to minimize some differences and to maximize others, depending upon the specific group. The generalization can be made, however, that *within every group each individual is deceived into living in a world which is only partly real, when, of all animals, he has the greatest potentiality of living in the real world, and of modifying the real world in ways which are to his advantage.*

The thesis that the individual perceives only part of the reality "available" to him is hardly an original creation of the present author. It has been expressed throughout the centuries in various forms, some much more adequate than the brief statement above. For example, the ancient and recurring statements that people are "asleep" or "blind," or that they are "actors" without realizing that they are acting, are expressions of more or less the same thesis, as are numerous more recent expositions by philosophers, ethnologists, psychologists, sociologists, general semanticists, novelists, psychiatrists, etc. Alan Watts (1961) prefers to say that the individual is "hypnotized" by the culture; Erich Fromm (1941) has also used the analogy with hypnosis in describing the individual's empty role-taking and alienation from parts of himself and from others.[3]

Alfred Korzybski (1948), Eric Hoffer (1951), and Ernest Schachtel (1947) have written about similar processes, though with different words and emphases.

In thus grouping together such a wide variety of formulations, I do not mean to deny important differences between them, nor to argue that the general thesis is correct simply because many learned people have held it, but to emphasize that it is continually "rediscovered" and expressed in ways that sometimes obscure the underlying similarities. It is probably our false pride and our status striving, as well as the impossibility of reading everything, which often prevent our seeing and acknowledging that others have been trying to express that which we believe (sometimes correctly) we can formulate more clearly and succinctly. My own preference for a formulation in terms of deception stems from the fact that in child-rearing practices, as in adult interactions, many concrete examples of intentional deception and of withholding of information which results in unintentional deception can be cited and corrected by telling the individuals concerned, in language they can understand, what one believes to be the truth. Comparisons with hypnosis and sleep, while valid, are both harder to exemplify and also less clear in terms of their implications; this is not to say that they are less important theoretically, or that they are not needed in a more complete account of socialization processes and remedies thereof.

IT IS LARGELY by means of language and definition of role that groups cast a veil of illusions over the individual. Language, especially, is a convenient vehicle for achieving some uniformity in illusions, as well as in valid perceptions, from one individual to another, in an especially deceptive and insidious manner (Schachtel, 1947; Adams, 1953). Definition of role is, however, at least a close second. Roles not only prescribe the "moves" which an individual is entitled to make in relationships with others; they penetrate the interior of the individual and prescribe his perceptions, thoughts, and feelings (Goffman, 1959; Sarbin, 1954). Role behavior is an expression of cognitive structure and *vice versa*.

If one examines any given processes of communication which are prescribed by roles and limited by language, one may become aware of something which is "not supposed" to be seen within the culture — namely, that the *processes under examination perpetuate the delusions and illusions of the members of the culture*. For example, the restrictions on communication in judicial processes tend to prevent the participants, including the defendant, from seeing that what is called "justice" is sometimes a hypocritical and tragic farce. On the other hand, a lawyer or a judge may, during the course of his career, gradually "wake up," and may continue to "play the game," and/or work toward judicial and legal reforms (Bazelon, 1960; Ploscowe, 1951).

Restrictions on communication very often serve the function of preserving false beliefs, and this function is frequently not recognized even by those who impose the restrictions. "The "excommunication" of an individual, for example, whether from a religious community, a professional group, or "society" in general, can permit false beliefs about the individual to be perpetuated. When comments

67

about an individual are made in his absence, for example, he has no chance to correct whatever false beliefs are expressed, or to contribute information which is lacking. *These false beliefs and incomplete information about excommunicated individuals play an extremely important part in the social life of the community.* This principle is partly recognized by those who refuse to form their beliefs about an individual on the basis of gossip and insist upon informing themselves firsthand, but the more general conservative function of exclusion is rarely perceived (Lemert, 1962).

◆   IT HAS BEEN RECOGNIZED for many years that "psychotic episodes" can be precipitated by insights into oneself. It was for this reason, in fact, that Freudians tended to avoid taking "pre-psychotics" into treatment, whereas Jung took the unpopular and "mystical" position that such episodes, preferably confined to the interviewing room, are the most effective, though admittedly hazardous, road to individuation.

The precipitation of psychotic episodes by insights into the outside world has been less well recognized, at least within the mental health professions. To acknowledge such a possibility is to acknowledge that the culture permits, teaches, or trains the individual to be blind or deluded; thus it locates pathology outside as well as inside the individual (and in his relation to the outside) and in particular it locates pathology in the most powerful institutions and authorities of the culture. Whereas the location of pathology within the individual is in accordance with the Western cultural tradition that the individual is "ignorant," "bad," "sinful," "deprived," or "depraved," except for the saving grace of outside forces, the location of pathology in the dominant institutions of the culture is hardly in accordance with the tradition of any culture. On the other hand, Western civilization, unlike some "primitive" societies, has contained and nourished also a tradition of critical examination of the world as well as of oneself, a tradition inevitably in conflict with institutions or cultural patterns which blind the individual. This duality is particularly obvious in northern U.S.A. culture, which from the days of the first Puritan settlers contained a strong trend toward critical self-examination — with surprising psychological sophistication — as well as strong conservative forces, without which no culture can survive (Smith, 1954).

It is not difficult to see how insights, whether into oneself or the outside world, can precipitate "psychotic" episodes, and why from that point onward the individual is likely to find it difficult to articulate with the culture. There are at least two ways in which an "insight" can trigger a neurological "jam session": (1) by arousing an intense emotion and thus altering the chemical composition of the blood and consequently the functioning of the brain, and (2) by a sudden collapse of boundaries between two or more cognitive structures previously kept separated from each other, within that particular individual's total set of cognitive structures. Cognitive structures are presumably related in some manner to the structure of neurological processes (Kohler, 1938; Hebb, 1949; Miller, Pribram, and Galanter, 1960). A sudden change in the former is therefore presumably accompanied by a sudden change in the latter.

THESE TWO MECHANISMS are not mutually exclusive, and perhaps in most episodes they work hand-in-hand. The most important insights are probably those in which two or more cognitive systems, each available to consciousness, are brought into relation. The defense mechanism which breaks down is *compartmentalization,* which has been relatively neglected in the literature, possibly because it is a defense *par excellence* of most people called "experts," "scholars," "intellectuals," "technicians," or "scientists." Theorists are usually very particular, for example, about what is "relevant" to their "discipline" or "specialty," what they are or are not supposed or required to know or to do in their roles, exactly how an idea should be worded and the great superiority of one wording over another, etc. From the fields of logic and mathematics many clear examples can be drawn of valid isolation of cognitive systems and of apparently slight changes in wording which do in fact produce enormous differences in implications or in efficiency, and also some examples of invalid compartmentalization and of quibbling over symbols which obscures the similarity of underlying conceptual structures.

The evidence for the breakdown of compartmentalization in psychotic episodes is both phenomenological and behavioral. Phenomenologically, things seem to "run together" in ways that may be alternately bewildering, amazing, inspiring, amusing, bizarre, uncanny, terrifying, etc. Speech during such episodes is what would be expected when decompartmentalization occurs. What the individual says does not "make sense" in a conventional way; he does not stick to the point and instead drags in matters which appear to observers to be completely irrelevant. In other words, a massive dedifferentiation of cognitive systems and linguistic habits occurs,

69

which may be as bewildering to the individual as to those with whom he may attempt to communicate.

For any given individual the massive cognitive dedifferentiations called "psychotic episodes" result in more valid perceptions and beliefs in certain respects — the individual has now seen through some of his delusions and illusions, idiosyncratic and/or culturally taught, but they usually result in new delusions and illusions and in even less accurate perceptions and beliefs in some respects than before. Cognitive processes such as memory, attention span, control over impulsivity, and especially judgment are often impaired for much longer periods than the acute episodes themselves, and euphoric or dysphoric emotions may continue, often appearing "inappropriate" to others and sometimes to the person himself. The way in which the individual is classified according to the official psychiatric nomenclature depends upon the stage and circumstances during which he is examined, as well as who examines him, etc.

As each individual has lived in a somewhat different phenomenal world and has belonged to a different set of groups-of-reference from every other individual, and is subjected to a different environment and sequence of external events during his episodes, the *individual differences and communication difficulties among those who have experienced psychotic episodes tend to be much greater than among those who have not,* especially as the insights and ideas developed are often among those which cannot be expressed within the vocabulary of the individual or, even worse, among those which the language of the culture tends to militate against or rule out of existence or awareness. The kindness which a long-term patient may show toward a new one in a mental hospital is perhaps usually accompanied not by an understanding of that individual but simply by the realization that his phenomenal world, whatever it was, has collapsed, as did the long-term patient's world at some time in the past.

A GENERAL PRINCIPLE of social psychology is that members of groups are usually less open in their communications to outsiders than to other members of their own groups, i.e., tend to give less full and accurate information, to voice their convictions or doubts less freely, etc.[4] The importance of this principle for the field of so-called "mental illness" can hardly be overemphasized, because the labelling of an individual as "mentally ill," "emotionally disturbed," "psychotic," "schizophrenic," "paranoid," etc., immediately moves the individual either entirely outside the group, or at least toward the periphery. Whereas the designated patient often needs fuller and more accurate information than before, the information he receives is usually both less complete and less accurate. At the time when he is suffering most from feelings of alienation, he is likely to be treated in such a way as to increase his alienation, especially as he may behave in a way that is especially unattractive or repellent to others. Any demand for additional information is easily construed as "paranoid" by those who see no reason for his lack of trust, and who are thus blind without realizing it (Goffman, 1961). When people lie or withhold relevant information they usually, if not always, do so imperfectly; in other words, they emit incongruent messages. These incongruent messages often place the receiver into a "double bind" (Bateson, *et al.*, 1956). *Lying and withholding of relevant information are perhaps the major causes of "mental illness," as well as the major ways in which such "illnesses" are perpetuated.*

Jung emphasized long ago that the road to individuation is narrow as a razor's edge, fraught with peril, and that only a few fail to lose their way. As an individual begins to see things as they are, in a way he has not done before — to see clearly not only his own blind and seamy past but also the stupidity, irrationality, cruelty, and blindness of his own culture and groups-of-reference, he must have not only great tolerance for pain, including feelings of alienation and uncanny emotions; unless he has advantages such as knowledge, power, status (albeit this is a two-edged sword), devoted friends and relatives, and financial independence, the burden is likely to be beyond the endurance of any human being. The restriction of the "sacred" mushrooms to high-caste individuals, found in some societies, makes considerable sense in this respect.

The solution found in Zen Buddhism and formulated clearly by Alan Watts of becoming a "joker," i.e., one who has seen through the arbitrariness or absurdity of social "games" but is able to "play" them anyway, is helpful but not sufficient, because, as Watts would presumably agree, *some social "games" must not be played but broken up,* if we are to avoid a complete Hell on Earth. For example, the "game" of "blame the Jews," "played" in Nazi Germany and in many previous and subsequent times and places, e.g., in Western Europe during the 14th century, when the Black Death was blamed on the Jews, must be broken up, although to be a "joker" might under some conditions be necessary as a device enabling one to operate underground in a different way, i.e., decently.

71

Some patients who refuse to leave mental hospitals are no longer interested in the "games" which people on the outside insist upon "playing," among these "games" being those of "blame it on the ex-patients," "be kind to ex-patients but be careful about trusting them or telling them the truth," "one step forward, one step back," "your private life is my business," "last things first, first things last," "if you don't believe it, pretend you do anyway," "don't let your right hand know what your left hand is doing," "be both prudish and pornographic," "be both mechanistic and mystical," "sentence first, trial afterward," "be both a coward and a gentleman," etc.[5] Some patients also have a partly justifiable punitive attitude toward society — "since you say I'm crazy, you can pay my room and board, indefinitely."

All the psychedelic or "mind-manifesting" drugs attack the defense of compartmentalization and thus make it possible for an individual to see through some of the absurdities, including status systems, of his own behavior, and of his own culture and groups-of-reference.[6] This, I believe, is the most important basis for attempts to ban or restrict the uses of these drugs, even more than the fact that, unlike alcohol, they make possible great pleasure without subsequent punishment, contrary to the long-standing "moral" dicta of Western civilization. The distinction, however, between "transcendental experiences" and "experimental psychoses" is, in my opinion, extremely unfortunate, and has resulted in a failure to recognize the great contribution that can be made by these drugs to an understanding of what we have been calling "psychosis." Several years ago the author heard Harold Abramson remark that *every time someone takes a large dose of LSD-25 he undergoes an experimental psychosis.* At that time I thought Dr. Abramson, who had worked extensively with this drug for several years, old-fashioned, and privately congratulated myself on being more informed and up-to-date, or even ahead-of-my-time. Now I am in complete agreement with his statement, granted that the term "experimental psychosis" can give a very misleading impression about drug experiences and that an "experimental psychosis" and a "real psychosis" are usually very different in some very important respects.[7]

The fact that an experience is extravagantly satisfying, in terms of emotions, sensations, and fantasy, complete with technicolor and sound-track, creatively and productively loaded with valid insights, does not justify our not labelling it "psychotic," unless we are to drop the word altogether. To avoid using the word "psychotic," reserving the latter only for the frightened, suspicious, obviously deluded, depressed, constricted, or empty experiences, is to overlook what mental health experts — with the exception of Jung and a few other voices crying in the wilderness — have traditionally minimized, i.e., the *constructive* aspects of "psychosis." That "psychotic" experiences can be emotionally gratifying is grudgingly recognized in many descriptions of patients, but seldom does one find even a grudging recognition of the possible beneficial effects of these emotional orgies. The views of religious mysticism which have been held by most psychologists and psychiatrists make this one-sidedness particularly obvious. There is virtually no recognition of the possible value of *dysphoric* emotions. When it comes to cognition, there is again very little recognition of the constructive or creative aspects of psychosis, despite the repeated lesson from history that people who put forth truly new ideas — or old ideas which are unpopular or unfashionable — have often if not usually been said to be "insane," and that there has often been some truth in such accusations.[8] In fact, labelling the innovator as "insane" has been a standard method of fighting genuinely new ideas, as opposed to old ideas whose deceptive rewordings are eagerly accepted as the latest fashion. It was the irrationality of this kind of opposition to new ideas which led William James to remark that one of the least important objections that can be made to any theory is that the man who invented it was insane. James's remark can be generalized: *one of the least important objections that can be made to any statement whatsoever is that the man who made it is "psychotic" or "mentally ill" or "emotionally disturbed."* By "least important objection" we understand that we are concerned with the *validity of the statement* and not with the question of giving the individual power over others, setting him up as a model for others to attempt to emulate, or encouraging the wholesale acceptance of everything he has said, or will say in the future.

Hell is at least as instructive as Heaven, and out of the Hell called "experimental psychosis" can come changes in the individual which are just as valuable or even more so than those arising from "transcendental experiences." The tendency to give the patient or subject as gratifying and "wonderful" an experience as possible, to protect him from later trouble, and to assert that those who have "bad experiences" or later conflict have not taken the drug in a "proper" context or with the "proper" preparation is a form of conservatism; the preceding word is not intended, however, to assign this attitude to the lowest regions of Hell. It is kind to help people to grow, change, or regress (in the service of the ego, of course) gradually and relatively painlessly, but *it should not be assumed that gradual and painless change is always possible, or even necessarily desirable*. In a world as irrational as ours, to be fully human one must be capable of taking great and sudden pain.

Although raptures about "transcendental experiences" often focus primarily on the visual splendors and lofty insights into the meaning of existence and the universe and the increase in aesthetic sensitivity, the real source of enthusiasm is much more likely to be the strong feelings and bodily sensations which are aroused, often for the first time in many years or since the individual was very young. The ban on emotional expression, especially in Anglo-Saxon cultures and especially among men, makes the enthusiasm and wonder arising from drug-induced states readily understandable, because without emotional expression the emotions themselves wither away.[9] To attribute one's enthusiasm to feelings and sensations is less congruent with these cultures than to praise the "higher level" processes. The same has been true in religious mysticism, although it has been pointed out many times that the bodily sensations in religious mysticism have become painfully obvious on occasion, e.g., when saints have "gone wild" and shouted that they desired the body of Jesus.[10] In revivalism, also, emotional gratification is apparently the most important source of enthusiasm, although to the individual who has been "saved" the cognitive "insights" are believed to be the primary source (Sargant, 1957). Some individuals who have been "saved" have frequently felt good for months and have been able to live comfortably without searching for feeling through "sin," only to "fall from grace" eventually. Similarly, following gratifying emotional orgies during drug sessions, many subjects have been able to live for a time in their usual routine manner without boredom, eventually to crave another gratifying orgy, which may be conceptualized primarily as an opportunity to rise to a "higher" level of existence or knowledge, etc. The same can be said of many individuals who have experienced intense emotions during "depth" psychotherapy. The search for "meaning" in life is usually in large part a search for feeling; unless the individual becomes aware of the nature of his search, he may spend his life in a never-ending pursuit of cognitive "insights" or "understandings," like those scholars and scientists who keep searching for a "discovery" when their greatest needs would be met by standing up openly for what they already know or believe, thus exposing themselves to the danger and excitement of external conflict.[11]

All paths to individuation, whether through "psychosis," drug states, psychotherapy, Zen Buddhism, general semantics, philosophy, solitary confinement, Catholicism, Calvinism, thinking and reading on one's own, etc., are effective only if the individual can accept the chaff with the wheat, only if he can look squarely at the horrors of the world as well as its joys and beauty, can tolerate a variety of emotions (and thus supply his body with a variety of drugs), and can summon up the courage to act in accordance with his moral principles as well as his more obvious needs, and thus have some self-respect. In a society as hypocritical as ours is today, *the most socially unacceptable and dangerous acts are those which are most in accordance with the private moral convictions of the individual.* This is true not only for "intellectuals" and "worldly" people, but for "peasants" and "small-minded" people as well, because there are powerful individuals and groups on most sides of most fences, and because there is widespread cynicism about "fighting City Hall" and about standing up openly for one's private knowledge and convictions.

WESTERN CIVILIZATION has gone through a number of cycles or spirals which can be described as (1) the setting up of rules or "games"; (2) the development of hypocrisy, i.e., a discrepancy between the way things are — and are privately known to be, especially by those having access to large amounts of accurate information — and the way they are publicly acknowledged to be; and (3) the reduction of some forms of hypocrisy and the setting up of "new" rules. All three phases are present at any one time, with one or another phase dominant with respect to a given set of rules. Hypocrisy develops when official rules make satisfaction in living difficult or impossible — as, e.g., excessive official restrictions on emotional expression, sexual conduct, open conflict, excessive definition of role, etc.

In eliminating or reducing hypocrisy a *standardization* or *normalization* of the population has in past times occurred, and such normalizations have been extremely cruel and unjust, as certain individuals and groups have served as totem animals, taking on the projected collective guilt of the tribe, arising from hypocrisy, among other sources.[12] The "new" rules have tended to be the old rules in disguised form, or modified versions which have been even worse; some forms of hypocrisy are retained and new forms are created.

To a limited degree one must agree with the prophets of doom (Spengler, Toynbee, Sorokin) that Western civilization has been rolling downhill (Geyl, 1958). The normalization may occur under various headings: in southern France (Languedoc) in the 13th and 14th centuries and in many other areas during the same and succeeding centuries, under the heading of eliminating "heresy"; in Calvin's Geneva during the 16th century, under the heading of turning the citizens into sincere and honest "Christians"; throughout Western Europe during the 16th and 17th centuries, under the heading of eliminating "witchcraft"; and in 20th century Russia and Germany, under the heading of developing good "Communists" and "Nazis," respectively. *Each of these headings concealed certain normalizations which would have been impossible or more difficult to carry out if seen clearly for what they were.*

Secrecy has been of obvious advantage in normalizations. A second weapon is a principle made explicit by the inquisitors, by Calvin, and by the Communists and Nazis, which can be stated as follows: *a person who is off the norm in one respect is likely to be off the norm in another respect.* For example, a person who dressed oddly was suspect as a heretic. One of the most cruel of the inquisitors, Robert le Bugre, a reformed Patarin (Cathar), claimed to be able to detect a heretic by the manner in which he moved.[13] Although ordinary citizens could help in rooting out heresy by informing anonymously on anyone who seemed "off the norm," *only an ideologist (inquisitor) could determine whether the individual was actually a heretic.* Since statistical studies were even worse than they are today, the "norms" themselves could be located conveniently in the fantasies of the ideologists, and could also be decreed by them to a considerable extent, as they gained power. Thus, the ideologists were able, in all these times and places, to "normalize" the population along whatever lines they desired or thought necessary. Languedoc had a culture distinctly different from that of northern Europe, and was in general more advanced. Under the heading of eliminating "heresy" it was transformed in the direction of northern France — the southerners, including devout Catholics, had to be "normalized."[14] The elimination of "witchcraft," from the latter part of the 15th to the early part of the 18th century, was, among other things, the virtual liquidation of the remnants of a religion many centuries older than Christianity.[15] Calvin, who had been called the "accusative case" by his more aristocratic and perhaps more ruthless and dishonest schoolmates, transformed the image of man a step downward from that of the Catholic theologians, from "deprived" to "depraved," and liquidated or drove away the old aristocratic families of Geneva, many of whom belonged to the political party known as "Libertines." (It is worth noting that although Calvin never set foot in the New World, he has been probably as important to the development of the U. S. A. as any other man of modern times.[16]) The early Communist ideologists planned freedom in personal life and the "withering away of the state," but as class warfare progressed it was discovered that sex "immorality" was incompatible with being a good Communist, and that the State was helpful in keeping the masses in their proper places (Reich, 1962). During the Nazi revolution the Prussian military leaders, the old aristocracy, had to become even more cold and cruel than they had been before and to revise their standards of honor in the direction of those of a middle class individual much more cynically contemptuous of average human beings than they were.

During and immediately following a normalization, no one is allowed to be himself, as no one fits the "ideal" which is officially held and enforced; thus, alienation from parts of oneself is produced, with resulting fear and hatred which are then displaced toward those who are discernibly "different," i.e., outsiders, who are made into scapegoats. The great cruelty during normalization can be at least partly explained on the basis of this kind of process.

The drastic ideological changes and shifts of power which occur during normalization increase the frequency of psychotic episodes and other disturbances. *Mental illness is thus mixed in with religious, class, ideological, racial, and ethnic warfare.* The thesis that many of the "witches" were "mentally ill" is not incompatible with the thesis that many were followers of the Old Religion, or that many were members of the old landed gentry, who sometimes cling to old religions, especially out in the provinces, or that many were poor and ignorant. When one considers the widespread existence of practices such as forcing children to watch as their grandmothers or mothers were burned alive (Lea, 1939) — this was done by German Lutherans — it would seem strange if "mental illness" were not prevalent during that period. These children probably saw, without being able to formulate their perception clearly, that they were in the hands of destructive giant robots unaware of their irrational cruelty. Many of the children being labelled "schizophrenic" today may have had similar perceptions.

77

Both hypocrisy and the reduction of hypocrisy tend to increase the incidence of mental and emotional disturbances. During both phases behavior tends to be formal, secretive, and robot-like; people feel alienated and distrustful. Information "leaks out" or is deliberately provided, and *the people who are most likely to be precipitated into psychotic episodes (by sudden insights) are those from whom certain facts have been carefully concealed, in other words, women, especially old women.* When normalization starts, many people are "scared stiff" and thus are even more robot-like, suspicious, and cautious. The "schizophrenic" perception of individuals as mechanical puppets is probably a valid perception; the "schizophrenic" sees the robotization that Fromm (1941) and others have described. This perception can also be attained by means of the psychedelic drugs.

The greatly increased exposure to facts and ideas, through mass communication media, travel in foreign countries, etc., can greatly increase the frequency of psychotic episodes, according to the present theory. It is interesting, for example, that an "uneducated" person in a small town can purchase a paperback in a five-and-ten which can reveal to him that some of the peculiar ideas which for years he has taken as a sign of his secret insanity or depravity have been written about by Plato, Whitehead, Russell, Freud, Fromm, Carnap, etc.[17]

Hypocrisy is an unstable social condition, as everyone has to operate in a fog, but the reduction of hypocrisy can in theory be brought about by openly allowing people to be different and human, without a normalization. If our country avoids a normalization, it will be the first accomplishment of this kind in the history of Western civilization; nevertheless, there is reason for hope. Normalization requires the consolidation of power, and it is much more difficult to consolidate power in the U.S.A. than in any of the previous times and places, for the following reasons: there are two major cultures (with many influential sub-cultures), two major political parties, several large communication media, many powerful individuals and groups, and there are many checks and balances on an over-concentration of power within government. Furthermore, women, who find it more difficult to be deliberately cruel than do men, have much more power. Nevertheless, there is danger, as indicated by the following signs of the times: the tendency for activities to go "underground," so that it is difficult to obtain information which one believes that he has a right to know;[18] the ridicule of old women (most of whom have done the best they could with what they have known); the emphasis on the public importance of one's private life; the attacks on fraternal organizations; the attacks on the old religion of Christianity; and the formation of new secret societies.[19]

There are those who wish to normalize this country under the heading of having only "good Americans"; others wish to normalize under the heading of eliminating or preventing "mental illness" (Szasz, 1961; Gross, 1962). An example of the first is an item which appeared in the *New York Times Western Edition* on Nov. 1, 1962, headed "Ideological split fills Amarillo with bitterness and suspicion." Among its other activities, the John Birch Society had attempted to purge schools and libraries of "Communist" reading matter. Several books, however, were removed for alleged "obscenities"; among these were four Pulitzer Prize novels and George Orwell's *Nineteen Eighty-Four,* a satire on collectivist society. Thus, under the self-deceptive heading of "eliminating Communism" comes a "clean-up," even though the Russians are apparently much "cleaner" than Americans and have objected to the "immoral" behavior of Americans visiting their country. All the previous normalizations have included "clean-ups" — that is why Europe is so clean. "Sex perversion," for example, was "cleaned up" in Germany by the inquisitors and later by the Nazis; these "clean-ups" account for the current absence of "sex perversion" in that country, just as the "clean-up" of prostitution in San Francisco in the 1930's accounts for the current absence of prostitution in that fair city. What has been virtually eliminated in "clean-ups" has not been "unclean" acts, which have if anything increased as exclusive pursuits, but love and friendship, which cowards envy and take satisfaction in destroying, reducing everyone else to their own empty and lonely condition. Any "lower" animal which could be taught to revile or be alienated from parts of its own body and the bodies of other members of its own species could easily be seen to be "mean and crazy." There are few data on this point; an experiment by Birch (1956) is relevant. In this experiment, hoods were placed around the necks of pregnant rats so that they were prevented from the usual self-licking of the anogenital region which is increased during pregnancy. When their young were born, these mother rats, with hoods removed, ate most of their pups and failed to nourish the rest adequately; none survived. The most "mean and crazy" humans, however, have not been female.

The possibility that normalization could occur under the heading of "eliminating mental illness" is illustrated by a remark made by a leading psychoanalyst, Dr. Bernard Diamond, in addressing the Santa Clara County Mental Health Association — "A person who is off the norm in one respect is likely to be off in another respect." This is the principle referred to earlier, made explicit by the inquisitors and later by Nazi and Communists. Dr. Diamond himself is a relatively outspoken defender of the rights of individuals to live their private lives in the manner they choose rather than the manner he would choose for them; his statement, however, could easily be used in the service of tyranny by experts or others more power-hungry. Szasz (1961) has made a brief comparison between institutional psychiatrists and inquisitors, but even better analogies can be drawn between some psychotherapists in clinics and in private practice, and inquisitors. Members of the public, e.g., teachers and physicians, are encouraged to watch for "subtle signs of mental illness" (signs of heresy, signs of witchcraft) and to refer or report such individuals to the proper authorities for help, and outpatient treatment is now offered on an involuntary, as well as a voluntary, basis. Psychiatrists may be able to achieve much more power than they have at present, but if they do not align themselves on the side of the rights of individuals, they will become even more hated and feared than were the inquisitors. This remark should not be construed as an endorsement of "rights" such as walking down the street shouting insults or making scary faces, physical assault, vandalism, urinating on a busy street in broad daylight, etc. If we are to preserve our freedoms, however, *involuntary* confinement resulting from such acts should be for a stated maximum length of time, not an indefinite stretch the termination of which is to be decided by an ideologist.

DURING CULTURAL REVOLUTIONS the dominant ideologists provide the rationalization for normalization. Psychology (broadly defined) is now, as before, a focal point of ideological controversy. Modern psychodynamic theories (and some learning theories and theories of interpersonal relations) share with medieval theology (the psychology of that era) the following characteristics: (1) complexity; (2) formulation in learned language unknown to the vast majority of people; (3) the appearance of objectivity, at the same time allowing sufficient concealed and self-deceptive subjectivity to be used in the service of the ideologists; (4) the principle of reversal, so that someone or something can be shown by the ideologist to be "in reality" just the opposite from what he or it appears to be to the unlearned observer; and (5) an emphasis on sex and other puzzling and troublesome aspects of human or extra-human relationships such as status, power, or control. These are highly desirable characteristics for an ideology which can be used to divide, conquer, and establish tyranny.

Concepts which would interfere with normalization and with those forms of hypocrisy which are retained or created tend to become extinct or to be considered inadequate, irrational, or old-fashioned. Among these concepts are courage, honor, decency, integrity, loyalty, truth, friendship, honesty, love, kindness, fun, and fair-play.[20] These concepts have been largely ignored in the psychology of our time, as the reader can check for himself by examining the subject index of *Psychological Abstracts,* which covers many "disciplines" in addition to psychology and includes foreign as well as domestic references. For example, during the 36 years of its publication, the index lists nine references under "courage," the latest being in 1948.[21]

Ideologies preserve certain attitudes and ideas within the culture and eliminate others. Old ideas and attitudes are reworded and claimed to be new discoveries by the ideologists, especially those who are ignorant of history and of the sociology of knowledge. The dominant ideology of the U. S. A. has been Calvinism, and some psychological theories and methodologies (as well as some varieties of "common sense") are more-or-less disguised forms of Calvinism (Fromm, 1941). Calvinism had several facets, including a mean and crazy aspect exemplified by the beheading of a child in Calvin's Geneva for striking one of his parents, thus upholding "parental authority." This mean and crazy aspect of Calvinism was carried to the U.S.A. in many ways, e.g., in the old Connecticut "blue laws" which gave fathers the legal right to kill disobedient sons (Dollard & Miller, 1950). Calvin outlawed most types of pleasure, even in the privacy of one's own home, and this aspect of Calvinism was also imported (Smith, 1954).[22]

Individuals who oppose powerful social institutions are sometimes labelled "insane." An instructive example is Thomas of Apulia, who in the 14th century, when Western Europe resembled an old-fashioned asylum, preached that what was needed was more love and less theology and Church ritual, that the reign of the Holy Ghost had supplanted that of the Father and Son, and that he was the envoy of the Holy Ghost sent to reform the world. The learned theologians of the University of Paris burned his book, and he was pronounced insane by medical alienists and committed to life imprisonment, probably as a means of discrediting his work (crowds had been listening to him) more than as a "humane" alternative to the stake. Yet men like Thomas have been relatively sane, whereas *"homo normalis,"* as Wilhelm Reich (1949) called him, has often been mean and crazy, and this has been especially true of his cynical leaders.

One method of reducing hypocrisy and at the same time preventing normalization is to defend the right to be "crazy" in the sense of (1) seeking and loving the truth;[23] (2) loving people instead of hating them;[24] (3) openly respecting the rights of others to be different from oneself and one's own friends or colleagues; (4) living primarily in accordance with values other than status, power, security, or material possessions; (5) openly challenging powerful authorities and institutions; and (6) being a socially unacceptable truth-teller instead of a socially acceptable liar.

◆ ◆ ◆

Summary

A theory of psychosis as a sudden and drastic change in cognitive structure has been presented. The ways in which socialization, including deception, creates cognitive structures which change rapidly upon exposure to new information have been described. The psychedelic drugs attack compartmentalization and thus produce insights into some of the absurdities within the individual and also within the social structure in which he is embedded. The constructive aspects of psychosis, "experimental" or real, have been greatly neglected in the literature. Psychology is a focal point in ideological conflict, as it has been in past cultural revolutions. Normalization, i.e., the reduction or elimination of certain individual differences and human qualities, has accompanied the reduction of hypocrisy in previous cultural revolutions, but there are reasons to believe that hypocrisy can be reduced in the U. S. A. without such normalization. Suggestions are made for the accomplishment of this objective.

FOOTNOTES

[1] The ideas expressed herein are in large part the result of the observations and experiences of the author during the two years of his tenure as USPHS Fellow, 1958-1960, and as a staff member of NIMH Project MY-2621, located at the Mental Research Institute, Palo Alto Medical Research Foundation, Don D. Jackson, Principal Investigator, James Terrill, Staff Psychologist, Charles Savage and Jerome Oremland, Research Associates. Grateful acknowledgment is made to Thomas Gonda, Department of Psychiatry, Stanford University, who sponsored my fellowship application, and to Leo Hollister, Richard Hamister and John Sears, who cooperated in the biweekly administration of LSD-25 to two hospitalized patients over a period of many months at the VA Hospital, Palo Alto. The views expressed herein are emphatically the sole responsibility of the author, who experienced a psychotic

reaction lasting several months following a 200 μg LSD-25 session, without hospitalization, and one year later managed to experience a spectacular psychotic episode without benefit of drugs, resulting in one month's hospitalization. The statements herein are by no means free of the biases or values of the author; for example, I do not like to see people kept deceived or locked up for years in order to help preserve respectability, the sex mores, or status systems. I have no complaints whatsoever concerning my own treatment, and I consider myself extremely fortunate indeed.

2 The epistemological position of the author is similar to and perhaps identical with that taken by the founders of Gestalt psychology long ago and recently discovered by many others. See, for example, Koffka, 1935, and Kohler, 1938.

3 A beautiful and moving literary expression of the idea that people are only half-awake is found in Thornton Wilder's play, *Our Town.* Al Hubbard, one of the pioneer workers with LSD-25, expressed this idea very well by the informal remark, "Most people are walking in their sleep; turn them around, start them in the opposite direction, and they wouldn't even know the difference."

4 This statement assumes that group membership is *defined* in other ways; in other words, the statement is intended as an empirical assertion, not as a tautology. Important exceptions sometimes occur when anonymity is guaranteed, when the recipient of information is sworn to secrecy, etc. The free exchange of "confidential" information about designated "patients" between "experts" whose group membership is defined in terms of being "expert," accounts for the feeling of alienation which some "experts" have toward their "patients," to whom these "experts" never say anything which they believe would not be "good" for the "patient." Such "experts" are very similar to many other politicians.

5 " 'No, no!' said the Queen. 'Sentence first — verdict afterwards.'
" 'Stuff and nonsense!' said Alice loudly. 'The idea of having the sentence first'
" 'Hold your tongue!' said the Queen, turning purple. . . ." (quoted by Jourdain (1918, p. 96) from *Alice's Adventures in Wonderland.*)

6 Unfortunately these drugs have sometimes resulted in new status systems which compete in absurdity with any others in existence, including those in psychoanalytic circles.

7 It is especially important that the subject understand that the drug is responsible for his craziness or his loftiness and that his craziness or his loftiness will be only temporary. When drugs are given without the subject's knowledge, as, e.g., certain criminals have been reported to have done in India with a mixture of marijuana and datura, the "experimental psychosis" can become very real indeed. See Osmond and Hoffer (1958).

8 Sir Isaac Newton is an example of someone who became "psychotic" after putting forth a new idea, experimentally demonstrable, and seeing how his learned colleagues in the Royal Academy reacted. He did not publish again for about 20 years, meanwhile writing "metaphysics" (which is kept locked up, a source of embarrassment to physicists).

9 Smith (1954) tells of the history of what the early Puritans called the heresy of Antinomianism, of giving way to subjective conviction, emotion, and impulsivity. Southerners were considered generally tainted with this terrible heresy. It survives as a form of "mental illness" or a "sign" of mental illness, especially according to northern experts.

10 It has usually not been noted that such a desire may be very rational in a world in which men consider some parts of their bodies "dirty" and look upon virginity as the "highest" state of womanhood.

11 Much of what is called "epistemology" and "methodology" is a complex

and deceptive rationalization of cowardice. This has been particularly obvious in the field of philosophy, in which the convenient though double-edged idea developed very early that one cannot know or communicate anything — "Nothing is; or, if anything is, it cannot be known; or, if anything is and can be known, it cannot be communicated," (Gorgias, ca. 500 B.C.). The principle is also readily discernible in psychology, history, and the social sciences. One form of this principle was called the "good taste psychosis" by Harry Elmer Barnes, who added that the good taste psychosis among respectable historians was the greatest enemy of truth in his field.

[12] Among these have been especially the following: women, children, old people, followers of old religions, the old aristocracy, people in the "provinces," uneducated people, especially of the "lower classes," Jews, Gypsies, and people who are "odd," who don't "fit in." Most of these totem animals cannot easily fight back; that explains their selection as totem animals. Remnants of the old aristocracy who have managed to retain some power are discredited on the basis of their "bad" sex lives, or allegations thereof.

[13] The English word "bugger," and similar vernacular expressions in French and Italian, stem from the word "Bugres," by which the Cathari were designated because of their Bulgarian origin. The full significance of this derivation is not known to the present author, but Robert's cruelty illustrates how dangerous it can be to reform someone. He was finally locked up himself.

[14] Current attempts to describe southern U. S. A. character structure in pathological terms can be partly understiod in terms of the general phenomenon of acculturating conquered territory. This is not to say that these attempts are invalid, but that northern character structure is also pathological, though in a different way. The northern treatment of Negroes, for example, is at least as irrational as the southern treatment, though in a way which differs behaviorally and psychodynamically. There has never been a culture that has not created pathological character structures, i.e., all "national character structures" are pathological in some ways and to some extent.

[15] Christianity as actually practiced was by no means always clearly distinct from the Cult of the Horned God, just as in contemporary Latin America Christianity is not always distinct from the indigenous Indian religions.

[16] One of the author's grandiose delusions during his real psychosis was that he was a reincarnation of John Calvin, among other historical figures. My conviction that it would be salutary to lock everyone in solitary confinement at least once during his lifetime shows that this delusion, like most, has at least a grain of truth. I was also tortured by the delusion that I was an actual descendent of that mean hypocrite, John Knox, the founder of Scottish Presbyterianism.

[17] Many philosophers, e.g., Nietzsche, Schopenhauer, Wittgenstein, have gone "insane." It seems probable that they saw through the absurdities of their own cultures, i.e., they ate of the forbidden fruit of the tree of knowledge (cf. May, 1961).

[18] Several writers, e.g., Hanson Baldwin, have recently written of the prevalence of the mentality that values secrecy even when it is clearly unnecessary.

[19] The secret patriotic societies of the 1840's and 1850's, members of which were called "Know Nothings" by outsiders, are interesting antecedents of such societies at the present time.

[20] A reputable psychologist has been unable to find a publisher for a manuscript on love behavior, containing empirical data of a non-obscene variety. One publisher informed him that the topic was not of sufficient interest. When a professor of psychology at one of our leading universities

announced that a graduate student was planning a dissertation on the subject of friendship, another member of the department exclaimed in surprise, "Friendship! — What kind of damned topic is that?" The Association for Humanistic Psychology has been formed to attempt to encourage interest and research in these and related concepts.

21 John F. Kennedy (1956) and Sir Compton Mackenzie (1962) have written interesting books on the subject of moral courage, but their works are not abstracted, as they are not members of our learned groups.

22 For example, whereas the State of California has outlawed drunkenness only in public places, the City of San Jose has an ordinance against being drunk anywhere within the city limits, including one's own home. It is true that no attempt is made to enforce this ordinance, but neither is it repealed as absurd. The State statute is used discriminately: "respectable" citizens found drunk in public places are either left alone or escorted discreetly to their homes, whereas "lower" class people are often thrown into the "drunk" tank or taken involuntarily to a mental hospital, etc. This is an example, though not one of the worst, of hypocrisy as defined earlier.

23 Translated into what is sometimes considered "scientific" psychodynamic theory, this means that someone has repressed his desire to sleep with the null class. The idea that the concept of truth is dispensable is an old idea, "discovered" by various scientists and philosophers of this century. La Barre (1954) gives one form of this idea, stating that truth in mathematics is relative to what is called "mathematics" within the culture. This is similar to the view of mathematics presented to psychologists by S. S. Stevens (1951), with a different formulation. It is correct for parts of mathematics but not for other parts, especially the oldest parts such as the theory of numbers (Myhill, 1952, 1960).

One of the most deflating papers ever written is that by Ness (1938). In this paper Ness demonstrated that people, selected more-or-less haphazardly off the street, expressed all the concepts of truth to be found among the writings of philosophers. One can imagine how this discovery endeared him to his learned colleagues.

On loving psychology, see Bugental (1962).

24 Although I do not love everybody, I try not to hate anyone. Sometimes, however, I apparently do not try hard enough; I would be delighted to read in the newspaper that certain "experts" had been eaten by crows, and that some of the oversized cowards in high public and private office had fallen overboard on one of their many voyages, been caught in nets, sliced up and boiled down for whale oil. In baboon societies the larger and stronger males remain on the outskirts, as the colony moves along the ground, and thus are the first to encounter danger. This demonstrates that large baboons tend to have more courage and *noblesse oblige* than many large men. There are, nevertheless, some large men of the right type — these are the ones who are not afraid of someone who shows that he is not afraid of them. Mr. Crawford Greenwalt is an example of a man in a high position who could do a great deal more for this country than criticize the psychological testing industry (Gross, 1962). Like Gross, he fails to see, or at least to say, that this horrendous industry is carrying out the directives of more powerful agents and of impersonal social forces.

References

Adams, J. K. Concepts as operators. *Psychol. Rev.*, 1953, 60, 241-251.

Adams, J. K. Differentiation and dedifferentiation in healthy functioning. *J. Human. Psychol.*, 1961, 1, No. 2, 30-38.

THE PSYCHEDELIC READER

Adams, J. K. The overemphasis on sex in Western civilization — a point of view. *J. Human. Psychol.*, 1963, *3*, No. 1, 54-75.

Anonymous. A new theory of schizophrenia. *J. Abnorm. Soc. Psychol.*, 1958, *57*, 226-236.

Asch, S. *Social Psychology.* New York: Prentice-Hall, 1952.

Bateson, G., Jackson, D. D., Haley, J., and Weakland, J. H. Toward a theory of schizophrenia. *Behavioral Sci.*, 1956, *1*, 251-264.

Bazelon, D. L. Crime and insanity. In *The mentally ill offender: a symposium.* Sacramento: Dept. of Mental Hygiene, 1960.

Beers, C. W. *A mind that found itself.* New York: Doubleday, 1921.

Birch, H. G. Sources of order in the maternal behavior of animals. *Amer. J. Orthopsych.*, 1956, *26*, 279-284.

Boisen, A. T. *The exploration of the inner world.* Chicago, New York: Willett, Clark, 1936.

Bugental, J. F. T. Precognitions of a fossil. *J. Human. Psychol.* 1962, *2*, No. 2, 38-46.

Bugental, J. F. T. Self-fragmentation as a resistance to self-actualization. *Rev. Exist. Psychol. & Psychiat.*, 1962, *2*, 241-248.

Carnap, R. *Meaning and necessity.* Chicago: Univ. of Chicago, 1947.

Carroll, L. *Alice's adventures in Wonderland, Through the looking-glass,* and *The hunting of the snark.* New York: Modern Library.

Chandler, A. L. and Hartman, M. A. Lysergic acid diethylamdie (LSD-25) as a facilitating agent in psychotherapy. *AMA Arch. Gen. Psychiatry*, 1960, *2*, 286-299.

Cohen, S. Notes on the hallucinogenic state. *Int. Rec. Med.*, 1960, *173*, 380-387.

Dobbs, Z., *et al. Keynes at Harvard.* Revised edition. New York: Veritas Foundation, 1962.

Dollard, J. & Miller, N. *Personality and psychotherapy.* New York: Mc-Graw-Hill, 1950.

Fromm, E. *Escape from freedom.* New York: Farrar & Rinehart, 1941.

Geyl, P. *Debates with historians.* New York: Meridian Books, 1958.

Goffman, E. *Asylums.* Garden City, N. Y.: Doubleday-Anchor, 1961.

Goffman, E. *Presentation of self in everyday life.* Garden City, N. Y.: Doubleday-Anchor, 1959.

Gross, M. L. *The brain watchers.* New York: Random House, 1962.

Hebb, D. O. *The organization of behavior.* New York: Wiley 1949.

Hoffer, E. *The true believer.* New York: Harper, 1951.

Jourdain, P. E. B. *The philosophy of Mr. B*rtr*nd R*ss*l.* London: Allen & Unwin, 1918.

Jung, C. *Two essays on analytical psychology*. New York: Meridian Books, 1956.

Kelly, G. A. *The psychology of personal constructs*. New York: Norton, 1955.

Kennedy, J. F. *Profiles in courage*. New York: Harper, 1956.

Kesey, K. *One flew over the cuckoo's nest*. New York: Viking, 1962.

Krech, D. & Crutchfield, R. S. *Theory and problems of social psychology*. New York: McGraw-Hill, 1948.

Kohler, W. *The place of value in a world of facts*. New York: Liverright, 1938.

Koffka, K. *Principles of Gestalt psychology*. New York: Harcourt-Brace, 1935.

Korzybski, A. *Science and sanity*. Third edition. Lakeville, Conn.: International Non-Aristotelian Library, 1948.

La Barre, W. *The human animal*. Chicago: University of Chicago, 1954.

Lea, H. C. *History of sacerdotal celibacy in the Christian Church*. Third edition, revised. London: Williams & Norgate, 1907.

Lea, H. C. *The inquisition of the middle ages*. New York: Macmillian, 1961. (An abridged version of a much longer work first published in 1887-1888.)

Lea, H. C. *Materials toward a history of witchcraft*. Philadelphia: Univ. of Pennsylvania, 1939. New York, London: Thomas Yoseloff, 1957.

Lemert, E. M. Paranoia and the dynamics of exclusion. *Sociometry*, 1962, *25*, 2-20.

Mackenzie, C. *Certain aspects of moral courage*. New York: Doubleday, 1962.

Matthew, *et al*. *The New Testament*.

May, R. The meaning of the Oedipus myth. *Rev. Exist. Psychol. and Psychiat.*, 1961, *1*, 44-52.

McReynolds, P. Anxiety, perception, and schizophrenia. In Jackson, D.D. (Ed.), *The etiology of schizophrenia*. New York: Basic Books, 1960.

Mills, C. W. *Power, politics, and people*. New York: Ballantine, 1963.

Myhill, J. Some philosophical implications of mathematical logic. *Rev. Metaphysics*, 1952, *6*, 165-198.

Myhill, J. Some remarks on the notion of proof. *J. Philos.*, 1960, *57*, 461-471.

Ness, A. 'Truth' as conceived by those who are not professional philosophers. *Skrifter Utgitt av Det. Norske Videnskaps-Akademi i Oslo, II Hist.-Filos. Klasse*, 1938, No. 4.

O'Brien, B. *Operators and things*. Cambridge, Mass.: Arlington Books, 1958.

Osmond, H. A review of the clinical effects of psychotomimetic agents. *Annals New York Acad. Sci.*, 1957, *66*, 418-443.

THE PSYCHEDELIC READER

Osmond, H. & Hoffer, A. The case of Mr. Kovish. *J. Ment. Sci.*, 1958, *104*, 302-325.

Plato. A touchstone for courage. *Psychedelic Rev.,* 1963, *1*, No. 1, 43-46.

Ploscowe, M. *Sex and the law.* New York: Prentice-Hall, 1951.

Reich, W. *Character analysis.* New York: Orgone Institute Press, 1949.

Reich, W. *The sexual revolution.* Fourth edition. New York: Noonday Press, 1962.

Sarbin, T. R. Role theory. In Lindzey, G. (Ed.), *Handbook of social psychology.* Cambridge, Mass.: Addison-Wesley, 1954.

Sargant, W. *Battle for the mind.* Baltimore: Penguin Books, 1961.

Schachtel, E. On memory and childhood amnesia. *Psychiatry,* 1947, *10,* 1-26.

Smith, C. P. *Yankees and God.* New York: Hermitage House, 1954.

Stevens, S. S. Mathematics, measurement, and psychophysics. In Stevens, S. S. (Ed.), *Handbook of experimental psychology.* New York: Wiley, 1951.

Sullivan, H. S. *Schizophrenia as a human process.* New York: Norton, 1962.

Szasz, T. S. *The myth of mental illness.* New York: Hoeber-Harper, 1961.

Taylor, G. Rattray. *Sex in history.* New York: Vanguard, 1954.

Terrill, J., Savage, C., & Jackson, D. D. LSD, transcendence and the new beginning. *J. Nerv. Ment. Disease,* 1962, *135,* 425-439.

Watts, A. W. *Psychotherapy east and west.* New York: Pantheon Books, 1961.

Wilder, T. N. *Our town.* New York: Coward-McCann, 1938.

Botanical Sources of

The New World Narcotics ❖

RICHARD EVANS SCHULTES

Man has learned to rely upon the plant kingdom not only for life's neces-
sities but also its amenities and ameliorants, in virtually every part of the world.
None of the ameliorants has had a more absorbing history nor better shows
man's cleverness and ingenuity than those which we call the *narcotics*.

The very word "narcotic" has taken on a sinister meaning in American
culture. There is probably no field — save perhaps religion and politics —
so replete with popular misinformation and purposeful misrepresentation. This
condition is general, yes, even universal, insofar as the public is concerned.
But its paralysis has invaded even our technical circles. The misuse of the
terms "habit-forming" and "addictive," for example, is found even amongst
our students. It is a fact that there are but two plant narcotics known to
cause addiction and to be physically, morally and socially so dangerous that
they must be strictly controlled — this fact is lost to most people, for whom
it is enough that a substance be called a *narcotic* to draw away aghast.

I use the term "narcotic" in its classic sense. It comes from the Greek
"to benumb" and, therefore, broadly applies to any substance (howsoever
stimulating in one or several stages of its physiological activity) which may
benumb the body.

The use of narcotics is always in some way connected with escape from
reality. From their most primitive uses to their applications in modern medicine, this is true. All narcotics, sometime in their history, have been linked
to religion or magic. This is so even of such narcotics as tobacco, coca and
opium which have suffered secularization — which have come out of the
temple, so to speak, have left the priestly class and have been taken up by
the common man. It is interesting here to note that, when problems do arise
from the employment of narcotics, they arise after the narcotics have passed
from ceremonial to purely hedonic or recreational use. This historical background can explain much, especially when we realize that there are still some

* A composite of two lectures ("Native narcotics of the New World" and
"Botany attacks the hallucinogens") delivered in the Third Lecture Series,
1960, College of Pharmacy, University of Texas, and published in the Texas
Journal of Pharmacy 2 (1961) 141-185. Slight changes from the original
text have been made in several places, and additional information has been
added to bring the treatment of the subject up to date.

89

narcotics used by primitive peoples only in a religious or magic context: peyote is a good example. This is why the botanist who goes out to search for new narcotics in primitive societies must be versed in and sympathetic to anthropological or ethnological fields — and we have come to refer to this type of scientist as an ethnobotanist.

None of the New World narcotics, save tobacco and coca, has assumed a place of importance in modern civilization, and many are still rather unfamiliar even to our botanists, chemists and pharmacologists. It is for this reason that I have chosen, even at the risk of seeming rather superficial, to say a few words about each of the native New World narcotics, with almost all of which I have had personal experience in the field over a long period. By doing this, I hope to give you an overall picture of what we may term the "narcotic complex" of New World peoples. For sundry of these, the literature, though recondite, is extensive, covering many fields of research; but for the greater number, bibliographic sources are few and pertain to only one or two fields of investigation. Reference to tobacco and alcohol, both native American narcotics, will be omitted from this brief article.

The identification of the source plants of American narcotics has interested me since 1936. Consequently it is natural, I suppose, that my remarks should be heavily botanical. That the final and complete understanding of narcotic plants rests solely and fundamentally on a knowledge of their botanical sources makes it obvious that the first step must be made in the direction of botany or ethnobotany. Convinced of the importance of this step, I have studied narcotic plants among North American Indians in Oklahoma, have made several trips into the Mazatec, Chinantec and Zapotec Indian country of northeastern Oaxaca, Mexico, and lived almost without interruption, from 1941 to 1953, in the northwest Amazon and the northern Andes of South America.

For some of the plants mentioned, there are no chemical, much less pharmaceutical, data. For some, even, there are still serious problems concerning their botanical source or sources. Here, then, lies one of the most promising fields for research, for we know that tropical America still holds secrets in connection with narcotic plants.

For general purposes, there is probably no more serviceable classification of the plants man uses in his striving for temporary relief from reality than that proposed by the German toxicologist, Louis Lewin.

Of Lewin's five categories, i.e., *Excitantia, Inebriantia, Hypnotica, Euphorica, Phantastica,* none has stirred deeper interest through the ages, and none has foretokened a greater field for discovery for the present and future, than the *Phantastica.* There have recently been proposed very learned and intricate words to distinguish the several kinds of narcotics. Our modern terminology has come to call these the *hallucinogens,* the *psychotomimetics,* or the *psychedelics.* Differing from the psychotropic drugs, which normally act only to calm or to stimulate, the hallucinogens or psychedelics act on the

Botanical Sources of The New World Narcotics

central nervous system to bring about a dream-like state, marked (as Hofmann points out) by extreme alteration in the "sphere of experience, in the perception of reality, changes even of space and time and in consciousness of self." They invariably induce a series of visual hallucinations, often in kaleidoscopic movement and usually in rather indescribably brilliant and rich colors, frequently accompanied by auditory and other hallucinations and a variety of synesthesias. Notwithstanding this mushrooming new nomenclature, it seems to me difficult to find a simpler and more serviceable classification than that of Lewin.

It is of interest that the New World is very much richer in narcotic plants than the Old and that the New World boasts at least 40 species of hallucinogenic or phantastica narcotics as opposed to half a dozen species native to the Old World.

It is clear that medical and psychological research into these strange agents, at a painfully embryonic state at the present time, promises more than we are able fully to comprehend. Powerful new tools for psychiatry may be only one of the results of such investigations. But research into the effects of these substances on the human mind must be carried out carefully, without haste or superficiality and, above all, by the most qualified personnel, for what may be one of the most promising fields for progress ever within man's grasp can easily be jeopardized or utterly destroyed by irresponsible and inadequately planned research or by the manipulations of dilettantes.

Ayahuasca, Caapi, Yajé

One of the weirdest of our phantastica or hallucinogens is the drink of the western Amazon known as *ayahuasca, caapi* or *yajé*. Although not nearly so popularly known as peyote and, nowadays, as the sacred mushrooms, it has nonetheless inspired an undue share of sensational articles which have played fancifully with unfounded claims, especially concerning its presumed telepathic powers.

In spite of its extraordinarily bizarre ability to alter man's physical and mental state, this narcotic drink finally disclosed itself to prying European eyes only about a century ago. And it remains one of the most poorly understood American narcotics today.

The earliest mention of *ayahuasca* seems to be that of Villavicencio' in his geography of Ecuador, written in 1858. The source of the drug, he wrote, was a vine used "to foresee and to answer accurately in difficult cases, be it to reply opportunely to ambassadors from other tribes in a question of war; to decipher plans of the enemy through the medium of this magic drink and take proper steps for attack and defense; to ascertain, when a relative is sick, what sorcerer has put on the hex; to carry out a friendly visit to other tribes; to welcome foreign travellers or, at least, to make sure of the love of their womenfolk."

A few years earlier, in 1852, that tireless British plant explorer, Richard

Spruce, had discovered the Tukanoan Indians of the Uaupés in Amazonian Brazil using a liana known as *caapi* to induce intoxication. His observations were not published until the posthumous account of his travels appeared in 1908.

One of Spruce's greatest contributions to science was his precise identification of the source of *caapi* as a new species of the *Malpighiaceae* which was called *Banisteria Caapi*. The correct name is now *Banisteriopsis Caapi*, since it has been shown to be not a true *Banisteria*.

The natives of the upper Rio Negro of Brazil use it for prophetic and divinatory purposes and also to fortify the bravery of male adolescents about to undergo the severely painful *yurupari* ceremony for initiation into manhood. The narcosis amongst these peoples, with whom I have taken *caapi* many times, is pleasant, characterized, amongst other strange effects, by colored visual hallucinations. In excessive doses, it is said to bring on frighteningly nightmarish visions and a feeling of extremely reckless abandon, but consciousness is not lost nor is use of the limbs unduly affected.

Two years later, in 1854, Spruce encountered the intoxicant along the upper Orinoco, where the natives chewed the dry stem for the intoxicating effects. Again, in 1857, he came upon *ayahuasca* in the Peruvian Andes and concluded that it was "the identical species of the Uaupés, but under a different name."

Later explorers and travellers — Martius, Orton, Crévaux, Koch-Grünberg and others — referred to *ayahuasca, caapi* or *yajé* but in an incidental, even casual, manner. All agreed, however, that the source was a forest liana.

In the years following the early work, the area of use of *Banisteriopsis Caapi* was shown to extend to Peru and Bolivia, and several other species of the genus with the same use were likewise reported from the western Amazon. Of outstanding interest was the work in 1922 of Rusby and White in Bolivia and the publication by Morton in 1931 of notes collected by Klug in the Colombian Putumayo. Similarly, the work of the Russians Varonof and Juzepczuk in the Colombian Caquetá in 1925-6 added information of interest to the whole picture.

Serious complications, however, early entered the story of the correct identification of *ayahuasca, caapi* and *yajé*. Back in 1890, Magelli, a missionary in Ecuador, through a misuse of the native names for Jivaro intoxicants, confused our malpighiaceous vine-narcotics with one of the tree-species of *Datura*. The effects of the two psychotomimetics differ widely. This confusion, fortunately, did not enter the pharmacological or chemical literature.

A complication which has, however, sorely plagued both the botanical and the chemical literature, even as recently as 1957, stems from the days of Spruce. This meticulous observer noted, when he discovered caapi and identified its source, that another kind called *caapi-pinima* or "painted caapi" in the Rio Negro area might be "an apocynaceous twiner of the genus *Haemadictyon*, of which I saw only young shoots without any flowers." "The leaves," he wrote, "are of a shining green, painted with the strong blood-red veins. It is possibly the same species . . . distributed by Mr. Bentham under the name of *Haemadictyon amazonicum.* It may be the caapi-pinima which gives its nauseous taste to the caapi . . . and it is probably poisonous, but it is not essential to the narcotic effect of *Banisteria* . . . ." I have consulted Spruce's unpublished notes at the Royal Botanic Gardens at Kew and find that he stated that the caapi drink is made from the lower parts of the stems of *Banisteriopsis Caapi* "beaten in a mortar with the addition of water and a small quantity of the slender roots of the Apocynac (apparently a *Haemadictyon*) called caapi-pinima. . . . May not the peculiar effects of the caapi," he queried, "be owing rather to the roots of the *Haemadictyon* than to the stems of the *Banisteria?* The Indians, however, consider the latter the prime agent, at the same time admitting that the former is an essential ingredient."

It is clear that Spruce suspected that the apocynaceous vine might play a role in causing the intoxication. But he was not sure. Nor did he make any definite statement, being careful to point out that *Banisteriopsis* alone could produce hallucinogenic effects.

Recent botanical work has shown that the genus *Haemadictyon* is not distinct from *Prestonia. Haemadictyon amazonicum,* therefore, is now correctly called *Prestonia amazonica.* It is a species known from only one collection, that made by Spruce along the lower Amazon in Brazil. We must assume, consequently, that it is a very strict endemic.

Now, I have previously pointed out that the narcotic species of *Banisteriopsis* bear different vernacular names. In the northwestern Amazon of Brazil and in adjacent parts of Colombia, it is termed *caapi;* in Amazonian Bolivia, Peru and Ecuador, *ayahuasca;* along the eastern foothills of the Andes in Colombia and Ecuador, it is *yajé.*

For some unexplained reason, writers usually have assumed that ayahuasca and caapi refer to *Banisteriopsis* but that yajé refers to *Prestonia amazonica,* notwithstanding the fact that this apocynaceous species is not known in the region where yajé is prepared.

It was apparently the anthropologist, Reinberg, who, in 1921, first suggested that in Peru the source of ayahuasca and of yajé were different plants. He suggested tentatively that yajé might be *Prestonia* or a related genus. The following year, the Belgian horticulturist, Claes, said that the yajé of the Koregwahes of Colombia "might be" *Prestonia amazonica.* I have found no voucher specimens of Reinberg or of Claes' collections, but the pharmacologists Michiels and Clinquart, who worked on Claes' material, reported that it seemed to belong to *Prestonia amazonica.*

Another and an unnecessary complication arose when the Colombian chemist, Fischer, while admitting that no botanical identification of his material had been made, referred yajé to *Aristolochia;* and the French pharmacologist, Rouhier, at first accepted this determination. Later, however, Rouhier pointed out the similarity of the narcosis from ayahuasca and doubted the possibility that yajé could be *Prestonia amazonica.*

At about the same time, Barriga-Villalba and Albarracín, a Colombian chemist and pharmacologist, respectively, described yajé, on which they worked, as a "climbing shrub."

In 1927, two French pharmacologists, Perrot and Hamet, published an extensive review of what was then known botanically and chemically of this complex of intoxicants. Botanically, they pointed out that 1) yajé, ayahuasca and caapi referred to one species of plant — *Banisteriopsis Caapi* and that 2) no apocynaceous species is at all concerned with this narcotic complex.

In reply to Perrot and Hamet, the German botanist, Niedenzu, published several observations made from herbarium material. His specimens, of course, are no longer extant, for they were burned in the Berlin-Dahlem Botanical Garden during the last war, but his observations bear the stamp of authority, since Niedenzu was the outstanding specialist in the *Malpighiaceae.* His studies indicated that ayahuasca in Peru and Ecuador ought to be considered *Mascagnia psilophylla* var. *antifebrilis, Banisteriopsis quitensis* and *B. Caapi.* This introduced into the puzzle another genus, *Mascagnia,* albeit one closely allied to *Banisteriopsis.*

Another attempt to make order out of chaos came in 1930, when the French botanist, Gagnepain, stated 1) that ayahuasca was probably *Banisteriopsis Caapi,* but yajé could not be referable to this species; 2) that yajé seemed to approach *Prestonia amazonica;* 3) that material sent in from divergent regions by Reinberg and by Rivet seemed to represent the same malpighiaceous species. Gagnepain felt that yajé of Colombia was the same species as caapi of Brazil but that yajé of Ecuador was a different species of *Banisteriopsis.*

Hammerman, in 1929, basing his observations on the field studies of Varanof and Juzepczuk in Colombia, reported that Colombian yajé seemed to comprise several species of *Banisteriopsis,* though most of it was probably *B. quitensis.*

Perhaps the greatest single advance since Spruce's contribution occurred in 1931 when Morton described a new species of *Banisteriopsis* from southern Colombia, naming it *B. inebrians.* On the basis of meticulous field work and observations of the German plant explorer, Klug, Morton reported that at least three species are employed in this region: *Banisteriopsis Caapi, B. inebrians,* and *B. quitensis* and that *B. longialata* and *B. Rusbyana* may sometimes enter as additional ingredients.

During my 12 years of plant exploration in the Amazon Valley, I encountered ayahuasca, caapi and yajé and was able to partake of the hallucinogenic drink on a number of occasions with the natives. In all cases save one, the beverage was prepared with *Banisteriopsis,* regardless of the vernacular name that was employed for the drink.

94

Botanical Sources of The New World Narcotics

Along the eastern foothills of the Andes in Colombia, yajé is prepared as a concentrated decoction from day-long boiling of the rasped bark of *Banisteriopsis inebrians.* I saw no admixture with any other plant, yet the drink had a very strong psychotropic effect. Its intoxication had an initial stage of giddiness and nervousness, followed by profuse sweating and nausea. Then began a period of lassitude, during which a play of colors, at first mainly a hazy blue, increased in intensity. This eventually gave way to a deep sleep, interrupted by dreams and accompanied by a feverishness. No uncomfortable after-effects, save a severe diarrhea, were felt on the next day.

My studies indicate that the Kofán, Inga and Siona Indians of the Putumayo area do often employ the leaves of *Banisteriopsis Rusbyana,* known locally as *chagro-panga* or *oco-yajé,* as an admixture with the bark of *B. inebrians.* I collected *Banisteriopsis Rusbyana* several times, when natives pointed it out as the plant employed to make yajé stronger. The botanist, Cuatrecasas, has likewise found both species used together in the Putumayo.

Klug reported that these Indians "added to the *yajé* (*Banisteriopsis inebrians*) the leaves and young shoots of the branches of the *oco-yajé* or *chagra-panga* (No. 1971) (*B. Rusbyana*), and it is the addition of this plant which produces the 'bluish aureole' of their visions." The Colombian botanist, García-Barriga, noted their use of two admixtures, one of the amaranthaceous *Altenanthera Lehmanii,* the other an unidentified plant; he reported that the *Altenanthera,* when added to native beers or *chicha,* increased their intoxicating properties.

It is, I think, quite significant that the relatively intensive, though sporadic, botanical work in the Putumayo has not turned up *Prestonia* in connection with yajé. And I think we are justified in doubting that the yajé of this area is wholly or partly made from this apocynaceous vine. Nevertheless, we must not dismiss the possibility for other regions. There have been several serious intimations that *Prestonia* enters the narcotic complex. And, in 1957, the chemists Hochstein and Paradies analyzed ayahuasca from Peru, calling it *Banisteriopsis Caapi,* and, from the same region, yajé which they attributed to *Prestonia amazonica.* I have been unable to check the voucher herbarium specimens upon which, apparently, the Peruvian botanist, Ferreyra, made his determination. These chemists stated that the natives of the Rio Napo "commonly consume a mixed extract of the *B. Caapi* and *P. amazonica* leaves in the belief that the latter suppress the more unpleasant hallucinations associated with the pure *B. Caapi* extracts."

Much of my field work was done in the eastern part of the Colombian Amazon, near Brazil. Here *Banisteriopsis Caapi* is usually used alone, but sometimes the leaves of *B. Rusbyana* are added. I noted a few reports of admixtures, such as powdered tobacco or dried tobacco leaves and the crushed leaves of an apocynaceous tree, the toxic *Malouetia Tamaquarina.* The drink is invariably prepared as a cold water infusion in this region.

As far as I was able to judge from six or seven experiences with caapi, the effects differ little from those from the boiled concoction used in the

Putumayo. The intoxication is longer in setting in, and much more of the drink must be taken, but the symptoms of the intoxication and their intensity seem to me to be very similar.

It was my good fortune in 1948 to be able to witness the preparation and to partake of a narcotic caapi-drink amongst the nomadic Makus of the Rio Tikié near the Colombian boundary in Brazil. This is the same area in which Spruce worked a century ago. From the bark of a forest liana, a definitely hallucinogenic drink in the form of a cold water infusion, yellowish in hue and exceedingly bitter, is made. The liana represented an undescribed species of the malpighiaceous genus *Tetrapterys*, which I named *T. methystica*.

In summary, we may state that: a) the narcotic known in the western Amazon as *caapi, yajé* and *ayahuasca* is made basically from species of *Banisteriopsis* or from closely related malpighiaceous genera; b) the most widely employed species of *Banisteriopsis* are *B. Caapi, B. inebrians* and *B. Rusbyana,* but *B. quitensis* appears also to be a major source; c) the genus *Tetrapterys* is employed along the Colombia-Brazilian boundary, where only one species, *T. methystica,* is known to be used; d) *Mascagnia psilophylla* var. *antifebrilis* has been suggested as a source of ayahuasca, but the evidence is not strong; e) the identification of yajé as an *Aristolochia* is without foundation; f) *Prestonia amazonica* has frequently been named as a source of yajé; but there is little or no reliable evidence that it is ever employed, at least, as the prime ingredient, in preparing the narcotic; g) non-malpighiaceous plants are known occasionally, but apparently not frequently, to be added as admixtures together with *Banisteriopsis*.

If there be confusion in the botanical field, there is chaos in the chemical. This stems in great part, to be sure, from uncertainty as to precisely what the plants involved may be. The problem consequently is basically an ethnobotanical one.

An alkaloid was isolated from yajé in 1923 by Fischer who named it telepathine, but he gave neither structure nor other pertinent data. At the same time, Barriga-Villalba and Albarracín reported two alkaloids from specimens of yajé: *yajeine* and *yajeinine*. Later, in 1926, Michiels and Clinquart isolated *yajeine;* and Reutter reported *yajeine* and *yajeinine* from samples of yajé which, without herbarium specimens, he identified as *Prestonia amazonica*. In 1928, Lewin isolated what he called *banisterine;* this alkaloid, incidentally, was tried clinically in mental cases at that time.

In the same year, Wolfes, as well as Rumpf and Elger, claimed that both yajeine and banisterine were actually *harmine,* one of the indole derivatives found in the seeds and roots of *Peganum Harmala* of the family *Zygophyllaceae*. This point of view has been generally accepted. Although pharmacological similarities between the activity of these alkaloids and harmine are close, Hamet, while agreeing that telepathine, yajeine and banisterine are identical, felt that evidence was not yet sufficient to identify them with harmine.

Working, so far as I am aware, for the first time with accurately identified botanical materials, Chen and Chen demonstrated that the alkaloid of *Banisteriopsis Caapi* is harmine and that telepathine, yajeine, and banisterine are superfluous synonyms.

Recent chemical investigation has, however, apparently reopened the whole question. In 1953, working with material of *Banisteriopsis inebrians* which I collected in the Colombian Putumayo, O'Connell and Lynn found harmine in the stems and, in the leaves, "an alkaloid which was partly identified as harmine." Mors and Zaltzman, however, in 1954, questioned that harmine and yajeine were the same. Most recently, in 1957, Hochstein and Paradies, likewise on the basis of botanically determined materials, found that *Banisteriopsis Caapi* contains, in addition to harmine, the alkaloids *harmaline* and *d-tetrahydroharmine*, the three differing only in their state of oxidation and therefore of considerable biogenetic interest. They conclude that "in view of the low degree of psychotomimetic activity reported for harmine and the effectiveness ascribed to *B. Caapi* extracts, it seems likely that the harmaline or d-tetrahydroharmine may have substantial psychotomimetic activity in their own right."

This is how far 100 years has brought us. How much farther is there to go? Should we not step up the speed of our studies before time blots out much of the native lore of the western Amazon?

Datura and Other Solanaceous Plants

The well known intoxicating solanaceous genus, *Datura*, has two New World centers of aboriginal use. In the American Southwest (California, Arizona, New Mexico) and adjacent Mexico, several herbaceous species, chiefly *D. meteloides* and *D. inoxia* (the *toloache* of Mexico), have been a part of religious and magical rites from earliest times. They are still so employed. *Toloache*, reported as a narcotic by all of the early chronicles, is still widely employed in rural parts of northern and central Mexico.

In the Andes, from Colombia to Chile, and along the Pacific Coast of South America, where the Daturas are trees, a number of species are known to have been of extreme importance in some of the ancient civilizations, including the Incas and Chibchas, and are still valued in magico-religious and divinatory rites in isolated areas of Colombia, Ecuador and Peru. There is even a report of witch-doctors of the Ecuadorian highlands taking lessons recently from Jivaro medicine-men and re-introducing the use of *Datura* into the populous and now civilized Andean tribes. The important economic species are *Datura candida, D. sanguinea, D. aurea, D. dolichocarpa, D. suaveolens* and *D. arborea*. A recently discovered species, *Datura vulcanicola*, may also have been used.

The preparation and use of *Datura* differ widely. It is most generally taken in the form of pulverized seeds dropped into beverages such as *chicha* or native beers. Many South American Indians thus bring on the intoxication which is marked by an initial state of violence so furious that the partaker must be held down pending the arrival of the deep, disturbed sleep during which visual hallucinations, interpreted as spirit visitations, are experienced. This narcosis enables the witch-doctor to diagnose disease, to discover thieves and to prophesy the outcome of tribal affairs and hopes. The Jivaro value *Datura* in correcting very refractory children who are given the seeds in the hope that the spirits of their forefathers may come to admonish them. The Chibchas anciently gave women and slaves potions of *Datura* to induce stupor prior to their being buried alive with departed husbands or masters.

Accurate identification of the species used by the tribes for special purposes leaves much to be desired, but since most species are known to contain similar alkaloids — *hyoscyamine, scopolamine, atropine* — this is not such a serious problem as it is in the case of some other narcotics.

In one high mountain-girt valley in southern Colombia, inhabited by Kamsá and Ingano Indians, I collected in 1942 what, after 13 years of field and herbarium study, I decided was a new solanaceous genus, closely akin to the tree-Daturas. Apparently a strict endemic, this tree has 12-inch flowers and long slender leaves from which an infusion is made for use similar to that of the *Datura* species. *Methysticodendron Amesianum,* for that is what I called it, is stated to be more potent and more dangerous than the Daturas. Its chemical composition includes l-scopolamine and hyoscyamine, with evidence of the presence of very minor amounts of other alkaloids.

The Indians of this isolated Valley of Sibundoy may possess the most intricate narcotic consciousness of any peoples of the New World. In addition to several species of tree-Daturas and *Methysticodendron,* they recognize and keep through vegetative reproduction clones of Daturas which are variously atrophied as a result of virus infection. Some of these "races" are such monstrosities that it is difficult to discover the species to which they belong. The natives have special names for each clone. Since they are reputedly stronger, weaker, or in other ways different from healthy Daturas in their effects, they are conserved for very special uses by the witch-doctors. Here is an excellent problem never investigated but well worthy of research — are they really chemically different and, if so, is the difference associated with the virus infection?

The alkaloidal family *Solanaceae* is so excessively rich in genera and species in the Andean area that there would seem to be every probability that additional plants of the family may be found to be or to have been utilized as native narcotics. Only further field research will tell.

Mescal Beans

In Texas and other southwestern states and in adjacent Mexico, one of the characteristic plants of the drier areas is the shrubby *Sophora secundiflora.* The pods of this leguminose species bear dark red seeds known locally as *mescal beans* or, in Mexico, as *frijolitos.*

The genus *Sophora* is rich in alkaloids. The seeds of *Sophora secundiflora* have been found to contain *cytisine,* known also as *sophorine,* a crystalline alkaloid belonging pharmacologically to the same group as nicotine. Cytisine is highly poisonous. Its intoxication is characterized by nausea and convulsions, and death occurs as a result of respiratory failure.

In spite of its toxicity — or perhaps because of it — the seed of *Sophora secundiflora* was used formerly by Indian groups, especially in Texas and northern Mexico, as the basis for the Red Bean Dance. Various groups of the Plains Indians likewise employed the mescal bean in distinct patterns of use: as an oracular or divinatory medium, to induce visions in initiation rites and as a ceremonial emetic and stimulant. Its use today amongst the Kiowa and Comanche Indians as part of the ornamental dress of the leader of the peyote ceremony may point to its earlier employment as a narcotic, a role which it lost with the sweeping arrival of peyote which was so much safer and so much more spectacularly hallucinogenic.

References to the mescal beans go back to 1539, when Cabeza de Vaca spoke of them as objects of trade amongst the Indians of what is now Texas. They were mentioned in the mission literature of Texas as an oracular seed, and the Stephen Long Expedition in 1820 reported that the Arapaho and Iowa Indians used large red beans as a medicine and narcotic.

What interests us especially about *Sophora secundiflora* is how, in such a short period of time, its use has disappeared so completely that we have but a fragmentary knowledge of the whole picture. The same fate lies in store for other native narcotics, and it behooves us to act before aboriginal folklore be completely lost to us forever.

Ololiuqui and Tlitliltzen

The early chroniclers in Mexico, writing shortly after the Conquest, discovered a number of intoxicants as major factors in native religions. One of the strangest was *ololiuqui,* the seed of which was a vision-producing narcotic. Several sources described the plant as a vine and illustrated it. Hernandez, the King of Spain's personal physician who spent a number of years studying the medicinal plants, animals and stones of the new country, accurately illustrated ololiuqui as a morning glory in his work which was not published until 1651.

Religious persecution of the native cults by the newly arrived Roman Catholic authorities drove the use of the sacred narcotic plants into hiding. For four centuries, no morning glory with intoxicating principles ever came to light. In spite of the insistence of reliable Mexican botanists in the literature that ololiuqui actually was a member of the Convolvulaceae, the American economic botanist Safford asserted that it must be a species of *Datura*. He reasoned that 1) no morning glory was known to contain principles active on the central nervous system; 2) the flowers of the morning glories were tubular and similar to those of *Datura* and the Indians could have fooled Hernandez with a substitution; and 3) the narcosis described in the literature for ololiuqui coincided well with *Datura*-intoxication. Safford's identification

99

was readily accepted and, to this day, is well established in the scientific literature.

Nothing could have been further from the truth. In 1938, in the hills of Oaxaca, I found a convolvulaceous vine growing in the door-yard of a *curandero*. The seeds were employed as a sacred divinatory narcotic. As had been pointed out by Mexican botanists without the aid of voucher specimens, it was referable to the white-flowered morning glory, *Rivea corymbosa*. The few seeds available were examined by Santesson in Sweden who reported that in frogs they induced a kind of "half-narcosis" and who suggested that perhaps the active principle might be an alkaloid linked with a gluocoside.

In 1941, I published a modest survey of our knowledge of the ololiuqui plant, but nothing further was done until a Canadian psychiatrist, Osmond, became interested in the effects described for the narcotic. In 1955, he reported four experiments with ololiuqui, characterizing *Rivea*-intoxication as consisting of apathy and anergia together with heightened visual perception and increased hypnagogic phenomena. He found no mental confusion but instead an acute awareness combined with alteration of time perception, followed a few hours later by a period of calm, alert euphoria. We might well harken back at this point to Hernandez' statement that Aztec "priests communed with their gods . . . to receive a message from them, eating the seeds to induce a delirium when a thousand visions and satanic hallucinations appeared to them." It was so powerful that he wrote ". . . it will not be wrong to refrain from telling where it grows, for it matters little that this plant be here described or that Spaniards be made acquainted with it."

Recently, Wasson has established that the seeds of another morning glory, *Ipomoea violacea*, are employed in Oaxaca for the same purpose and in the same way as those of *Rivea corymbosa;* he has identified *Ipomoea violacea* as the *tlitliltzen* of the Aztecs.

For many years, chemists were unable to isolate any narcotic principle which could cause the characteristic intoxication, but in 1960, Hofmann was able to find the active constituents. They are the amides of lysergic acid and of d-lysergic acid, chanoclavine and clymoclavine, substances hitherto known only in the fungus ergot (*Claviceps purpurea*). They have been found in *Rivea corymbosa* as well as in *Ipomoea violacea*.

Peyote

Another of the sacred plants closely tied in with religious practices which the conquerors of Mexico encountered was the now famous *peyote* cactus, *Lophophora Williamsii*. The spineless heads of this small gray-green cactus with a long carrot-like root are sliced off and dried to form the so-called *mescal buttons*. The intoxication induced by eating mescal buttons is one of the most highly complex known and has been too often and expertly described in the literature to detail here. The most spectacular phase of this intoxication is made up of the kaleidoscopic play of richly colored visual hallucinations. It is primarily this extraordinary phase of the narcosis which has convinced Mexican and North American Indians that the plant is a divine messenger enabling the partaker to communicate with the gods without the medium of a priest and has occupied the serious attention of experimental psychologists now for a number of years.

Peyote goes back far in Mexican history. The chronicles of the Conquistadores are full of fanatic and vituperative condemnation of peyote as a diabolic root. Missionaries combated its use in native religions as a sacred element and compared the eating of the cactus with cannibalism.

Peyote survived, however, as a divine therapeutic agent and religious hallucinogen in northern Mexico, where the explorer Lumholtz in 1892 discovered its use in ceremonial dances amongst the Huichols and Tarahumares and sent back to Harvard University material upon which a definitive botanical determination was made.

During the last half of the past century, Indian tribes from the United States brought back knowledge of the peyote from their raids into northern Mexico. After 1880, peyote was accepted with great speed amongst many tribes in the United States as the central sacrament in a religious cult which incorporated both Christian and aboriginal elements. By 1922, the adherents to the peyote cult numbered some 13,300 and, for protection against fierce and often unjust persecution from missionary and political circles, it was legally incorporated as the Native American Church. There are now many more tribes, as far north as Saskatchewan, represented in the peyote cult in the United States and Canada; the figure has been put as high as a quarter of a million. Having attended peyote ceremonies in Oklahoma, I must say that I am impressed with the reverence and seriousness of the Indian in his practice of the peyote ceremony, the moral teachings of which are of the highest. Since science has not demonstrated that peyote is a dangerous and addictive narcotic, I personally can see no reason for political interference with its use in the American Indian religious rites.

There are some eight isoquinoline alkaloids in the peyote cactus. While all of them undoubtedly contribute to the characteristic peyote intoxication, one — *mescaline* — is responsible for the fantastic visual hallucinations.

So much has been written on the various aspects of peyote that I need not elaborate in this brief survey. What should concern us, however, is the advisability of intensive chemical and pharmacological investigations of the Cactaceae, especially of those genera allied to *Lophophora*. Alkaloids similar to or identical with those of *Lophophora* have been found in species of *Anhalonium* and *Ariocarpus,* but there seems never to have been carried out a concerted screening of the family. Of the more than twenty plants which, in Mexico, have been called "peyote," either because their physiological effects are similar or because they are used with *Lophophora Williamsii*, more than half belong to the *Cactaceae*. Here is one area, I believe, where the attention of chemists and pharmacologists is strongly indicated.

THE PSYCHEDELIC READER

Rapé dos Indios

In the central part of the Brazilian Amazon, along the upper Xingú, to be precise, a psychotomimetic snuff has recently been discovered. It is known in Portuguese only by the name *rapé dos indios* or "Indian snuff." Nothing has as yet been published. My source of information was the late Dr. George A. Black, botanical explorer of the Brazilian Amazon, where he lost his life in a rapids. Black informed me in a letter that this snuff is made from the fruit of the gigantic forest tree, *Olmedioperebea sclerophylla,* a member of the *Moraceae.* One could hardly have chosen a less likely source-family for an hallucinogen. Unfortunately, we have no information about its manner of use, and no chemical study has, to my knowledge, been carried out, so that we do not know anything as yet as to the nature of the active principle.

Salvia and Other Mints

A species of *Salvia,* of the Labiatae or Mint Family, has very recently been discovered by Wasson as an hallucinogenic narcotic in use in northeastern Oaxaca, Mexico. The species, *Salvia divinorum,* new to science, has the vernacular names *hojas de la pastora* or *hojas de María Pastora* in Spanish and *ska-Pastora* among the Mazatec Indians.

Although the plant and its properties are familiar to virtually all Mazatecs, there seem to have been no very early reports of the use of *Salvia divinorum* in magico-religious rites. Its area of diffusion comprises only the Mazatec country and possibly adjacent regions inhabited by Cuicatec and Chinantec Indians. The leaves are consumed, usually by chewing them directly, but the effects may be induced when the leaves are drunk in water after having been crushed. *Salvia* leaves are taken when the mushrooms are not available, their narcotic effects coming on quicker, but, while these are similar to the effects of the mushrooms, they are "less sweeping" and of shorter duration. The psychotomimetic properties have been adequately experienced in the field of Wasson and others in his party.

Wasson has recently identified *Salvia divinorum* as probably *the pipiltzintzintli* of the Aztecs.

The chemical constituent or constituents responsible for the narcotic effects of *Salvia divinorum* have not yet been determined. As a mint, of course, the plant would normally be rich in essential oils.

Coleus pumila and two "forms" of *C. Blumei,* both of the Mint Family and both species of Old World origin, have been pointed out by natives in the Mazatec country to be likewise psychotropic, but these lack field corroboration by critical researchers. As Wasson has stated, "it would seem . . . that we are on the threshold of the discovery of a complex of psychotropic plants in the Labiatae or Mint Family."

Botanical Sources of The New World Narcotics

Teonanacatc (teonanacatl)

The Spaniards, like most Europeans, are mycophobes — that is to say, they have an innate dislike of mushrooms. At the time of Spain's great expansion into the New World, they were fired by a religious fanaticism the like of which has never been seen since. We can, consequently, understand the utter disgust of the conquerors of Mexico when they discovered certain intoxicating mushrooms called *teonancatl*, "flesh of the gods," employed as a kind of sacrament or communion in Aztec religious rites.

Most of the early chroniclers were clerics, and they put special emphasis on the need for stamping out such loathsome pagan customs. The peyote cactus and the morning glory, ololiuqui, fell under their ban, too, but particular wrath was directed towards the mushrooms which, through the visions induced by the sacred powers residing in the plant, permitted the Indian to commune with the spirit world.

Sahagún, a Spanish friar, was one of the first Europeans to refer to teonanacate. He made several references to mushrooms "which are harmful and intoxicate like wine" so that those who eat of them "see visions, feel a faintness of heart and are provoked to lust." He detailed the effects in one reference, saying that the natives ate them with honey and "when they begin to be excited by them start dancing, singing, weeping." "Some," Sahagún continued, "do not want to sing but sit down . . . and see themselves dying in a vision; others see themselves being eaten by a wild beast; others imagine that they are capturing prisoners of war, that they are rich, that they possess many slaves, that they had committed adultery and were to have their heads crushed for the offence . . . and when the drunken state had passed, they talk over amongst themselves the visions which they have seen." In addition to the detailed reports, several editions of Sahagún's writing give crude illustrations of the sundry mushrooms employed.

There are four or five references to the sacred fungi in these early writings. According to Tezozomoc, for example, inebriating mushrooms were part of the coronation feast of Montezuma in 1502. Friar Motolinía, who died in 1569, mentioned the sacred psychotomimetic mushrooms in a work on pagan rites and idolatries. The physician, Hernandez, who studied the medicinal lore of Mexican natives for seven years, spoke of three kinds of mushrooms used as narcotics and worshiped. Of some, called *teyhuinti,* he wrote that they "cause not death but madness that on occasion is lasting, of which the symptom is a kind of uncontrolled laughter . . . these are deep yellow, acrid and of a not displeasing freshness. There are others again which, without inducing laughter, bring before the eyes all kinds of things, such as wars and the likeness of demons. Yet others there are not less desired by princes for their festivals and banquets, and these fetch a high price. With night-long vigils are they sought, awesome and terrifying. This kind is tawny and somewhat acrid."

Notwithstanding the relatively numerous and forceful Spanish reports, nothing was known about these mushrooms until very recently. The first attempt to determine them botanically was made in 1915, when the American botanist, Safford, asserted that teonanacate was, in reality, only the peyote cactus. The dried, brown, discoidal head or "button" of *Lophophora Williamsii*, he wrote, resembled "a dried mushroom so remarkably that, at first glance, it will even deceive a mycologist." Safford was led into this serious error first by his oft-stated belief that the Mexican Indians were deficient in botanical knowledge and secondly by the similarity of the effects of peyote and teonanacate. Safford's outstanding reputation stamped his conclusions with authority, and they became generally accepted.

Dr. Blas P. Reko, a physician who did extensive botanical collecting in Mexico, raised a lone voice in protest and, though he failed to produce specimens, wrote, as early as 1919 and 1923, that teonanacate in reality was a dung-fungus and was still employed in religious rites in Oaxaca.

In 1936, an engineer, Robert J. Weitlaner of Mexico City, secured a few specimens of a mushroom used in ceremonial divination in northeastern Oaxaca and sent them to the Harvard Botanical Museum. They were poorly preserved but it was possible to assign them to the genus *Panaeolus*. In 1938 and 1939, during the course of ethnobotanical field work in Oaxaca in the company of Reko, I collected *Panaeolus sphinctrinus* as one of the narcotic mushrooms employed by the Mazatec Indians of Huautla de Jiménez. During the same field studies, a specimen of *Stropharia cubensis* was likewise collected as one of the psychotomimetic mushrooms. In the time available, I was unable to witness a ceremony, and so few mushrooms were available because of the very dry season that it was not possible for me to take them experimentally : all were needed as voucher herbarium specimens.

I was able to publish two papers in which I suggested that *Panaeolus sphinctrinus* (*P. campanulatus* var. *sphinctrinus*) was probably the teonanacate or sacred mushroom of the Aztecs, and my work then took me to the Amazon Valley for twelve years, so that I never returned to Oaxaca to continue the research.

About fifteen years later, Mr. R. Gordon Wasson of New York and his wife, intensely interested amateur ethnomycologists, read my papers and decided to visit Oaxaca to pursue this fascinating phase of their life-long study of mushrooms. Their first trip was made in 1953. It has been followed by seven or eight expeditions to Oaxaca and other parts of Mexico. Wasson sensed the need for intensive study of all phases of the use of the sacred mushrooms, so he enlisted the collaboration of specialists. The resulting research, woven by Wasson into an intricately interrelated whole, will long hold a high place as an outstanding model of what can be accomplished by well planned and carefully executed ethnobotanical investigation. Amongst his collaborators, he numbers the French mycologist, Dr. Roger Heim, and the Sandoz pharmaceutical scientists under Hofmann. Wasson and his associates were able to witness and to take part in mushroom ceremonies and to eat of the mushrooms themselves.

Botanical Sources of The New World Narcotics

The work of the Wassons and Heim has indicated that a number of different species of *Basidiomycetes* are employed as sacred, psychotomimetic mushrooms in Mexico. This was expected, in view of the ancient chronicles, but the wealth of genera and species still used — and probably not all have been uncovered as yet — is unexpectedly great. Furthermore, a large percentage of those employed represent species new to science.

Wasson and Heim failed to find *Panaeolus* employed by their informants, but it must be remembered that different *curanderas* may use different mushrooms and that the purpose for which the intoxicant is taken in a given ritual or séance may likewise have a part in choice of the species. The following mushrooms make up the Wasson-Heim list of Mexican hallucinogens: *Canatharellaceae-Conocybe siliginoides*, growing on dead tree trunks; *Strophariaceae-Psilocybe mexicana*, a small tawny inhabitant of wet pastures, apparently the most highly prized by the users; *Psilocybe aztecorum*, called "children of the waters" by the Aztecs; *Psilocybe zapotecorum* of marshy ground and known by the Zapotecs as "crown of thorns mushroom"; *Psilocybe caerulescens* var. *mazatecorum*, the so-called "landslide mushroom" which grows on decaying sugar cane refuse; *Psilocybe caerulescens* var. *nigripes*, that has a native name meaning "mushroom of superior reason"; and *Stropharia cubensis*.

The interest stirred up in the scientific world by this work encouraged others to enter the field, but due primarily to the rapid nature of their work as compared to the sustained investigations of the Wasson group, they have contributed little to the total picture. The principal additions have been made by Singer and Guzman who, in 1957, visited Oaxaca and found several other species of *Psilocybe* used.

Undoubtedly there were many tribes in ancient Mexico who employed teonanacate, but we know with certainty only of the Chichimecas, who spoke Nahuatl. We know that today the sacred mushrooms are consumed by the Mazatecs, Chinantecs, Chatinos, Zapotecs, Mixtecs, and Mijes, all of Oaxaca; by the Nahoas of Mexico; and possibly by the Tarascans of Michoacan and the Otomis of Puebla.

The Wassons have uncovered much indirect evidence which they have interpreted, correctly I believe, to indicate a very great extent for the use of psychotropic mushrooms in Mexico and Guatemala, as well as an astonishing age for the mushroom cults. Certain frescoes from central Mexico, for example, dating back to 300 A.D., have designs which seem to put mushroom worship back that far. There are likewise the archaeological artifacts now called "mushroom stones" from the highland Maya of Guatemala, going back to 1000 B.C. Consisting of an upright stem with a man-like figure crowned with an umbrella-shaped top, these stone carvings have long baffled archaeologists who supposed them to be phallic symbols. It is now rather clear that they represented a kind of icon connected with mushroom worship.

The most important of the narcotic mushrooms of Oaxaca is *Psilocybe mexicana*. Besides the kaleidoscopic play of visual hallucinations in color, the outstanding symptoms of *Psilocybe*-intoxication are: muscular relaxation, flaccidity and mydriasis early in the narcosis, followed by a period of emotional disturbances such as extreme hilarity and difficulty in concentration. It is at this point that the visual and auditory hallucinations appear, eventually to be followed by lassitude and mental and physical depression, with serious alteration of time and space perception. One peculiarity of the narcosis which promises to be of interest in experimental psychiatry is the isolation of the subject from the world around him — that is, without a loss of consciousness, he is rendered completely indifferent to his environment which becomes unreal to him as his dreamlike state becomes real.

Heim and his colleague Cailleux succeeded in growing cultures of *Psilocybe mexicana* and other species. This opened the way for chemical study of the fungus in the Sandoz laboratories in Switzerland. Hofmann and his group there isolated white crystals which were soluble in water and methanol but almost insoluble in usual organic solvents. They called the substance *psilocybine* and found that it had an unusual chemical structure which research indicated to be an acidic phosphoric acid ester of 4-hydroxydimethyltryptamine. It is, therefore, allied to other naturally occurring compounds such as *bufotenine* and *serotonin*. Psilocybine is the first known naturally occurring indole derivative containing phosphorus. The discovery of such a substance has implications of great import, for example, for the study of biogenesis of the ergot alkaloids and for many other aspects of chemical investigation of the psychotropic indole alkaloids such as harmine and reserpine.

Psilocybe mexicana contains another indolic compound in minute amounts which, while closely allied to psilocybine is apparently not stable and has not yet been crystallized. It is called *psilocine*.

Since reporting on his preliminary work with *Psilocybe mexicana*, Hofmann has discovered psilocybine in other psychotomimetic species of this genus and in *Stropharia cubensis*. And I have heard unofficially that the same compound is suspected to occur in the genus *Panaeolus*.

Psilocybine is now under clinical examination as an aid in experimental psychiatry and in therapy, and promises to be as fruitful perhaps as lysergic acid has been.

Vinho de Jurumena

Another little known South American intoxicant is a beverage called *vinho de Jurumena,* prepared from the seeds of the leguminose *Mimosa hostilis.* Identification of this narcotic drink, employed by the Pancarú Indians in Pernambuco, Brazil, was made by Gonçalves de Lima, who described its role in the magico-religious ceremonies of this tribe. It is an hallucinogen and is believed to transport the soul to the spirit world.

The isolation of an alkaloid called *nigerine* was reported in 1946, but work completed last year indicates that nigerine is, in reality, N,N-dimethyltryptamine, the same constituent found in species of the closely related genus *Piptadenia.*

Yakee or Paricá

At the beginning of this century, the German ethnologist, Koch-Grünberg, mentioned an intoxicating snuff prepared from the bark of an unidentified tree by the Yekwana Indians of the headwaters of the Orinoco in Venezuela. There is every probability that this snuff was prepared from trees of the genus *Virola* of the *Myristicaceae,* the family to which our nutmeg belongs.

During my ethnobotanical field work in the Colombian Amazon, I learned of a particularly intoxicating snuff used only by the witch-doctors in several tribes. This was the *yakee* or *parica.* After eight years of search, I discovered that yakee was prepared from several species of *Virola, V. calophylla, V. calophylloidea* and, perhaps, *V. elongata.* The natives strip bark from the trunks before the sun has risen high enough to heat up the forest. A blood-red resin oozes from the inner surface of the bark. It is scraped off with a machete or knife and boiled in an earthen pot for hours until a thick paste is left. This paste is allowed to dry and is then pulverized, sifted through a fine cloth, and finally added to an equal amount of ashes of the stems of a wild cacao species. The ashes give the snuff consistency to withstand the excessive dampness of the air which might otherwise quickly "melt" the powdered resin-paste to a solid lump.

The active principle is undoubtedly the same essential oil — *myristicine* — that is common throughout the family and that makes our household nutmeg a dangerous narcotic when used in the appropriate amounts. Work on samples brought from the Colombian Amazon has not yet been completed. In the ethnological literature, yakee snuff has been consistently confused with both tobacco and yopo snuffs, so that it is difficult to get a clear picture from the literature of the extent of use of these three narcotics. We may say, however, that yakee is employed by tribes in the Colombian Vaupés and in the Orinoco drainage basin and in the upper Rio Negro basin in Brazil; if we are correct in ascribing the "bark snuff" reported by Koch-Grünberg to *Virola,* we should then include the headwaters of the Orinoco in Venezuela.

It may be interesting to append a few observations which I made personally after taking yakee. I took about one-third of a teaspoonful in two inhalations, using the characteristic V-shaped bird-bone snuffing tube. This represents about one-quarter the dose that a diagnosing medicine man will take to bring on an eventual state of unconsciousness.

The dose was snuffed at five o'clock one afternoon. Within fifteen minutes, a drawing sensation was felt over the eyes, followed very shortly by a strong tingling in fingers and toes. The drawing sensation in the forehead gave way to a strong and constant headache. Within a half hour, the feet and hands were numb and sensitivity of the fingertips had disappeared; walking was possible with difficulty, as with beri-beri. I felt nauseated until eight o'clock, and experienced lassitude and uneasiness. Shortly after eight, I lay

107

down in my hammock, overcome with a drowsiness, which, however, seemed to be accompanied by a muscular excitation except in the hands and feet. At about nine-thirty, I fell into a fitful sleep which continued, with frequent awakenings, until morning. The strong headache lasted until noon. A profuse sweating and what was probably a slight fever persisted throughout the night. The pupils were strongly dilated during the first few hours of the intoxication.

Though performed under primitive conditions in the jungle by myself, this experiment does, I think, indicate the great strength of the snuff as a psychotic agent. The witch-doctors see visions in color, but I was able to experience neither visual hallucinations nor color sensations. The large dose used by the witch-doctor is enough to put him into a deep but disturbed sleep, during which he sees visions and has dreams which, through the wild shouts emitted in his delirium, are interpreted by an assistant. That it is a dangerous practice is acknowledged by the witch-doctors themselves. They report the death, about 15 years ago, of one of their number from the Puinave tribe during a yakee-intoxication.

Yopo and Huilca

The snuffing of narcotics is widespread in aboriginal America, especially in South America. A number of different narcotics are involved, and there is still much to do to clarify all aspects of their botanical identity.

The most widely employed snuff, of course, is tobacco. From records in the literature, it is not always possible to distinguish when snuff is made from tobacco or from other plants, and this has caused much confusion.

The first scientific report concerning yopo or snuff from the leguminose *Piptadenia* is apparently that of Humboldt who, in 1801, saw the Otomacs along the Orinoco pulverize the seed of *Piptadenia peregrina,* mix the powder with quicklime and use it like tobacco snuff. Spruce gave us the earliest detailed report, however, when he wrote about *niopo* amongst the Guahibos of the Orinoco of Colombia.

The principal area of use of the *Piptadenia peregrina* snuff seems to be the Orinoco basin and Trinidad. Safford has identified the cohoba snuff of ancient Hispaniola as *Piptadenia peregrina,* and he seems to have good, even though indirect, evidence.

As practiced today in the Orinoco basin of Colombia and Venezuela, yopo-snuffing is a dangerous habit carried on, not by witch-doctors alone, but the whole population — men, women, children. The frightening intoxication first produces convulsive movements and distortions of the face and body muscles, then a desire to dance which is rapidly overwhelmed by an inability to control the limbs; it is at this point that a violent madness or a deep sleep disturbed by a nightmare of frightening sights takes over. The intoxication always ends in a long stupor. The use of yopo in daily life in the *llanos* area of Colombia and Venezuela may be relatively recent, for it was anciently employed only for specific purposes, such as to induce bravery before a battle, to give hunters keener sight and as an agent for prophesying, clairvoyance and divination.

Recent chemical work on carefully identified material has shown that the major alkaloid of a number of species of *Piptadenia* is *bufotcnine*. Present also may be another hallucinogenic alkaloid, *N,N-dimcthyltryptamine*. *Piptadenai colubrina*, a species closely allied to *P. peregrina*, has up to 2.1 percent of bufotenine.

Another species of *Piptadenia*, *P. macrocarpa*, is the source of a snuff of the Andean regions of Peru, where the plant is called *huilca*. Little of a definite nature seems to be known about *huilca* and its uses, but it is believed to have been the source of the strong, divinatory snuff of early Peru.

Coca

Although *coca*, the dried leaves of *Erythroxylon Coca*, does not constitute an hallucinogen, we should not terminate a discussion of South American narcotics without a mention, howsoever brief, of this very ancient drug. It belongs to Lewin's *Euphorica*, along with the opium poppy, *Papaver somniferum* of the Old World. I include these cursory remarks on coca merely because, by and large, it is, next to tobacco, America's most important narcotic and one which, even at this late date, deserves further study from many points of view. It is unquestionably, as employed by the Indians, one of the most maligned of narcotics.

There is no need to go into details which are easily available to all readers. The few lines which I shall devote to coca, the source of our *cocaine*, will discuss certain aspects not commonly found in the literature nor easily available to those who have not had personal experience in the field with the narcotic.

The chemical makeup of coca is extremely complex, with numerous alkaloids in six groups of the tropane series. The chemical literature usually attributes the source of coca to several species of *Erythroxylon*, but there seems to be little botanical reason for referring all of the slight geographical variants to different species. *Erythroxylon Coca* is a cultigen of long association with man, now unknown in the wild state and with a very wide altitudinal range.

Coca was a divine plant in pre-Colombian Andean cultures where it was once restricted to the priestly class but early escaped to the common man. Dried leaves have been found in Peruvian mummy bundles dating back at least 2000 years.

Coca chewing today is an integral part of the culture pattern in many isolated parts of the highlands of Colombia and in most highland parts of Peru, Bolivia and the northwesternmost corner of Argentina. Its use in highland Ecuador has all but died out. From the Andes, the habit spread into the lowland in most parts of the northwesternmost Amazon Valley in Colombia and Peru, where, however, it is employed in a rather different way. All highland groups chew the toasted leaves together with small pieces of lime or *lliptu*, of mineral, plant or animal origin. The Amazonian Indians pulverize the toasted coca leaves and mix the green powder with finely sifted ashes from leaves of the *Cecropia* tree; the resulting gray-green powder is packed over the gums and is not actually chewed but allowed to dissolve slowly and trickle down to the stomach. Most Indian coca-users keep the cheeks full of the material throughout their waking hours.

What is very commonly overlooked or even purposely ignored in many governmental and sociological circles is the fact that coca, as chewed by the native, is not of necessity physically, socially and morally dangerous enough to warrant prohibitive laws. It has nothing in common with cocaine addiction, and coca-chewing apparently does not lead to addiction. Peruvian Indians conscripted for the army where coca is forbidden are not unduly bothered by the lack of the narcotic. For the greater part of eight of my twelve years in exploration of the northwest Amazon, I used coca daily and found no desire for it when, back in the capital city, I had no supply. It is perhaps roughly comparable to the use of tobacco in our culture, and is certainly much less of a problem in the Andes than is alcohol in a mechanized society such as ours in the United States. Unwise legal prohibitions in certain Andean areas, aimed at extirpation of the coca-custom, have invariably driven the Indian — deprived in his inhospitable, cold altitudes of the euphoric coca — to the dangerously poisonous, locally distilled, alcoholic drinks, with an attendant rapid rise in crime of every description. As Taylor has wisely summed it up: "If medicine and addiction were its only uses, no one would bother to read what follows. But neither the addicts nor most doctors, nor many others, realize that the birth of cocaine was tended by the gods, nurtured in the high purity of the Andes without a taint of depravity, and was, if not divine, so considered for countless centuries. Even today, it has the touch of the miraculous."

* * * *

This brief discussion of native American narcotics of plant origin comprises but a very superficial panoramic view of the work that has been done on the hallucinogenic drugs and which has opened up such vistas of promise in both practical and academic fields of medical and biological research.

I have wanted to emphasize the part that many apparently unrelated fields may take in such an interdisciplinary attack. And I trust that we have been able to point out very specifically the two most important methods for the discovery of new drugs — on the one hand, examination of ancient records and interpretation of folklore; on the other, field work amongst primitive peoples who still live in close association with the plant world.

Certainly none of us could have been ready to accept some of the fantastic reports of the early writers on the unearthly effects produced by the sacred mushrooms. Now we know that they are true. We can no longer afford to ignore reports of any aboriginal use of a plant merely because they seem to fall beyond the limit of our credence. To do so would be tantamount to the closing of a door, forever to entomb a peculiar kind of native knowledge which might lead us along paths of immeasurable progress.

Hermann Hesse:

Poet of the Interior Journey

TIMOTHY LEARY

and

RALPH METZNER

HERMANN HESSE was born in July, 1877, in the little Swabian town of Calw, the son of Protestant missionaries. His home background and education were pietistic, intellectual, classical. He entered a theological seminary at the age of fourteen with the intention of taking orders, and left two years later. In Basel he learned the book trade and made his living as a bookseller and editor of classical German literary texts. He became acquainted with Jacob Burckhardt, the great Swiss historian and philosopher, who later served as the model for the portrait of Father Jacobus in *The Bead Game*. In 1914 Hesse's "unpatriotic" anti-war attitude brought him official censure and newspaper attacks. Two months after the outbreak of the war, an essay entitled "O Freunde, nicht diese Töne" (O Friends, not these tones) was published in the *Neue Zürcher Zeitung:* it was an appeal to the youth of Germany, deploring the stampede to disaster.

In 1911 he travelled in India. From 1914 to 1919 he lived in Bern, working in the German embassy as an assistant for prisoners of war. A series of personal crises accompanied the external crisis of the war: his father died; his youngest son fell seriously ill; his wife suffered a nervous breakdown and was hospitalized. In 1919, the year of the publication of *Demian,* he moved to the small village of Montagnola by the lake of Lugano and remained there till the end of his life. In 1923 he acquired Swiss citizenship, and in 1927 remarried. Hesse steeped himself in Indian and Chinese literature and philosophy, the latter particularly through the masterful translations of Chinese texts by Richard Wilhelm. In 1931 he remarried a third time and moved to another house in Montagnola which had been provided for him by his friend, H. C. Bodmer. In 1946 he was awarded the Nobel Prize; in 1962, at the age of 85, he died. Asked once what were the most important influences in his life, he said they were: "the Christian and completely non-nationalist spirit of my parents' home," the "reading of the great Chinese masters," and the figure of the historian Jacob Burckhardt.

Few writers have chronicled with such dispassionate lucidity and fearless honesty the progress of the soul through the stages of life. *Peter Camenzind* (1904), *Demian* (1919), *Siddhartha* (1922), *Steppenwolf* (1927), *Narziss und Goldmund* (1930), *Journey to the East* (1932), *Magister Ludi* (1943) — different versions of spiritual autobiography, different maps of the interior path. Each new step revises the picture of all the previous steps, each experience opens up new worlds of discovery in a constant effort to communicate the vision.

As John Cage is fond of reminding us, writing is one thing and reading is another. All writings, all authors are thoroughly misunderstood. Most wise men do not write because they know this. The wise man has penetrated through the verbal curtain, seen and known and felt the life-process. We owe him our gratitude when he remains with us and tries to induce us to share the joy.

The great writer is the wise man who feels compelled to translate the message into words. The message is, of course, around us and in us at all moments. Everything is a clue. Everything contains all the message. To pass it on in symbols is unnecessary but perhaps the greatest performance of man.

Wise men write (with deliberation) in the esoteric. It's the way of making a rose or a baby. The exoteric form is maya, *the hallucinatory facade. The meaning is within. The greatness of a*

112

*great book lies in the esoteric, the seed meaning concealed behind
the net of symbols. All great writers write the same book, changing
only the exoteric trappings of their time and tribe.*

HERMANN HESSE IS ONE OF THE GREAT WRITERS *of our time.
He wrote* Finnegan's Wake *in several German versions. In addition
to being a wise man, he could manipulate words well enough to win
the Nobel Prize.*

*Most readers miss the message of Hesse. Entranced by the
pretty dance of plot and theme, they overlook the seed message.
Hesse is a trickster. Like nature in April, he dresses up his code in
fancy plumage. The literary reader picks the fruit, eats quickly, and
tosses the core to the ground. But the seed, the electrical message,
the code is in the core.*

Take *Siddhartha*[1] — the primer for young Bodhisattvas, written when Hesse was forty-five. Watch the old magician warming up
to his work. We are introduced to a proud young man, strong, hand-
some, supple-limbed, graceful. Siddhartha is young and ambitious.
He seeks to attain the greatest prize of all — enlightenment. Cosmic
one-upmanship. He masters each of the other-worldly games. The
Vedas. Asceticism. Matches his wits against the Buddha himself.
Tantric worldly success. "We find consolations, we learn tricks with
which we deceive ourselves, but the essential thing — the way —
we do not find." "Wisdom is not communicable." "I can love a
stone, Govinda, and a tree or a piece of bark. These are things and
one can love things. But one cannot love words. . . . Nirvana is not
a thing; there is only the word Nirvana." Then in the last pages of
the book, Hermann Hesse, Nobel Prize novelist, uses words to describe the wonderful illumination of Govinda, who

> no longer saw the face of his friend Siddhartha. Instead he saw
> other faces, many faces, a long series, a continuous stream of faces
> — hundreds, thousands, which all came and disappeared and yet all
> seemed to be there at the same time, which all continually changed
> and renewed themselves and which were yet all Siddhartha. He saw
> the face of a fish, of a carp, with tremendous painfully opened mouth,
> a dying fish with dimmed eyes. He saw the face of a newly born
> child, red and full of wrinkles, ready to cry. He saw the face of a
> murderer, saw him plunge a knife into the body of a man; at the
> same moment he saw this criminal kneeling down, bound, and his head
> cut off by an executioner. He saw the naked bodies of men and

113

women in the postures and transports of passionate love. He saw corpses stretched out, still, cold, empty. He saw the heads of animals, boars, crocodiles, elephants, oxen, birds. He saw Krishna and Agni. He saw all these forms and faces in a thousand relationships to each other, all helping each other, loving, hating and destroying each other and become newly born. Each one was mortal, a passionate, painful example of all that is transitory. Yet none of them died, they only changed, were always reborn, continually had a new face: only time stood between one face and another. And all these forms and faces rested, flowed, reproduced, swam past and merged into each other, and over them all there was continually something thin, unreal and yet existing, stretched across like thin glass or ice, like a transparent skin, shell, form or mask of water — and this mask was Siddhartha's smiling face which Govinda touched with his lips at that moment. And Govinda saw that this mask-like smile, this smile of unity over the flowing forms, this smile of simultaneousness over the thousands of births and deaths — this smile of Siddhartha — was exactly the same as the calm, delicate, impenetrable, perhaps gracious, perhaps mocking, wise, thousand-fold smile of Gotama, the Buddha, as he had perceived it with awe a hundred times. It was in such a manner, Govinda knew, that the Perfect One smiled.

Those who have taken one of the psychedelic drugs may recognize Govinda's vision as a classic LSD sequence. The direct visual confrontation with the unity of all men, the unity of life. That Hesse can write words such as "unity," "love," "Nirvana," is easily understood. Every Hindu textbook gives you the jargon. But his description of the visual details of the cosmic vision, the retinal specifics, is more impressive. Whence came to Hesse these concrete sensations? The similarity to the consciousness-expanding drug experience is startling. The specific, concrete "is-ness" of the illuminated moment usually escapes the abstract philosopher of mysticism. Did Hesse reach this visionary state himself? By meditation? Spontaneously? Did H.H. the novelist himself use the chemical path to enlightenment?

The answer to these questions is suggested in the next lesson of the master: *Steppenwolf*[2] — a novel of crisis, pain, conflict, torture — at least on the surface. Hesse writes in a letter: "If my life were not a dangerous painful experiment, if I did not constantly skirt the abyss and feel the void under my feet, my life would have no meaning and I would not have been able to write anything." Most readers sophisticated in psychodynamics recognize the drama presented — the conflict between ego and id, between spirit and material civilization, the "wolfish, satanic instincts that lurk within even our civilized selves," as the jacket of the paperback edition has it. "These readers [writes Hesse] have completely overlooked that above the Steppenwolf and his problematical life there exists a second, higher, timeless world . . . which contrasts the suffering of the Steppenwolf with a transpersonal and transtemporal world of faith, that the book certainly tells of pain and suffering but is the story of a believer not a tale of despair."

As in *Siddhartha,* Hesse involves the reader in his fantastic tale, his ideas, his mental acrobatics, only to show at the end that the whole structure is illusory mind-play. The mental rug is suddenly pulled out from under the gullible psychodynamic reader. This Zen trick is evident on at least two levels in the *Steppenwolf.* First, in the little "Treatise," a brilliant portrait of Harry, the man with two souls: the man — refined, clever and interesting; and the wolf — savage, untamable, dangerous and strong. The treatise describes his swings of mood, his bursts of creativity, his ambivalent relationship to the bourgeoisie, his fascination with suicide, his inability to reconcile the two conflicting selves. A breathtakingly subtle psychological analysis. Then, the sleight of hand:

> . . . . There is . . . a fundamental delusion to make clear. All interpretation, all psychology, all attempts to make things comprehensible, require the medium of theories, mythologies and lies; and a self-respecting author should . . . dissipate these lies so far as may be in his power. . . . Harry consists of a hundred or a thousand selves, not of two. His life oscillates, as everyone's does, not merely between two poles, such as the body and the spirit, the saint and the sinner, but between thousands ....
> ....
> Man is an onion made up of a hundred integuments, a texture made up of many threads. The ancient Asiatics knew this well enough, and in the Buddhist Yoga an exact technique was devised for unmasking the illusion of the personality. The human merry-go-round sees many changes: the illusion that cost India the efforts of thousands of years to unmask is the same illusion that the West has labored just as hard to maintain and strengthen.

The dualistic self-image is described — the fascinating and compelling Freudian metaphor — and is then exposed as a delusion, a limited, pitiful perspective, a mind-game. The second example of

115

this trick occurs at the end of the book. We have followed Hesse in his descriptions of Harry, as he runs through a series of vain attempts to conquer his despair — through alcohol, through sex, through music, through friendship with the exotic musician Pablo — finally he enters the Magic Theater. "Price of Admission, your Mind." — In other words, a mind-loss experience.

> From a recess in the wall [Pablo] took three glasses and a quaint little bottle. . . . He filled the three glasses from the bottle and taking three long thin yellow cigarettes from the box and a box of matches from the pocket of his silk jacket he gave us a light. . . . Its effect was immeasurably enlivening and delightful — as though one were filled with gas and had no longer any gravity.

Pablo says:

> You were striving, were you not, for escape? You have a longing to forsake this world and its reality and to penetrate to a reality more native to you, to a world beyond time. . . . You know, of course, where this other world lies hidden. It is the world of your own soul that you seek. Only within yourself exists that other reality for which you long. . . . All I can give you is the opportunity, the impulse, the key. I help you to make your own world visible. . . . This . . . theater has as many doors into as many boxes as you please, ten or a hundred or a thousand, and behind each door exactly what you seek awaits you. . . . You have no doubt guessed long since that the conquest of time and the escape from reality, or however else it may be that you choose to describe your longing, means simply the wish to be relieved of your so-called personality. That is the prison where you lie. And if you enter the theatre as you are, you would see everything through the eyes of Harry and the old spectacles of the Steppenwolf. You are therefore requested to lay these spectacles aside and to be so kind as to leave your highly esteemed personality here in the cloak-room, where you will find it again when you wish. The pleasant dance from which you have just come, the treatise on the Steppenwolf, and the little stimulant that we have only this moment partaken of may have sufficiently prepared you.

It seems clear that Hesse is describing a psychedelic experience, a drug-induced loss of self, a journey to the inner world. Each door in the Magic Theatre has a sign on it, indicating the endless possibilities of the experience. A sign called "Jolly Hunting. Great Automobile Hunt" initiates a fantastic orgy of mechanical destruction in which Harry becomes a lustful murderer. A second sign reads: "Guidance in the Building-Up of the Personality. Success

Guaranteed," which indicates a kind of chess game in which the pieces are the part of the personality. Cosmic psychotherapy. "We demonstrate to anyone whose soul has fallen to pieces that he can rearrange these pieces of a previous self in what order he pleases, and so attain to an endless multiplicity of moves in the game of life." Another sign reads: "All Girls Are Yours," and carries Harry into inexhaustible sexual fantasies. The crisis of the Steppenwolf, his inner conflicts, his despair, his morbidity and unsatisfied longing are dissolved in a whirling kaleidoscope of hallucinations. "I knew that all the hundred thousand pieces of life's game were in my pocket. A glimpse of its meaning had stirred my reason and I was determined to begin the game afresh. I would sample its tortures once more and shudder again at its senselessness. I would traverse not once more, but often, the hell of my inner being. One day I would be a better hand at the game. One day I would learn how to laugh. Pablo was waiting for me, and Mozart too."

So Harry Haller, the Steppenwolf, had his psychedelic session, discovered instead of one reality, infinite realities within the brain. He is admitted into the select group of those who have passed through the verbal curtain into other modes of consciousness. He has joined the elite brotherhood of the illuminati.

And then what? Where do you go from there? How can the holy sense of unity and revelation be maintained? Does one sink back into the somnambulent world of rote passion, automated action, egocentricity? The poignant cry of ex-League member, H.H.: "That almost all of us — and also I, even I — should again lose myself in the soundless deserts of mapped out reality, just like officials and shop-assistants who, after a party or a Sunday outing, adapt themselves again to everyday business life!" These are issues faced by everyone who has passed into a deep, trans-ego experience. How can we preserve the freshness; illuminate each second of subsequent life? How can we maintain the ecstatic oneness with others?

Throughout the ages mystical groups have formed to provide social structure and support for transcendence. The magic circle. Often secret, always persecuted by the sleep-walking majority, these cults move quietly in the background shadows of history. The problem is, of course, the amount of structure surrounding the mystical spark. Too much, too soon, and you have priesthood ritual on your hands. And the flame is gone. Too little and the teaching function is lost, the interpersonal unity drifts into gaseous anarchy. The Bohemians. The Beats. The lonely arrogants.

Free from attachment to self, to social games, to anthropomorphic humanism, even to life itself, the illuminated soul can sustain the heightened charge of energy released by transcendent experiences. But such men are rare in any century. The rest of us seem to need support on the way. Men who attempt to pursue the psychedelic drug path on their own are underestimating the power and the scope of the nervous system. A variety of LSD casualties results: breakdown, confusion, grandiosity, prima-donna individualism, disorganized eccentricity, sincere knavery and retreat to conformity. It makes no more sense to blame the drug for such casualties than it does to blame the nuclear process for the bomb. Would it not be more accurate to lament our primitive tribal pressures towards personal power, success, individualism?

Huston Smith has remarked that of the eight-fold path of the Buddha, the ninth and greatest is Right Association. The transpersonal group. The consciousness-expansion community. Surround yourself after the vision, after the psychedelic session, with friends who share the goal, who can uplevel you by example or unitive love; who can help reinstate the illumination.

The sociology of transcendence. Hesse takes up the problem of the transpersonal community in the form of the League of Eastern Wayfarers.[3]

"It was my destiny to join in a great experience. Having had the good fortune to belong to the League, I was permitted to be a participant in a unique journey." The narrator, H.H., tells that the starting place of the journey was Germany, and the time shortly after World War I. ". . . our people at that time were lured by many phantoms, but there were also many real spiritual advances. There were Bacchanalian dance societies and Anabaptist groups, there was one thing after another that seemed to point to what was wonderful and beyond the veil." There were also scientific and artistic groups engaged in the exploration of consciousness-expanding drugs. Kurt Beringer's monograph, *Der Meskalinrausch*,[4] describes some of the scientific experiments and the creative applications. René

Hermann Hesse: Poet of the Interior Journey

Daumal's novel, *Le Mont Analogue,*[5] is a symbolic account of a similar league journey in France. The participants were experimenting widely with drugs such as hashish, mescaline and carbon tetrachloride.

Hesse never explicitly names any drugs in his writings, but the passages quoted earlier from the *Steppenwolf* are fairly unequivocal in stating that some chemical was involved and that it had a rather direct relationship to the subsequent experience. Now, after this first enlightenment, in *Journey to the East,* H.H. tells of subsequent visits to the Magical Theatre.

> . . . We not only wandered through Space, but also through time. We moved towards the East, but we also traveled into the Middle Ages and the Golden Age; we roamed through Italy or Switzerland, but at times we also spent the night in the 10th century and dwelt with the patriarchs or the fairies. During the times I remained alone, I often found again places and people of my own past. I wandered with my former betrothed along the edges of the forest of the Upper Rhine, caroused with friends of my youth in Tübingen, in Basle or in Florence, or I was a boy and went with my school-friends to catch butterflies or to watch an otter, or my company consisted of the beloved characters of my books; . . . For our goal was not only the East, or rather the East was not only a country and something geographical, but it was the home and youth of the soul, it was everywhere and nowhere, it was the union of all times.

Later the link between the Steppenwolf's drug liberation and the League becomes more specific:

> When something precious and irretrievable is lost, we have the feeling of having awakened from a dream. In my case this feeling is strangely correct, for my happiness did indeed arise from the same secret as the happiness in dreams; it arose from the freedom to experience everything imaginable simultaneously, to exchange outward and inward easily, to move Time and Space about like scenes in a theatre.

Hesse is always the esoteric hand, but there seems to be little doubt that beneath the surface of his Eastern allegory runs the history of a real-life psychedelic brotherhood. The visionary experiences described in *Journey to the East* are identified by location and name of participants. A recently published biography[6] traces the connections between these names and locations and Hesse's friends and activities at the time.

119

And again and again, in Swabia, at Bodensee, in Switzerland, everywhere, we met people who understood us, or were in some way thankful that we and our League and our Journey to the East existed. Amid the tramways and banks of Zürich we came across Noah's Ark guarded by several old dogs which all had the same name, and which were bravely guided across the dangerous depths of a calm period by Hans C., Noah's descendant, friend of the arts.

Hans C. Bodmer is Hesse's friend, to whom the book is dedicated, and who later bought the house in Montagnola for Hesse. He lived at the time in a house in Zürich named "The Ark."

One of the most beautiful experiences was the League's celebration in Bremgarten; the magic circle surrounded us closely there. Received by Max and Tilli, the lords of the castle. . . .

Castle Bremgarten, near Bern, was the house of Max Wassmer, where Hesse was often a guest. The "Black King" in Winterthur refers to another friend, Georg Reinhart, to whose house, "filled with secrets," Hesse was often invited. The names of artists and writers which occur in *Journey to the East,* are all either directly the names of actual historical persons or immediately derived from them: Lauscher, Klingsor, Paul Klee, Ninon (Hesse's wife), Hugo Wolf, Brentano, Lindhorst, etc. In other words, it appears likely that the scenes described are based on the actual experiences of a very close group of friends who met in each other's homes in Southern Germany and Switzerland and pursued the journey to what was "not only a country and something geographical, but it was the home and youth of the soul, it was everywhere and nowhere, it was the union of all times."

So the clues suggest that for a moment in "historical reality" a writer named Hermann Hesse and his friends wandered together through the limitless pageants of expanded consciousness, down through the evolutionary archives. Then, apparently, H.H. loses contact, slips back to his mind and his egocentric perspectives. ". . . the pilgrimage had shattered . . . the magic had then vanished more and more." He has stumbled out of the life-stream into robot rationality. H.H. wants to become an author, spin in words the story of his life. "I, in my simplicity, wanted to write the story of the League, I, who could not decipher or understand one-thousandth part of those millions of scripts, books, pictures and references in the archives!" Archives? The cortical library?

Hermann Hesse: Poet of the Interior Journey

What then was, is, the League? Is it the exoteric society with a golden-clad President, Leo, maker of ointments and herbal cures, and a Speaker, and a High Throne, and an extended council hall? These are but the exoteric trappings. Is not the League rather the "procession of believers and disciples . . . incessantly . . . moving towards the East, towards the Home of Light"? The eternal stream of life ever unfolding. The unity of the evolutionary process, too easily fragmented and frozen by illusions of individuality. ". . . a very slow, smooth but continuous flowing or melting; . . . It seemed that, in time, all the substance from one image would flow into the other and only one would remain. . . ."

Many who have made direct contact with the life-process through a psychedelic or spontaneous mystical experience find themselves yearning for a social structure. Some external form to do justice to transcendental experiences. Hermann Hesse again provides us with the esoteric instructions. Look within. The League is within. So is the two-billion-year-old historical archive, your brain. Play it out with those who will dance with you, but remember, the external differentiating forms are illusory. The union is internal. The League is in and around you at all times.

But to be human is to be rational. *Homo sapiens* wants to know. Here is the ancient tension. To be. To know. Well, the magician has a spell to weave here, too. The intellect divorced from old-fashioned neurosis, freed from egocentricity, from semantic reification. The mind illuminated by meditation ready to play with the lawful rhythm of concepts. The Bead Game.

The Bead Game (Magister Ludi),[7] begun in 1931, finished eleven years later, was published six months after its completion, but in Switzerland, not Germany. "In opposition to the present world I had to show the realm of mind and of spirit, show it as real and unconquerable; thus my work became a Utopia, the image was projected into the future, and to my surprise the world of Castalia emerged almost by itself. Without my knowledge, it was already preformed in my soul." Thus wrote Hesse in 1955. *The Bead Game* is the synthesis and end-point of Hesse's developing thought; all the strands begun in *Siddhartha, Journey to the East, Steppenwolf* are woven together into a vision of a future society of mystic game-players. The "players with pearls of glass" are an élite of intellectual mystics who, analogously to the monastic orders of the Middle Ages,

THE PSYCHEDELIC READER

have created a mountain retreat to preserve cultural and spiritual values. The core of their practice is the bead game, "a device that comprises the complete contents and values of our culture." The game consists in the manipulation of a complex archive of symbols and formulae, based in their structure on music and mathematics, by means of which all knowledge, science, art and culture can be represented.

> This Game of games . . . has developed into a kind of universal speech, through the medium of which the players are enabled to express values in lucid symbols and to place them in relation to each other. . . . A Game can originate, for example, from a given astronomical configuration, a theme from a Bach fugue, a phrase of Leibnitz or from the Upanishads, and the fundamental idea awakened can, according to the intention and talent of the player, either proceed further and be built up or enriched through assonances to relative concepts. While a moderate beginner can, through these symbols, formulate parallels between a piece of classical music and the formula of a natural law, the adept and Master of the Game can lead the opening theme into the freedom of boundless combinations.

The old dream of a *universitas,* a synthesis of human knowledge, combining analysis and intuition, science and art, the play of the free intellect, governed by aesthetic and structural analogies, not by the demands of application and technology. Again, on the intellectual plane, the problem is always just how much structure the mind game should have. If there are no overall goals or rules, we have ever-increasing specialization and dispersion, breakdown in communication, a Babel of cultures, multiple constrictions of the range in favor of deepening the specialized field. Psychology. If there is too much structure or over-investment in the game-goals, we have dogmatism, stifling conformity, ever-increasing triviality of concerns, adulation of sheer techniques, virtuosity at the expense of understanding. Psychoanalysis.

In the history of the bead game, the author explains, the practice of meditation was introduced by the League of Eastern Wayfarers in reaction against mere intellectual virtuosity. After each move in the game a period of silent meditation was observed; the origins and meaning of the symbols involved were slowly absorbed by the players. Joseph Knecht, the Game Master, whose life is described in the book, sums up the effect as follows:

122

Hermann Hesse: Poet of the Interior Journey

> The Game, as I interpret it, encompasses the player at the conclusion of his meditation in the same way as the surface of a sphere encloses its centre, and leaves him with the feeling of having resolved the fortuitous and chaotic world into one that is symmetrical and harmonious.

Groups which attempt to apply psychedelic experiences to social living will find in the story of Castalia all the features and problems which such attempts inevitably encounter: the need for a new language or set of symbols to do justice to the incredible complexity and power of the human cerebral machinery; the central importance of maintaining direct contact with the regenerative forces of the life-process through meditation or other methods of altering consciousness: the crucial and essentially insoluble problem of the relation of the mystic community to the world at large. Can the order remain an educative, spiritual force in the society, or must it degenerate through isolation and inattention to a detached, alienated group of idealists? Every major and minor social renaissance has had to face this problem. Hesse's answer is clear: the last part of the book consists of three tales, allegedly written by Knecht, describing his life in different incarnations. In each one the hero devotes himself wholeheartedly to the service and pursuit of an idealist, spiritual goal, only to recognize at the end that he has become the slave of his own delusions. In "The Indian Life" this is clearest: Dasa, the young Brahmin, meets a yogi who asks him to fetch water; by the stream Dasa falls asleep. Later he marries, becomes a prince, has children, wages war, pursues learning, is defeated, hurt, humiliated, imprisoned, dies and — wakes up by the stream in the forest to discover that everything had been an illusion.

> Everything had been displaced in time and everything had been telescoped within the twinkling of an eye: everything was a dream, even that which had seemed dire truth and perhaps also all that which had happened previously — the story of the prince's son Dasa, his cowherd's life, his marriage, his revenge upon Nala and his sojourn with the Yogi. They were all pictures such as one may admire on a carved palace wall, where flowers, stars, birds, apes and gods can be seen portrayed in bas-relief. Was not all that which he had most recently experienced and now had before his eyes — this awakening out of his dream of princehood, war and prison, this standing by the spring, this water bowl which he had just shaken, along with the thoughts he was now thinking — ultimately woven of the same stuff? Was it not dream, illusion, Maya? And what he was about to live in the

future, see with his eyes and feel with his hands until death should come — was that of other stuff, of some other fashion? It was a game and a delusion, foam and dream, it was Maya, the whole beautiful, dreadful, enchanting and desperate kaleidoscope of life with its burning joys and sorrows.

The life of Joseph Knecht is described as a series of awakenings from the time he is "called" to enter the Castalian hierarchy ("Knecht" in German means "servant"), through his period as Magister Ludi, to his eventual renunciation of the order and the game. Castalia is essentially the League, frozen into a social institution. Again the trickster involves us in his magnificent utopian vision, the "Game of games," only to show at the end of the transience of this form as of all others. Having reached the highest position possible in the order Knecht resigns his post. He warns the order of its lack of contact with the outside world and points out that Castalia, like any other social form, is limited in time. In his justificatory speech he refers to "a kind of spiritual experience which I have undergone from time to time and which I call 'awakening.' . . ."

> I have never thought of these awakenings as manifestations of a God or a demon or even of an absolute truth. What gives them weight and credibility is not their contact with truth, their high origin, their divinity or anything in that nature, but their reality. They are monstrously real in their presence and inescapability, like some violent bodily pain or surprising natural phenomenon. . . . My life, as I saw it, was to be a transcendence, a progress from step to step, a series of realms to be traversed and left behind one after another, just as a piece of music perfects, completes and leaves behind theme after theme, tempo after tempo, never tired, never sleeping, always aware and always perfect in the present. I had noticed that, coincidental with the experience of awakening, there actually were such steps and realms, and that each time a life stage was coming to an end it was fraught with decay and a desire for death before leading to a new realm, and awakening and to a new beginning.

The mystic or visionary is always in opposition to or outside of social institutions, and even if the institution is the most perfect imaginable, the Game of games, even if it is the one created by oneself, this too is transient, limited, another realm to be traversed. After leaving Castalia, Knecht wanders off on foot:

> It was all perfectly new again, mysterious and of great promise; everything that had once been could be revived, and much that was

new besides. It seemed ages since the day and the world had looked so beautiful, innocent and undismayed. The joy of freedom and independence flowed through his veins like a strong potion, and he recalled how long it was since he had left this precious sensation, this lovely and enchanting illusion !"

So there it is. The saga of H.H. The critics tell us that Hesse is the master novelist. Well, maybe. But the novel is a social form, and the social in Hesse is exoteric. At another level Hesse is the master guide to the psychedelic experience and its application. Before your LSD session, read *Siddhartha* and *Steppenwolf*. The last part of the *Steppenwolf* is a priceless manual.

Then when you face the problem of integrating your visions with the plastic-doll routine of your life, study *Journey to the East*. Find yourself a magic circle. League members await you on all sides. With more psychedelic experience, you will grapple with the problem of language and communication, and your thoughts and your actions will be multiplied in creative complexity as you learn how to play with the interdisciplinary symbols, the multi-level metaphors. *The Bead Game.*

But always — Hesse reminds us — stay close to the internal core. The mystic formulae, the League, the staggeringly rich intellectual potentials are deadening traps if the internal flame is not kept burning. The flame is of course always there, within and without, surrounding us, keeping us alive. Our only task is to keep tuned in.

REFERENCES

1 *Siddhartha.* (Transl. Hilda Rosner.) New York: New Directions, 1951. New Directions Paperbooks, 1957. (Quotes from pp. 20, 144, 147, 151-53.) [*Siddhartha*. Eine indische Dichtung. Berlin: S. Fischer, 1922.]

2 *Steppenwolf.* (Transl. Basil Creighton.) New York: Holt (1929); Ungar (1957); Random House [Modern Library] (1963). (Quotes from pp. vi, 62, 63, 66-7, 197-99, 217, 246.) [*Der Steppenwolf*. Berlin: S. Fischer, 1927.]

3 *The Journey to the East.* (Transl. Hilda Rosner.) New York: Noonday Press Paperback, 1957. (Quotes from pp. 31, 3, 10, 27-8, 29, 96, 118. Translation occasionally emended.) [*Die Morgenlandfahrt*. Eine Erzählung. Berlin: S. Fischer, 1932.]

4 Kurt Beringer: *Der Meskalinrausch*, seine Geschichte und Erscheinungsweise. Berlin: Springer, 1927.

[5] René Daumal: *Mount Analogue.* An Authentic Narrative. (Transl. and intro. by Roger Shattuck; postface by Véra Daumal.) London: Vincent Stuart, 1959. New York: Pantheon, 1960. [*Le mont analogue.* Préface par Rolland de Renéville, récit véridique. Paris: Librairie Gallimard, 1952.]

[6] Bernhard Zeller: *Hermann Hesse: Eine Chronik in Bildern.* Frankfurt a.M.: Suhrkamp, 1960.

[7] *Magister Ludi (The Bead Game).* (Transl. Mervyn Savill.) New York: Holt (1949); Ungar Paperback (1957). (Quotes from pp. 17, 39, 10, 500-1, 355-6, 359, 367.) [*Das Glasperlenspiel.* Versuch einer Lebensbeschreibung des Magister Ludi Josef Knecht samt Knechts hinterlassenen Schriften. 2 vv. Zürich: Fretz & Wasmuth, 1943. Frankfurt a.M.: Suhrkamp, 1961.]

[A complete listing of Hesse's works and the critical literature on him is available in Helmut Waibler's *Hermann Hesse: Eine Bibliographie.* Bern und München: Francke, 1962. Pp. 350.]

Did Hesse use mind-changing drugs?

Although the argument of the preceding commentary does not depend on the answer to this question, there are sufficient clues in Hesse's writings to make the matter of some historical and literary interest. In Germany, at the time Hesse was writing, considerable research on mescaline was going on. This has been reported in a monograph by Kurt Beringer *Der Meskalinrausch.* Much of the material was also analyzed in Heinrich Klüver's monograph, *Mescal,* the first book on mescaline published in English.*

In response to our inquiry, Professor Klüver, now at the University of Chicago, has written:

> To my knowledge Hermann Hesse never took mescaline (I once raised this question in Switzerland). I do not know whether he even knew of the mescaline experiments going on under the direction of Beringer in Heidelberg. You know, of course, that Hesse (and his family) was intimately acquainted with the world and ideas of India. This no doubt has colored many scenes in his books.

Readers of the journal who have any further information bearing on this question are invited to communicate with the editors.

---

* *Mescal.* The 'Divine' Plant and Its Psychological Effects. London: Kegan Paul, Trench & Trubner, 1928. (To be reprinted late 1964, Univ. of Chicago Press.)

Psychometabolism

SIR JULIAN HUXLEY[1]

As a mere biologist, I felt somewhat alarmed on being asked to talk on psychological matters to a gathering of psychiatrists. I eventually decided to approach the subject in the general perspective of evolution, and to speak about the role of mind as an operative factor in the evolutionary process.

If we look at the process of biological evolution as a whole, we will see that it tends toward the production of types which can utilize more of the world's space and material resources more efficiently. To achieve this, new types of metabolic utilization appear. The most fundamental metabolic divergence was that between green plants and animals. Later, there developed many new types of metabolic systems, capable of utilizing new materials. Termites, with the aid of their intestinal protozoa, can utilize wood; ruminants can utilize cellulose with the aid of their bacterial flora and protozoan fauna. Sometimes greater efficiency of exploitation is attained by symbiosis. The most famous case of such symbiosis between complementary metabolic systems is that of the lichens, which are mixed organisms, part algae and part fungi.

It is important to note that these metabolic novelties may produce results which affect the further course of evolution, by altering or even increasing the material resources available for future generations. Thus during much more than half the period of life's evolution on earth, there was no wood. When abundant wood was eventually produced by large green terrestrial plants, it provided the material for a new type of metabolic exploitation by termites. Again, once terrestrial vertebrates had produced keratin in bulk, the opportunity arose for the evolution of clothes-moths. This type of cybernetic feedback is a regular feature of the evolutionary process.

The other major tendency in biological evolution is manifested in the evolution of mind, a trend towards a higher degree of awareness. This is especially marked in the later stages of the process in the dominant types of animals, notably insects, spiders and vertebrates, and is of course mediated by their brains. Brains can be regarded as psychometabolic organs. Just as the physiological metabolic systems of organisms utilize the raw material provided by the physiochemical resources of the environment and metabolize them into special material substances, so brains, more highly developed, utilize the raw materials of simple experience and transform them into special systems of organized awareness.

This at once brings up the perennial problem of the relation between mind and body. We must first remember that the only primary reality we know is our own subjective experience. We can only *deduce* that other human beings have similar subjective experiences. This is perfectly legitimate, both logically and scientifically. It is also necessary pragmatically; life could not go on otherwise. We are sometimes able to detect and prove differences in other people's possibilities of subjective awareness, as, for example, with color-blindness or "taste-blindness." But in general we quite legitimately deduce that other human beings are conscious and have minds similar to ours, because they are made in the same sort of way and behave in the same sort of way, and because that is the only basis for understanding them and co-existing with them.

The only satisfactory approach to the general problem is an evolutionary one. We begin with man as an organization of *Weltstoff* — the stuff of which the universe is made. The human organization has two aspects: first, a material one when seen from the outside, and secondly a mental or subjective one when experienced from the inside. We are simultaneously and indissolubly both matter and mind.

Extending our survey to higher animals, it is not only scientifically legitimate but obvious that we must ascribe subjective awareness to them, as Darwin did in his great book *The Expression of Emotions in Man and Animals*. It is all too obvious for the higher apes. It is equally legitimate to say that mammals such as dogs must possess a marked degree of subjective awareness; otherwise, indeed, we should not be able to interpret their behavior at all. We can extend the principle to lower vertebrates with a high though lesser degree of certainty. Indeed, I do not see how you can refuse some sort of subjective awareness to higher invertebrates such as bees and ants. This, however, poses an extremely interesting neurological problem — how are bees and ants capable of their extremely complex behavioral activities? For instance, bees have a symbolic language, yet their brain is no bigger than a pin's head, with a number of neurons many orders of magnitude lower than that in any vertebrate brain.

The legitimacy and indeed the necessity of extending the capacity for awareness to less complex organizations than our human selves is equally obvious when we consider our own development. After all, we all start as a fertilized ovum whose behavior gives no evidence of awareness. Unless we believe that an entity like a "soul" or "mind" is somehow inserted into the human embryo from outside at some stage, we must conclude that this capacity for subjective awareness arises naturally and gradually in the course of development out of some dim original potentiality.

In this connection an analogy with bioelectricity is useful. As any zoologist knows, there are several genera of electric fish. Some are capable of giving quite severe shocks, while others, which are inhabitants of muddy waters where vision is not of much use, emit electric pulses by means of which they detect objects at a distance and so can steer themselves. (In passing, it is interesting that Galen mentions that electro-shock treatment was employed in antiquity — torpedo fish were used as a cure for headache and various other disorders.) A century ago, the electrical properties of these fish were supposed to be unique, and the problem of their evolutionary origin was a great puzzle to Darwin. However, we now know that the activities of every living cell in the body are accompanied by minute electrical changes: such changes occur every time a gland secretes or a muscle contracts. These are accidental epiphenomena, in the sense that they are not of direct biological advantage to the organism, but are merely consequences of the way living substance is made. In electric fish, on the other hand, certain tissues (muscular in some cases, glandular in others), have been modified so as to amplify and summate these minute electrical changes until they reach an intensity which is of biological significance.

This provides a perfectly good analogy with the evolution of mind. In this view, every living organism has what I may call a "mentoid" or potentially mental aspect, something of the nature of subjective awareness which is merely a consequence of the way it is made, and confers no biological advantage in its life. Brains, on the other hand, are organs where a large number of impulses from many different kinds of sense-organs, extero-, intero-, and proprioceptive, are brought together in some kind of closed-circuit system and can interact and combine there without issuing directly in motor activity, as with reflex systems. Brains are thus a mechanism for intensifying, amplifying and organizing life's original dim subjectivity to a level where it becomes significant in the life of the organism.

Today, we can be certain that biological evolution has taken place primarily, and indeed almost wholly, by means of the mechanism of natural selection. This means that no important character can evolve unless it is of biological advantage. This being so, mind cannot be just a useless epiphenomenon; it must be of significance and confer biological advantage. It does so by giving the organism a fuller awareness of both outer and inner situations, thus providing better guidance for behavior in the chaos and complexity of existence.

One way in which it does this is that, in some unexplained way, it generates qualitative distinction out of quantitative difference. The sensation of blue is irreducibly different from red. The difference between blue and red depends on quantitative differences in the frequency of the light-waves reaching the retina and of the impulses passing up the optic nerves, but, as sensations, blueness and redness are qualitatively distinct. Biologically, this permits readier discrimination between objects: it is much easier to discriminate between two qualitatively different colors than between two quantitatively different shades of gray.

Discrimination is similarly aided by the radical qualitative differences between the different modalities of sensation — sight, hearing, touch, smell, and so on — which again are irreducible in terms of any common factor. Again, it is essential to be able to discriminate potentially damaging situations and objects from those which are potentially enjoyable and useful, and this has been achieved through the radical qualitative difference between the sensations of pleasure and of pain. Similarly, it is valuable to discriminate between threatening or dangerous situations and desirable or useful ones: this has been achieved by the evolution of sharp quantitative differences in our "built-in" emotions — fear as against curiosity, for example, or sexual attraction as against hostility.

Finally, the central organ of awareness, the brain, has the astonishing capacity of integrating an enormous number of separate, and often disparate, elements of experience into an organized pattern of which the animal is aware as a whole, and which it experiences as different from all other such patterns. One of the ways in which experience is integrated is in memory; another way is in mental organizations for directing future behavior.

This integration of sensory information into organized patterns which can be readily discriminated in awareness may produce extraordinary results. Some of the most extraordinary are concerned with the way in which animals find their way about. For instance, we now know that migrating birds find their way by steering with the sun if they are day migrants and by the constellations if they are night migrants. Of course, they can only do this by means of some extremely elaborate computer system in their brains — though this is no more elaborate than the computer system in our own brains which enables us, while playing tennis, to anticipate our opponent's stroke with appropriate movements of our own. In both cases, however, the computer system is only the mechanism of the action; the organism must in some way be aware of the situation as a whole in order to put the computer system into operation. This instantaneous awareness of total situations is a psychometabolic activity of decisive importance for successful behavior.

Many interesting psychometabolic organizations operate in higher animals. Frequently, learning capacity is grafted onto an innate response. A good example is found in the English Robin, which is quite different from the American Robin, a smaller bird with a brighter red breast. In the breeding season, the sight of a red-breasted rival will stimulate hostility in a male Robin in occupancy of a territory. The same effect is produced by a stuffed dummy; even if the dummy's head, tail and wings are removed, leaving only a fragment of body with a patch of red feathers, this will be attacked in the same way. The sight of the red breast is a simple sign-stimulus which releases a built-in mechanism of attack. On the other hand, the system can be modified by the further psychometabolic activity of learning. A male Robin will learn to accept a female as mate even though she too has a red breast; and eventually, through becoming aware of slight differences in behavior, he will learn to discriminate between his individual mate and other female Robins, though they are indistinguishable to the human observer.

Just as the evolution of new kinds of material metabolism can provide the material basis for further biological change, so the evolution of new kinds or modes of awareness has effects on later evolution. Let me again take color and pattern as an example. As soon as there were organisms which came into existence possessing the capacity for colored pattern-vision, new and adaptive patterns began to evolve, both in members of the same species and in other species. Such characters are called allaesthetic; they have evolved in relation to the sensory capacity of other organisms. Patterns of warning coloration in insects, for instance, could not have evolved except in relation to the color-vision of the predators of the insects; and the striking color-patterns seen in the sexual display of birds could not have evolved unless birds were capable of color-vision and pattern-discrimination. Striking examples of allaesthetic characters are found in flower-color. Bees are completely red-blind, but they can see ultraviolet. In consequence, there is a total absence of pure scarlet flowers pollinated by bees. Some pure scarlet flowers exist, but they are all pollinated by birds, because birds can see red. Conversely, if bee-pollinated flowers are photographed by ultraviolet light, patterns are often revealed which are invisible to our eyes, but are of functional importance in guiding the bees to the nectar: they have been evolved in relation to this capacity of bees to see ultra-violet.

Let me return to the simple visual patterns serving to release specific behavior, which have come into prominence through the work of men like Lorenz and Tinbergen and Thorpe. The newly hatched Herring-gull pecks at its parent's bill, which then regurgitates food for it. Tinbergen showed that if the newly hatched young is tested before it has even seen an adult bird, it will peck just as well at a colored cardboard model as at the real parent's beak. The pattern of the beak — yellow with a red spot at the tip of the lower mandible — acts as a sign-stimulus operating the mechanism releasing the pecking reaction.

The whole system is "innate" — genetically determined. But its operation can be modified. As mentioned earlier, the normal beak is yellow, fairly elongated and with a red spot near the end of the lower mandible. A model without any spot has very little effect on the young. One with a spot of another color than red will be less efficient than the normal pattern, but more so than a model without any spot. Shortening the beak will make the model less effective, while a model which is not in the least like a normal beak, but is a very elongated rectangle with a very bright red spot near its end, will elicit a *supernormal* response — it will induce the young to peck at it more vigorously than they will at their own parent's beak.

We find similar phenomena in human beings. Here again, we find allaesthetic characters. In the evolution of man, both color and form have been employed as sign-stimuli, releasing sexual behavior or at least promoting sexual attraction. The red color of lips and cheeks is obviously of value in sexual selection, and its supernormal enhancement by rouge and lipstick is the basis for a large portion of the lucrative cosmetics industry. The form of the female breast is also a sexual sign-stimulus: its enhancement is the basis for the manufacture of brassieres, and its supernormal exaggeration has given rise to the article known as "falsies."

Ethology, as the study of animal behavior is now called, has led to some illuminating facts about the results of conflict situations. If a bird's aggressive impulses are stimulated by the presence of a rival, it often shows what is called an "intention movement" before it actually starts fighting — it gets itself into readiness for fighting. Similarly, if it is frightened, but before it actually flies off, it often shows an "intention movement" preparatory to flight. Sometimes a situation occurs in which two such emotional forces or drives are opposed in conflict. For instance, early in the breeding season, when the birds begin to mate up, the close proximity of another individual still elicits a certain amount of hostility and/or fear. Accordingly the male bird, as he approaches the female, is simultaneously animated by sexual attraction, hostility and fear. The result is a compromise attitude, intermediate between the intention movements of approach and of fleeing. Since such compromise attitudes are a regular feature of sexual approach in early breeding season, they have been utilized and polished up (if I may speak metaphorically) by natural selection and turned into functional sign-stimuli, which release sexual behavior-patterns in the mate. Attitudes which originate as mere consequences of a conflict become ritualized and converted into something of biological importance in their own right.

Another surprising consequence of conflict is what ethologists call "displacement activity." Apparently, when two conflicting drives are operating at high intensity, instead of just canceling each other out, the excess nervous tension (if I may again speak metaphorically) spills over into some quite irrelevant activity. In bird courtship, the frequent conflict between hostility and fear, instead of leading to a compromise attitude, may spill over into so-called displacement preening: the birds "make as if" to preen themselves, but do not really do so. Here again, actions which start as mere consequences may be seized on by natural selection and converted into functional sign-stimuli. Thus the displacement preening attitude of many species of

133

duck has been exaggerated, and the parts of the plumage to which it is directed have come to be adorned with bright colors, so that it has come to play a significant role as a releaser of mating behavior.

As Tinbergen and Lorenz have shown, these facts have relevance for man. Human beings show many displacement activities, such as scratching their heads when puzzled. More basically, conflict and the reconciliation of conflict in meaningful activity are of fundamental importance in human mental development, and are one of the chief concerns of psychiatrists. In man, instead of conflicting drives resulting in overt compromise attitudes, they often continue to operate internally. This results in a conflict of what we may call "intention urges" — urges or drives toward aggression, or fear, or sexual attraction; but whatever the conflict is based on, it is not overtly manifested in action. The problem is this: can these conflicting urges be reconciled internally and converted into something which combines the energy of both drives in a single and functionally valuable "superdrive"? Or are their energies going to remain locked up, so to speak, in functionally useless conflict? Or is half the energy of the conflicting drives going to be wasted by the repression of one of them?

In man there are very few examples of built-in sign-stimuli acting as releasers. The best-known is the so-called smile reflex of the human infant, which Spitz and others have studied. Even a crude model of a smiling human face will elicit a smile from the human infant at a certain early stage of life. Later, this becomes a more sophisticated reaction: learning enters in and you have to have a real face with a real smile, or at least a reasonable representation of them. The interesting thing about the smile reaction is that it is a self-reinforcing process. When the infant smiles at the mother, even if she is not smiling, she will smile back in return, and vice versa. The self-reinforcing process establishes and helps to strengthen the emotional bond between mother and infant.

This establishment of emotional bonds between members of a species is obviously of the greatest importance in evolution. Once again there are traces of it in sub-human creatures. My first important piece of behavior study was on the courtship behavior of a British bird, the Great Crested Grebe. In this species, both sexes develop elaborate sexual adornments in the breeding season and employ them in mutual displays. It is quite clear that, in addition to their stimulative function, these displays serve as an emotional bond between the members of the pair. They serve to keep the pair associated throughout the whole season, during which the young need to be looked after by both parents.

The bases of such emotional bonds are sometimes very interesting. In his fascinating studies of monkeys, Professor Harlow of Wisconsin took new-born monkeys away from their real mothers and gave them pairs of surrogate mothers. Both possessed an iron framework and a crude model of a face; one of them, the feeding mother, was provided with a bottle of milk which was the baby monkey's only source of food; the other, or furry mother, merely was covered with a furry material. In contradiction to psychoanalytic theory, the baby monkey chose to spend much more time with the furry mother, who did not satisfy its hunger but gave it a feeling of protection and an agreeable tactile sensation. It will be extremely interesting to see what happens to these monkeys after they have been brought up entirely by artificial mother surrogates. Can they be made to reaffirm an emotional bond with a real female monkey or a human surrogate? [2]

Besides bonds between members of a mated pair, and those between parent and offspring, there are familial bonds and the extremely interesting social bonds that operate in organized animal societies. Konrad Lorenz's delightful and important book, *King Solomon's Ring,* gives an account of some of these. I have only time to mention one, but one which is of great interest. The wolf-pack is an organized society of proverbially aggressive animals, but when a bigger or higher-ranking wolf is quarreling with a smaller or younger one, and the smaller one feels that he is in danger of being beaten and hurt, he will adopt a special "appeasement attitude," deliberately displaying his most vulnerable part. This acts as a sign-stimulus which definitely inhibits further aggressive behavior on the part of the larger wolf, or, if you prefer, releases a non-aggressive pattern of behavior. However angry he may have been, he just finds himself unable to go on attacking the smaller animal which is advertising its defenselessness. An ethologist friend of mine has applied this fact to human situations. He has twice recently avoided punishment for motoring offenses by assuming a cringing self-deprecatory "appeasement attitude." In one case an aggrieved car-owner didn't even take his name and address; in the other a policeman wouldn't give him a ticket. I recommend this as a very useful piece of applied psychology, but it needs histrionic skill.

Finally there are the bonds between generations. These become of increasing importance in higher vertebrates. In some birds and mammals we see the beginnings of what one must call tradition, the handing down of the results of experience from one generation to the next. Originally this occurs only across a gap of one generation: thus among many carnivores, like foxes and lions, the young learn hunting from their parents, usually from the mother. But in the case of the Japanese monkey, we see the beginnings of cumulative tradition. The animals go about in large troops and each troop has its own food-tradition (as well as its own type of social structure): different troops have slightly different ranges of foods. Occasionally there will be an innovation. In one case young monkeys were what we call in human terms "naughty" and persisted in eating a forbidden food, even when their elders tried to stop them. Eventually the new habit spread to other juveniles, then to their mothers, then to the dominant males, and finally to the subdominant males: the process took over three years. In another case a new food habit (eating wheat) was begun by the dominant male, and then spread rapidly to females and juveniles. This is the real beginning of culture in the anthropological sense, based on the cumulative transmission of experience, including some novel experiments.

Then there are many examples of normally unrealized possibilities, cases where evolution has produced organizations which possess potentialities that are not actually realized in the normal life of the species. One of the best known cases is the counting ability of birds. Professor Otto Koehler, in Germany, found that Jackdaws have just as good a capacity for non-verbal counting as human beings. They can distinguish between sets of objects according to their number alone, up to seven, which is the limit of non-verbal counting for most humans. Of course, if we employ verbal counting — 1 - 2 - 3 - 4 - 5 - 6 and so on — we can distinguish very large numbers; but without it we cannot do any better than Jackdaws. Yet, as far as we know, this ability to count non-verbally up to seven is not utilized by Jackdaws in nature.

Another example comes from a species of titmouse, *Parus coeruleus*, the Blue Tit. In England and Western Europe after the last war there was a veritable epidemic of milk-bottle opening by these birds, pecking off the cardboard lids and drinking the cream. This was something no Blue Tit had ever done before.

In this case, individual variation was also involved. Careful analysis showed that the habit had spread from three separate foci: there must have been three individual tit geniuses who discovered how to open milk-bottles, and the practice spread by some form of imitation or learning.

The amount of individual variability is quite high in all higher vertebrates and may be of decisive importance for the success of the species. Thus, in the Blue Tit, this valuable habit was originated by a handful of exceptional individuals. Distinctive individual variability also occurs, but in a rather different context, in Bowerbirds. Bowerbirds are of extreme interest because they show the beginning of aesthetic preference. For instance, Satin Bowerbirds not only prefer blue objects to put in front of their bowers, but reject red ones and remove them to a distance. In subjective terms, they dislike red and prefer blue. Not only that, but the males will deliberately paint the bases of the twigs composing their bowers with a mixture of berry juices and charcoal chewed up in their mouths, using a stick in their beak as a kind of brush. However, only a minority of the males do this, and still fewer individuals have learned to indulge their preference for blue objects by stealing blue bags from human houses.

The realization of such latent possibilities depends on environmental conditions. As we have just seen, man has no greater capacity for non-verbal mathematics than a Jackdaw. But in modern societies, with the aid of symbolic language and proper training, many men have the capacity for higher mathematics, although this could not have been any use to primitive man when he first evolved.

Let me take a very different example. When I was in Africa two years ago, I had the good fortune to see the famous lioness, Elsa, which Mrs. Adamson brought up and then released into the wild, where she had mated with a wild lion and produced three cubs. It was really extraordinary to see how something that one must call a human-like personality had been elicited by love and interest and devoted care from this wild and aggressive creature.

Unused potentialities are often implicit in the motor structures of animals. It is on the basis of their unrivaled manipulative abilities that chimpanzees and human beings are so intelligent. The same applies to elephants. They too are exceptionally intelligent, and can manipulate objects almost as delicately as can apes or human beings. Since they do this with trunks instead of hands, I propose to call their ability *trombipulative* (I am sure that Dr. Johnson would have approved the term). But whatever we call it, it is on the basis of this ability that they have become so extremely intelligent and have developed such an elaborate social life.

(One elephantine incident, though irrelevant to my present argument, will I think interest this psychiatric gathering. When my wife and I were in the Murchison Falls Park in Uganda, the Warden told us that some months earlier he had heard an unusual type of excited screaming by an elephant. He came around a corner to find a middle-aged elephant bull approaching a younger male with homosexual intentions. The younger male was rejecting these improper advances; eventually the older bull became so frustrated that he lay on his back, rolled on the ground, and trumpeted. The younger male thereupon sat down on his haunches and just looked at the other; upon which the Warden laughed so loud that both the elephants took fright and ran off!)

Thus, if I may sum up my argument, during the biological evolution of animals, the upper level of organization of awareness has been steadily raised. This has led to a steady increase in the extent and elaboration of what we may call the animal's significant world, that part of the universe which has meaning for the organism. Think of the difference between the significant worlds of an amoeba and a flatworm, of a flatworm and a fish, of a fish and a higher mammal, of a higher mammal and ourselves.

THIS BRINGS ME TO MY REAL SUBJECT. Throughout evolution, the animal, with the aid of various bodily organs, utilizes the raw materials of its food, drink, and inspired air and transforms them into characteristic biochemical patterns which canalize and direct its physiological activities. This is metabolism. But with the aid of its brain, its organ of awareness or mind, it utilizes the raw material of its subjective experience and transforms it into characteristic patterns of awareness which then canalize and help to direct its behavior. This I venture to call psychometabolism.

During the latter stages of evolution, an increasingly efficient type of psychometabolism is superposed on and added to the universal physiological metabolism. Eventually, about 10 million years ago, purely biological evolution reached a limit, and the breakthrough to new advance was only brought about by the further elaboration of the psychometabolic apparatus of mind and brain. This gave rise to man: it endowed him with a second method of heredity based on the transmission of experience, and launched him on a new phase of evolution operating by cumulative tradition based on ideas and knowledge. Both novelties are of course superposed on the biological methods of transmission and evolution, which he also possesses.

In man, organizations of awareness become part of the evolutionary process by being incorporated in cultural tradition. Accordingly, in human evolution totally new kinds of organization are produced: organizations such as works of art, moral codes, scientific ideas, legal systems, and religions. We men are better able to evaluate, to comprehend, to grasp far more complex total patterns and situations than any other organism. We are capable of many things that no other animal is capable of: conscious reflection, the idea of self, of death, and of the future in general; we have the capacity of framing conscious purposes which can then be translated into action, and of constructing values as norms for our activities. The result is that evolution in the psychosocial phase is primarily cultural and only to a minor extent genetic.

Of course all these new types of organization evolve like everything else. The science of comparative religion shows how religions have evolved and are still evolving. The history of science studies the evolution of scientific ideas and how they become operative in the psychosocial process.

Our mental or psychometabolic organizations fall into two main categories: those for dealing with the outer world and establishing a relation with external objects; and those for dealing with our inner world and relating our perceptions and concepts and emotional drives to each other and integrating them into a more or less harmonious whole. The ultimate aim is to deal with all kinds of conflict and to reduce mental friction, so as to get the maximum flow of what is often called mental energy.

Here I want to put in a plea against the physicists' bad semantic habit of appropriating terms from common human usage and restricting their employment to physicochemical phenomena. In the strict physicist view, it is no longer permissible for a biologist to use the term "mental energy"; for the physicists, energy is something exclusively material and mathematically definable in terms of mass, velocity and the like. But the biologist and the psychologist also need a terminology. There *is* something operating in the awareness-

139

organization of man and higher animals which is analogous to energy in the physical sense, and can operate with different degrees of intensity. For this, we may perhaps use the term *psychergy*, without committing ourselves to any views as to its precise nature.

A major job for all disciplines concerned with human affairs, whether biochemistry, psychology, psychiatry or social anthropology, is to investigate the extraordinary mechanisms underlying the organization and operation of awareness, so as to lay the foundation for and promote the realization of more meaningful and more effective possibilities in the psycho-social process of human evolution.

When we look at animal behavior, it is clear that differences in possibilities of awareness between different species are primarily genetic. One species of bird prefers blue, another does not: the sign-stimulus which will release adaptive patterns of action in one species of bird, will not do so in another. There is obviously a genetic basis for the difference.

Equally obviously, there is a genetic basis for the difference between the genetically exceptional individual and the bulk of the species. All great advances in human history are due to the thought or action of a few exceptional individuals, though they take effect through the mass of people and in relation to the general social background. We have seen how, already in birds and mammals, the exceptional individual can be of some importance in the life of the species. In man, the exceptional individual can be of decisive importance.

Today, many workers in psychology and psychiatry and other behavioral and social sciences resist or even deny the idea that genetic factors are important for behavior. I am sure that they are wrong. Of course environmental factors, including learning, are always operative, but so are genetic factors. To take an example, genetic differences in psychosomatic organization and somatotype are obviously correlated with differences in temperament, and these with different reactions to stress and proneness to different diseases.

Frequently, it is not so much complete genetic determination we have got to think about, but rather proneness to this or that reaction, a tendency to develop in this or that way. This comes out very clearly in regard to cancer: every different inbred strain of mice has a different degree of proneness for a different type of cancer — sometimes 40%, sometimes 80%, in a few cases 100%. Professor Roger Williams of Texas has coined a new word, *propetology,* to denote genetic proneness. A science of propetology is badly needed.

The old-fashioned behaviorists simply denied any influence to genetic factors. For them everything was due to learning; and I am afraid that a number of ethologists and students of behavior, especially in America, still stick to that point of view. They forget that even the *capacity* to learn, to learn at all, to learn at a definite time, to learn one kind of thing rather than another, to learn more or less quickly, must have some genetic basis.

One of the most curious discoveries of the past 30 or 40 years has been that of the sensory morphisms, where a considerable proportion of the population has a sensory awareness different from that of the "normal" majority. The best known cause is a taste-morphism. Phenylthiocarbamide (PTC) tastes very bitter to the majority of human beings, but a minority of about 25%, varying somewhat in different ethnic groups, cannot taste it at all except in exceedingly high concentrations. As R. A. Fisher pointed out in his great book, *The Genetical Basis of Natural Selection,* in 1930, two sharply contrasted genetic characters like this cannot coexist indefinitely in a population unless there is a balance of biological advantage and disadvantage between them. Thus whenever we find such balanced polymorphisms, or *morphisms* as they are more simply called, we know that there must be some selective balance involved. Quite recently it has been shown that PTC taste-morphism is correlated with thyroid function; here we begin to get some inkling of what advantage or disadvantage there may be.

Years ago, Fisher, Ford, and I tested all the captive chimpanzees in England for PTC sensitivity. We found, to our delight, that within the limits of statistical error they had the same proportion of non-tasters as human beings. People asked, "How did you find out?" Actually it was quite simple; we offered them a sugar solution containing PTC. If they were non-tasters, they drank it up and put the cup out for more; if they were tasters, they spat it in our faces: it was an all-or-nothing reaction. The fact that both chimpanzees and man react alike means that this balanced morphism must have been in existence in the higher primates for at least 10 million years.

There are a number of these sensory morphisms in man. There is a sex-linked morphism with regard to the smell of hydrogen cyanide, HCN; about 18% of males are insensitive to it, which can be dangerous in a chemical works or laboratory. There is another smell-blindness with regard to the scent of Freesias. I personally am one of the considerable minority of human beings unable to smell Freesias; I can smell any other flower, but am absolutely insensitive to the particular smell of even the most fragrant Freesias. There are visual morphisms; the best known is red-green color-blindness, which is also sex-linked. Another appears to be myopia. I remember years ago discussing with Professor H. J. Muller the puzzling fact of the considerable incidence of apparently genetic myopia in modern populations. However, he pointed out that during a considerable period of human history, from the time when people began doing fine, close work and up to the period when spectacles were invented, myopia would confer certain advantages. The short-sighted man would not only be employed on well-paid work, but would usually not be sent to war, so that there was less likelihood of his being killed. This would balance the obvious disadvantage of myopia in other aspects of life.

There are some very interesting biological problems concerning sensitivity to pain. Some human mutants are apparently insensitive to pain altogether and may incur terrible injuries because damaging agencies do not hurt them; but these are very rare. On the other hand, giraffes have mouth-cavities and tongues which appear to be surprisingly insensitive to pain. I always thought that they used their beautiful long tongues to strip the leaves off the extremely thorny acacia trees on which they often feed without getting pricked; but apparently this is not so. Recently in the London Zoo, giraffes have been tested with spiny hawthorn branches: they accept them and chew them just as readily as soft foliage. This surprising fact is worth further investigation.

At the other end of the psychometabolic scale from sensation, we have problems like schizophrenia. Apparently this too must involve a balanced morphism. First, in all countries and races there are about 1% of schizophrenic people; secondly, the disease appears to have a strong genetic basis; and thirdly, as already mentioned, genetic theory makes it plain that a clearly disadvantageous genetic character like this cannot persist in this frequency in a population unless it is balanced by some compensating advantage. In this case it appears that the advantage is that schizophrenic individuals are considerably less sensitive than normal persons to histamine, are much less prone to suffer from operative and wound shock, and do not suffer nearly so much from various allergies. Meanwhile, there are indications that some chemical substance, apparently something like adrenochrome or adrenolutin, is the genetically-determined basis for schizophrenia, and in any case there is a chromatographically detectable so-called "mauve-factor" in the urine of schizophrenics.

This biochemical abnormality presumably causes the abnormality of perception found in schizophrenics. The way the schizophrenic psychometabolizes his sensory experience and relates his sensations to build meaningful perceptions, is disordered. Accordingly he is subject to disorders of sensation and of all sorts of perception, including disorders of perception of time and space, and of association. Apparently, schizophrenic individuals show much less consistency in association tests than do normal people. The schizophrenic's world is neither consistently meaningful nor stable: this naturally puts him out of joint with his fellow human beings and makes communication with them difficult and frustrating, so that he retires much more into his own private world.

Hallucinogens like mescaline, lysergic acid, and psilocybin (from a Mexican fungus) appear to exert similar dislocating effects on perception, even in incredibly low doses. In addition, they can produce totally new types of experience: some of their effects can elicit something quite new from the human mind. They may have unpleasant effects if the subject is in a wrong psychological state, and exceedingly pleasant and rewarding effects if he is in a right one. But in either case they may reveal possibilities of experience which the subject did not know existed at all. For this reason the term *psychedelic,* or mind-revealing, has been suggested for this type of psychotropic drug. In many ways their effect closely resembles a very brief but acute schizophrenia: perception is disordered in a way very like that seen in schizophrenic patients.

In psychedelic drugs we have a remarkable opportunity for interesting research. Nobody, so far as I know, has done any work on their effects on different types of psychologically normal people — people of high and low IQ, of different somatotypes, of different affective dispositions, on verbalizers and visualizers. This would be of extraordinary interest: we might find out not merely how to cure some defect, but how to promote creativity by enhancing the creative imagination.

Another problem is to discover whether psychedelics modify or enhance dreaming. The study of dreaming has received a great impetus since the recent discovery that dreaming is necessary for good mental health. If people are prevented from dreaming night after night, their mental health begins to suffer. Dreaming, it seems, provides a satisfactory way of psychometabolizing various facts and experiences that have proved resistant to the integrating efforts of our waking psychometabolic activity. Unconscious mechanisms take revenge and provide an outlet in dreams.

Early detection is another facet of the schizophrenia problem. Here too, study and research are obviously needed. Granted that there is a genetic proneness to schizophrenia, it should be possible in many cases to detect its symptoms in quite early stages of life. This could clearly best be done in the schools, so that it will be important to establish a close link between psychiatrists and school teachers. The teachers would pick out the children who are prone to schizophrenia; while the psychiatrists would then suggest appropriate methods of education and training to prevent the disease from developing.

Indeed, the subject of education in general clearly needs overhauling, in the light of the two views of the human organism that I have been advocating. Today, we have hardly begun to think of how to educate the organism as a whole — the mind-body, the joint psychophysiological mechanism which we call the human child. We confine ourselves almost entirely to mental education through verbal means, with the crude physical education of games and physical training added as something quite separate. As my brother Aldous has stressed, we need non-verbal education as well, and education of the entire mind-body instead of "mind" and "body" separately.

It is not only in regard to schizophrenia that we are confronted with situations which demand immediate remedial measures, but later find ourselves impelled to adopt a preventive or a constructive attitude. Medical history is largely the story of people trying to cope with disease, then attempting to prevent disease from arising, and finally turning their knowledge to good account in the promotion of positive health. The same is true of the psychological approach. The psychiatrist starts with the mentally diseased person, tries to cure him, or at least to prevent his disease developing further, but in the course of this remedial process, he acquires knowledge which can be of extreme importance in building up a more fruitful normal personality. However, to achieve this, a new approach is needed. Psychiatry usually attempts to analyze the causes of the diseased condition and discover its origins. The very term *psychoanalysis* commits the Freudian practitioner to this approach. This is important, but is certainly not sufficient. All important biological phenomena are irreversible processes, whose end-results are biologically more significant than their origins. Accordingly, we must study the whole process, its end-results as well as its origins, its total pattern as well as its elements.

In psychology, pure and applied, medical and educational, our main aim should be to discover how to regulate the processes of psychometabolism so that they integrate experience in a more effective and less wasteful way and produce a more fruitful end-organization. For instance, I am sure that a study of the origin and strengthening of emotional bonds will repay a great deal of effort. Let me take John Bowlby's work as an example. He studied the development of children who had been deprived of maternal care (including care by a mother substitute) during a critical period of early life, and therefore were unable to form the primary affectional bond between infant and parent. Such children proved incapable of forming further emotional bonds and of developing a normal affectional and moral organization. This whole problem of building up affectional bonds, whether between members of a family or a social group, is fundamental for human life.

The overriding psychometabolic problem, of course, is how the developing human being can integrate his interior life, whether by reconciling emotional or intellectual conflict in a higher synthesis, or by reconciling diversity in a more embracing unity. Let me take the creative arts as an example. Thus the poet must reconcile diverse and even conflicting meanings in a single work of art and, indeed, must employ multivalent or multi-significant words and phrases in the process. Good poems and paintings are among the highest products of man's psychometabolic activities. Milton's line, "Then feed on thoughts that voluntary move harmonious numbers . . ." beautifully expresses this psychometabolic concept of artistic creation, while Lowe's celebrated critical study, *The Road to Xanadu*, shows how Coleridge psychometabolized the raw materials of his personal experience, his reading and his conversations and discussions, and was able to integrate them into a single poem, "Kubla Khan," with amazing emotional impact.

145

As an example of the emotional impact exercised by great art, let me recall a story of Bertrand Russell. When he was an undergraduate at Cambridge, he and a friend were going up his staircase in College and the friend quoted Blake's famous poem, "Tiger, Tiger!, Burning Bright." Bertrand Russell had never heard or read this before, and was so overcome that he had to lean against the wall to prevent himself falling.

On the other hand, we all know that many poems and works of art fail sadly to achieve this desirable result. The way in which an operatively effective unitary pattern of intellectual, emotional and moral elements can be built up, certainly deserves study, not merely in art, but also in morality, religion, and love.

Mysticism is another psychometabolic activity which needs much further research. A really scientific study of the great mystics of the past, of their modern successors, of Yoga and other similar movements, undoubtedly would be of great value. The scientist need not, indeed must not, accept at their face value the claims of mysticism, for instance, of achieving union with God or the Absolute. But some mystics have certainly obtained results of great value and importance: they have been able to achieve an interior state of peace and strength which combines profound tranquillity and high psychological energy.

There is also the still much neglected subject of hypnotism and hypnosis, with all its implications. One of the darker chapters in the history of science and medicine is the way in which the pioneer hypnotists were attacked and often hounded out of the medical profession. Even today, there is still clearly a great deal to be discovered in this strange and exciting subject.

The field of the psychiatrist and the psychologist today is nothing less than the comprehensive study of hypnosis, drugs, education, mysticism, and the subconscious, of mental disease and mental health, of the relation between normal and abnormal or supernormal experience. Backed by the concept of psychometabolism and the fact of the increasing importance of psychological organization of experience during evolution, they will be working for a better integration of all the psychological forces operating in man's life — emotional, imaginative, intellectual and moral — in such a way as to minimize conflict and to maximize creativity. In so doing, they will be in harmony with the only desirable direction that our scientific vision indicates for the future evolution of man — a direction making for increased fulfillment of individual human beings and fuller achievemen by human societies.

---

[1] 31 Pond Street, Hampstead N.W. 3, London, England. Reprinted, with permission of author and publisher, from *Journal of Neuropsychiatry*, Vol. 3, Supplement No. 1, August, 1962. (Special Supplement: Symposium, "Newer Psychotropic Drugs and Human Behavior," San Francisco, April 28-29, 1962.)

[2] I have later learned that such monkeys suffer irreversible emotional damage and grow up permanently abnormal. Something of the sort occurs with the human babies, deprived of adequate maternal love and care during a critical period of their infancy, as John Bowlby has shown.

REFERENCES

EVOLUTION:

Huxley, Julian: *Evolution, The Modern Synthesis,* G. Allen and Unwin, Ltd., London, 1942; Harper, New York, 1943.

Huxley, Julian: *Evolution in Action,* Harper, New York, 1953.

Huxley, Julian: *The Humanist Frame,* Harper, New York, Chap. 1, 1961.

EVOLUTION OF MIND:

Darwin, Charles: *The Expression of the Emotions in Man and Animals,* London, 1872. Rev. & abridged by Surgeon-Rear-Admiral C. M. Beadnell, Watts & Co., London, 1934. Philosophical Library, New York, 1955.

Frisch, K. von: *Bees, Their Vision, Chemical Senses and Language,* Cornell University Press, Ithaca, New York, 1950.

Frisch, K. von: *The Dancing Bees,* Harcourt Brace, New York, 1955.

BRAIN AND MIND:

Hebb, D. O.: *The Organization of Behavior,* Wiley, New York, 1949.

ALLAESTHETIC CHARACTERS:

Huxley, Julian: *Evolution, the Modern Synthesis,* Harper & Brothers, New York, p. 289, 1943.

Cott, H. B.: *Adaptive Coloration in Animals,* Methuen & Co., London, 1940.

INSTINCT, RELEASERS, LEARNING, IMPRINTING, ETC.:

Lorenz, Konrad: *King Solomon's Ring,* Methuen & Co., London, 1952.

Tinbergen, N.: *The Study of Instinct,* Clarendon Press, Oxford, 1951.

Thorpe, W. H.: *Learning and Instinct in Animals,* Methuen & Co., London, 1956.

Köhler, O.: "The Ability of Birds to 'Count,'" *Bull. Anim. Behaviour,* 9:41, 1950.

CULTURAL TRADITION IN MONKEYS:

Dobzhansky, Th.: *Mankind Evolving, The Evolution of the Human Species,* Yale University Press, New Haven, Connecticut, p. 212, 1962.

EMOTIONAL BONDS:

Harlow, H. F., and Zimmermann, R. R.: "The Development of Affectional Responses in Infant Monkeys," *Proc. Amer. Philos. Soc.,* 102:501-9, 1958.

Huxley, J. S.: "The Courtship Habits of the Great Crested Grebe, etc.," *Proc. Zool. Soc.,* p. 492, 1914.

THE PSYCHEDELIC READER

Scott, J. P.: "Critical Periods in the Development of Social Behavior in Puppies," *Psychosomatic Medicine*, 20 :42, 1958.
Bowlby, J.: "Maternal Care and Mental Health," *Bull. World Health Organization*, 1951.
Bowlby, J.: "An Ethological Approach to Research in Child Development," *Brit. J. Med. Psychol.*, 30 :230, 1957.
Bowlby, J.: "The Nature of the Child's Tie to His Mother," *Int. Jour. Psychoanalysis*, 39, Pt. 5, 350-373, 1958.

ORIGINS OF ART, ETC.:
Rensch, B.: *Homo Sapiens: vom Tier zum Halbgott*, Göttingen, 1959.
Huxley, J. S.: "Origins of Human Graphic Art," *Nature*, 149 :637, 1942.
Marshall, A. J.: *Bowerbirds*, Clarendon Press, Oxford, 1954.
Morris, D.: *The Biology of Art*, Methuen & Co., London, 1962.

EXCEPTIONAL INDIVIDUALS:
Hinde, R. A., and Fisher, J.: "Further Observations on the Opening of Milk Bottles by Birds," *Brit. Birds*, 44 :306, 1952.
Marshall, A. J.: *Bowerbirds*, Clarendon Press, Oxford, 1954.

ORIENTATION MECHANISMS:
Thorpe, W. H.: Learning and Instinct in Animals, Methuen & Co., London, p. 326, 1956.
Matthews, G. V. T.: *Bird Navigation*, Cambridge University Press, 1955.

POTENTIALITIES:
Adamson, Joy: *Born Free*, Collins, London, 1960.
Adamson, Joy: *Living Free*, Collins, London, 1961.
Carr, N.: *Return to the Wild*, Collins, London, 1962.
Maxwell, G.: *Ring of Bright Water*, Longmans, London and New York, 1960.

MORPHISM:
Fisher, R. A.: *The Genetical Theory of Natural Selection*, Clarendon Press, Oxford, 1930.
Fisher, R. A., Ford, E. B., and Huxley, J. S.: "Taste-Testing and Anthropoid Apes," *Nature*, 144 :750, 1939.
Huxley, J. S.: "Morphism and Evolution," *Heredity*, 9 :1, 1955.

PSYCHEDELIC DRUGS, SCHIZOPHRENIA, ETC.:
Huxley, A. L.: *The Doors of Perception*, Harper, New York, 1954.
Hoffer, A., and Osmond, H.: *The Chemical Basis of Clinical Psychiatry*, Charles C. Thomas, Springfield, Illinois, U.S.A., 1960.
Hoffer, A., and Osmond, H.: *Journal of Neuropsychiatry*, 2 :306-370, 1961.
Ropp, R. S. de: *Drugs and the Mind*, St. Martin's Press, New York, p. 182, 1957.

PSYCHOMETABOLISM AND POETRY:
Lowes, J. L.: *The Road to Xanadu*, [Rev. ed.] Boston [etc.] Houghton [pref. 1930] Vintage Books, New York, 1959.

Some Comments Concerning Dosage Levels Of Psychedelic Compounds For Psychotherapeutic Experiences

GARY FISHER

SUGGESTIONS FOR DOSAGE are best made for initial experiences, since an individual's receptivity and sensitivity to drugs is so variable that only experimentation with various dosages can determine for any individual the amount of drug that he will require for any particular experience desired. At the outset it should be made clear that this writer does not consider dosage to be the crucial factor in the experience the subject will have. Factors such as the individual's fear of self-exposure; his need to maintain a favorable impression of himself at all times; his willingness to learn; his ability to "go with" changing states of consciousness; the rigidity of belief patterns; the amount of insecurity about his personal worth; his preparation and intent as he goes into the session; his trust in individuals in general and particularly his confidence in the people with him; the wisdom of those who share the experience with him; and the persistence with which he defines himself — all these factors, and many more, are the crucial ones in determining the kind of experience an individual will have with the psychedelic compounds.

In spite of such a host of conditions, however, we have found that dosage does help or hinder the operation of these factors. Another word of caution: a particular dosage does not guarantee a particular reaction. The variability of response to the drugs is enormous, largely because what is most important for a particular person to learn at a particular time will vary tremendously, and thus the experience will differ accordingly.

The comments here offered concerning dosage are considered an integral part of the philosophy of psychedelic treatment outlined

149

elsewhere (e.g., Blewett & Chwelos, 1958; Chwelos, Blewett, Smith and Hoffer, 1959; IFIF, 1963; Leary, 1962; MacLean, MacDonald, Bryne & Hubbard, 1961; Savage, Terrill & Jackson, 1962; Sherwood, Stolaroff & Harman, 1962; Van Dusen, 1961; Watts, 1962). Briefly, the treatment philosophy has as its goal a radical change in personality structure, with attendant changes in values, goals, motivation, beliefs and behavior. This sought-for change is characterized by the individual's developing an attitude toward himself which enables him to begin to experience himself and the world about him in a positive, creative manner in which he assumes total responsibility for his own state of being. Sherwood, Stolaroff & Harman (1962) state:

> The concept underlying this approach is that an individual can have a single experience which is so profound and impressive that his life experiences in the months and years that follow become a continuing growth process. . . .

> There appears to emerge a universal central perception, apparently independent of subjects' previous philosophical or theological inclinations, which plays a dominant role in the healing process. This central perception, apparently of all who penetrate deeply in their explorations, is that behind the apparent multiplicity of things in the world of science and common sense there is a single reality, in speaking of which it seems appropriate to use such words as infinite and eternal. All beings are seen to be united in this Being. . . .

Much of the "psychotherapeutic" changes are seen to occur as a process of the following kind of experience:

> The individual's conviction that he is, in essence, an imperishable self rather than a destructible ego, brings about the most profound reorientation at the deeper levels of personality. He perceives illimitable worth in this essential self, and it becomes easier to accept the previously known self as an imperfect reflection of this. The many conflicts which are rooted in lack of self-acceptance are cut off at the source, and the associated neurotic behavior patterns die away. (p. 77)

It must be remembered that the impressions conveyed concerning the efficacy and characteristics of the various drugs come from the writer's experience with them and contain all the biases and prejudices inherent in any clinician's working model. The material is presented in the spirit of sharing experience gained in working with the psychedelic compounds in order to offer guideposts to those new in the field, and to offer the experienced some additional information on dosage and on technique of treatment.

Dosage Levels of Psychedelic Compounds

Pre-treatment medication:

If the session is to be run in the morning and if the subject is particularly apprehensive, it is wise to give him some mild bedtime sedative. The main reason for this is to prevent a restless and fitful night where he remains in a twilight sleep and where the cortical activity is very fast and fragmented.

We have found it wise for the individual to eat very lightly the day before his session and to have an especially light dinner the evening before the session day. If he can spend this day quietly, in peaceful surroundings with his guide (guru, therapist) and session mates, this is excellent. The subject should not eat the morning of the session, and he should also abstain from juices and coffee.

If the subject is apprehensive in the morning, and if this apprehension persists or is unusually severe, the subject should be instructed to take early morning medication. We have found librium to be a very useful drug at this stage. It should be noted that it is highly improbable that an individual will not have some degree of anxiety preceding a first psychedelic session. Indeed, in this writer's experience, it is only the very chronically psychotic individual who will show no demonstrable anxiety prior to a session. What is specifically referred to here is undue anxiety which is debilitating and which interferes with the functioning of the individual to the extent that a snowball phenomenon is initiated, wherein he becomes anxious and his anxiety makes him more frightened until he loses all perspective about the forthcoming experience. When this occurs, or it seems likely to occur, we have found it most effective to abort the reaction by early medication with librium. The dosage depends on the individual's sensitivity to drugs. Our usage of librium has been from 10 mg to 35 mg. A person's sensitivity to drugs can be roughly gauged by his sensitivity to other drugs. For instance, some people need 2½ grains of aspirin to ease a headache whereas others need 15 to 20 grains. Individuals' sensitivity to drugs varies tremendously. For example, given an equal amount of psychological rigidity and resistance (clinically estimated), we have seen two individuals vary in drug requirements by a ratio of 1 to 10 (e.g., one individual being able to have a certain degree of experience with $25\mu g$ LSD, whereas his clinically controlled partner required 250 μg).

If the individual does not have undue anxiety in his early morning hours, we then recommend giving 10 mg to 20 mg librium as the first drug in the session. Ten to fifteen minutes later 5 mg methedrine is given, followed 20 minutes later by psilocybin. The dosage of psilocybin again varies, but our range for first session experience has been from 6 mg to 16 mg. Twenty minutes following the administration of psilocybin, LSD-25 is given. Again the dosage varies, but the most effective range we have found is from 300 to 500 μg. The effect of this staggered dosage is to ease the subject gently into the state of fluid expanded consciousness. One of the effects of librium is to relax the musculature so that any somatic effects the subject begins to have from the psilocybin will not be imposed on a rigid, tense and therefore painful musculature system. If the body can become relaxed, loose, pliable and comfortable, then any somatic effects that emerge from the psychedelics will be experienced in a comfortable soma which will lead to an acceptance of these effects, rather than a resistance to them which would occur in a tense organism. Resistance results in the experiencing of pain, either somatically or psychically. When the organism is in a fluid state, impinging or emerging somatic changes take place and are experienced in this pleasant somatic setting. One very effective technique is to massage the individual early in the session. With quiet, relaxing music, soft lighting and comfortable, secure session mates, a very slow, deliberate body and head massage brings the individual into a relaxed, protective and nurturing environment, in which alarm and panic are hard to manufacture.

The methedrine serves to stimulate and activate the individual in this warm setting. Some individuals respond with too much thought activity to amphetamines, and if this can be determined prior to the session, then the methedrine should be omitted. With most people, however, this small amount of methedrine serves to produce an effect of heightened interest and fascination with the panorama of experiences that begin to come into consciousness. We have found the use of psilocybin prior to LSD to be beneficial in that psilocybin has a smooth, mellow, affectual tone. The initial effects are subtle, more gradual and more manipulatable than LSD. These techniques are all in the service of minimizing the likelihood of the individual's becoming overwhelmed too quickly with his changing state of consciousness, attempting to abort the reaction and becoming panicked when he is unable to do so. *Every precaution should be taken so that the individual does not attempt to shut off the developing consciousness expansion.* By the time the LSD begins to take effect, the individual has become relaxed, has begun to enjoy the increased sense perceptions and has become fascinated with the world of awareness that is beginning to open to him. The deep and profound experiences released by the LSD then flow uninterrupted, in an ever widening scope.

Adding drug during the session:

We have experimented with boosting with various drugs and with various dosages and time intervals. To date, our recommendation is that, given an initial adequate dosage, boosting is to be avoided. The primary season for this attitude is as follows: the individual will learn first what he needs to learn first, and boosting is often the result of a prejudiced set of the guide as to what the subject should be learning or experiencing. Secondly, boosting often indicates to the subject that it is the drug, after all, that is going to do the work (an attitude which we believe is to be avoided at all costs) and that the guide has lost faith in the individual's ability to work out his own resolutions to his conflicts and problems. Another important facet is that the individual often will take a stand early in the session concerning what he is willing and what he is not willing to do, and will stick to it despite efforts of the guide and despite boosters. Often this taking of a stand or position and sticking to it is a very important experience for the subject as he learns so deeply what and where his commitments get him, and has the opportunity to translate this experience into daily living so that he can see the fruits of his daily attitudes.

If the guide decides to boost, however, then we recommend that he use *at least as much as the initial dose of LSD* and that the boosting be done within the initial three hours. That is, if the individual has been given 350 μg LSD, then he should be boosted with an additional 350 μg, and it is preferable that it be given i.m. In our experience it is expedient to give a booster if the individual becomes completely entangled in an area in which he is in a circular bind wherein he is incapable of perspective and of conceiving any alternative solutions to his conflict. This usually involves some decision-making in which the individual sees that all old attitudes and patterns of behavior leave him with unsatisfactory solutions. In these cases the individual simply bounces from one old reaction pattern to another, without benefit. The solution is then outside the person's limit of entertained possibilities. In these cases, additional drug may be helpful to get him out of his bind, so that heretofore unimagined answers are forthcoming. Some experimenters who have had experience using dimethyltryptamine in these instances where additional drug is indicated, state that the use of this drug in quantities of 50 mg to 60 mg i.m. is very effective.

We have also found it useful to give librium when the individual gets into extreme states of agitation which pyramid, and from which there is no release — in terms of time, we would consider 40 to 50 minutes of extreme agitation and distress to be beyond the point of therapeutic usefulness. Librium used i.m. in dosages of from 50 mg to 100 mg is very helpful in allaying the extreme agitation and anxiety without bringing the individual out of the consciousness-expanded state. Librium in this respect is better than thorazine, the latter to be used when one wishes to terminate a session. This writer has found it necessary to terminate sessions on infrequent occasions. Dosage of from 25 mg to 100 mg is usually sufficient.

We have also found it helpful to use both librium and methedrine in the latter phases of sessions. Sometimes after a thoroughly exhausting emotionally charged session, it is difficult for the individual to orient himself to various "levels" of experience and phenomena, especially to the level of "usual" consciousness. Individuals may go from one level to another quite rapidly, trying to understand or rationalize these various levels, but to no avail, since the endeavor is premature. At these times we have found it helpful to use methedrine in dosages of 5 mg to 10 mg. This has the effect of smoothing out the experience and keeping the individual in a more expanded consciousness state for a longer period of time and with a gradual lowering of this expanded consciousness over an extended period. When the individual is becoming more integrated in his experience, we then use librium again in dosages from 10 mg to 25 mg as a relaxant and for a gradual soothing and calming effect. Often if there has been somatic tension during the day, this dosage of librium helps to loosen up, relax, and make the individual more comfortable.

Use of Psilocybin:

It is this author's opinion that it is not desirable to begin an individual's psychedelic experiences with psilocybin. The reason for this is that psilocybin does not have as great a potential as LSD for breaking through the resistances to expanded states of consciousness. It is best to use the most potent material available to increase the probability that an individual will be able to overcome his resistance and attain a state of cosmic (expanded) awareness. Psilocybin, although a powerful psychedelic, does not have the breadth of power of LSD. The experience of getting involved and encumbered with one's old, inadequate, value system or uncreative basic assumptions about life is to be avoided, and the most powerful agent to break these attitudinal sets is to be used when available. Dosage requirements are always to be viewed against this philosophical framework. If LSD is not available for an initial psychedelic experience, dosages of from 50 mg to 70 mg psilocybin are recommended. For initial psilocybin experiences following LSD experiences, dosages of 15 mg to 30 mg are usually sufficient.

Use of Mescaline:

Since this writer has had limited experience with mescaline, the reader is referred to Unger's (1963) review for detailed information. Low dosages of mescaline are considered to be in the range of from 100 mg to 200 mg, whereas for a standard psychedelic experience, dosages from 500 mg to 800 mg may be used. Dosages in excess of one gram are to be avoided because of toxicity. When mescaline and LSD are used together, the recommended dosage is: 200 mg to 400 mg mescaline with 100 μg to 300 μg LSD. Opinion differs with respect to the subjective effects of mescaline: some find it smoother, more mellow and giving a more prolonged descending experience than LSD, whereas others find it harsh, rough and producing unpleasant somatic effects.

Unger (1963) states:

Although the conclusion was delayed by both dissimilarities in their chemical structure and differing modes of introduction to the scientific community, it is now rather commonly adjudged that the subjective effects of mescaline, LSD-25, and psilocybin are similar, equivalent, or indistinguishable. (p. 112)

That the gross subjective effects are similar, no one would dispute. But it is this writer's impression that there are many distinguishing subjective differences among the drugs. Unger's conclusion stems mainly from experimental subjects who had limited experience with each drug. In those subjects who have had considerable experience with all three drugs, it is commonly reported that, rather than being indistinguishable, there are many distinctive experiential characteristics of each drug. This writer is not familiar, however, with any research where experienced subjects have attempted to specify which of the psychedelics was given to them in a blind trial.

Table 1 gives dosage levels (low, standard and high) and lethal dose for the drugs, LSD, psilocybin and mescaline.

TABLE 1

Dosage Levels for Some of the Psychedelic Compounds

Drug	Low Dosage	Standard Initial Psychedelic Experience	Highest Known Given to Man	LD 50 mg/kg*
LSD	25 μg - 75 μg	300 μg - 500 μg	1600 μg	Mice: iv 50 Rats: iv 16.5
Psilocybin	2 mg - 8 mg	20 mg - 40 mg	120 mg	Mice: iv 285
Mescaline	100 mg - 200 mg	500 mg - 800 mg	1500 mg	Mice: ip 500

*LD 50 mg/kg: Median Lethal Dose; 50% of subjects expire with this dosage expressed in milligram per kilogram of body weight.

Use of small dosages with experienced subjects:

This writer has often noted that experienced subjects tend to restrict themselves to a dosage level which they have found will induce a psychedelic experience. It is our opinion that this level is often unnecessarily high, and we suggest that experienced individuals experiment with smaller dosages. It is common experience that a subject finds that he needs a smaller amount of material to induce a psychedelic experience after he has had a few experiences with the larger dosage levels. However, individuals will often continue to use dosages of from 100 to 200 μg LSD. It is hypothesized that as dosage is decreased, variables of the environment and the clarity of mind prior to the session become increasingly important. Consequently, prior to small dosage sessions, a period of meditation is highly useful to enable the individual to relax and to clear his consciousness of irrelevancies. Dosages as low as 10 μg to 25 μg LSD or one mg to two mg of psilocybin have been found to produce rather amazing states of expanded consciousness.

Dosage Levels of Psychedelic Compounds

Use of small amounts of drugs for an initial experience:

One approach to be used with very anxious and frightened subjects will now be discussed. This approach can be used with any individual, of course, but with the majority of individuals it is not necessary and not even desirable. The main disadvantage of this approach is that it can build up resistance and make the desired breakthrough into cosmic consciousness more difficult. If, however, an individual is extremely apprehensive or frightened at the prospect of the psychedelic experience, and yet psychedelic treatment is indicated, small amounts of drug in a specially created atmosphere can be most helpful. Dosages of from 25 μg to 75 μg LSD are suggested, and for some subjects who are extremely drug-sensitive, even smaller amounts may be used. The idea is to create a hypnotic-like atmosphere in which the subject thoroughly enjoys himself and begins to eperience his sense modalities to their fullest possible limits. It is better with this approach to have the subject with just one guide, rather than the two or four session mates employed with the larger dosages. This guide is very active in producing and directing a comfortable, relaxed and enjoyable experience. There should be absolutely no interruptions, and the subject should be assured of this before the session begins. Special attention is paid to the decor of the room, with soft lighting and pastel shades predominating. A simply appointed room with selected objects is best. These objects are selected according to their artistic and aesthetic value. Objects with various combinations and values of color, shape and texture should be selected. Objects which have been found to be most useful are: a single flower (a red rose, a pansy, a sunflower, a violet), fresh fruit (one orange, one banana, one nectarine, a small bunch of grapes), whole grain bread and cheese. Music, of course, is most useful, and attention should be paid to the subject's favorite selections and composers. The music of Wagner, Sibelius, Saint-Saens, Richard Strauss, Liszt, Chopin, Mozart, Tchaikovsky, Mahler and Grieg is suggested. Other forms of music are also very helpful for mood change, such as Indian music, progressive jazz, Gregorian chants, Negro spirituals and the Blues. Simple figurines are useful — some made from wood and others from stone. Delicate perfumes and incense can be employed, and precious jewels are excellent. A variety of textures should be made available to the subject. Laura Huxley's record, mentioned in her book, *You Are Not the Target*, is an especially good one to play during the session, as she creates a beautiful, ecstatic and safe world for the

157

psychedelic voyager to explore. Any stimulus which will enhance the subject's completely experiencing his senses should be employed.

The guide presents these objects to the subject and helps to call his attention to the beauty of each object. In this respect it is very beneficial for the guide to take a small amount of the drug himself so that his state of expanded awareness can be shared by the subject. The guide's enjoyment of his surroundings entices the subject into the guide's world, and the more the guide is able to reach a state of ecstatic wonder, the more he can share experiences available to the subject. The guide goes about to create a state of beauty and delight to the subject—with any method at his disposal.

Somatic changes can be dealt with by having the subject communicate their first occurrence to the guide, who then suggests, perhaps in a hypnotic-like manner, that the subject gently, then thoroughly, experience these sensations as pure sensation and take the label off the sensation (e.g., pain) and simply experience it as it is. In this way the subject ceases to resist the somatically experienced sensations, and they then become delightful phenomena and cease to be painful. (Pain, either physical or psychical, is always caused by resistance to some naturally occurring phenomenon.)

The purpose of the whole experience is for the person to *learn* to experience himself and the things about him with fulfillment and joy. Having a good time and experiencing beauty *is* therapeutic. This approach is to help the individual to release his tensions, to experience his body in a delightful way, to enjoy music, to see vivid colors, to absorb works of art, to eat fruit and bread, to look at trees, flowers — to be in awe of beauty. This is a good introduction to psychedelics. It is a good introduction to one's guide in a sharing experience. In this setting the guide must be an active participant, a constant companion, and a directing initiator into pleasant and beautiful experiences.

REFERENCES

Blewett, D. B., and Chwelos, N., *Handbook for the Therapeutic Use of Lysergic Acid Diethylamide-25: Individual and Group Procedures.* Mimeographed, 1958, Saskatchewan. (In press.)

Chwelos, N., Blewett, D. B., Smith, C., and Hoffer, A., Use of d-lysergic acid diethylamide in the treatment of alcoholism. *Quart. J. Stud. Alcohol,* 1959, *20,* 577-590.

Dosage Levels of Psychedelic Compounds

Huxley, A., *The Doors of Perception.* N. Y.: Harper, 1954. (Reprinted 1962, with Huxley's *Heaven and Hell,* Harper Colophon paperbacks; hardcovor edition, early 1964.)

Huxley, L. A., *You Are Not the Target.* Foreword by A. Huxley. N. Y.: Farrar, Straus & Co., 1963. (The record titles, "Rainbow Walk" and "Your Favorite Flower," are part of a series available from: Recipes for Living and Loving, Columbia Special Products, Box 500, Pico Rivera, California.)

Leary, T., How to change behavior. In Nielsen, G. S., ed., *Clinical Psychology.* Proc. 14th Session, Intern. Congr. Appl. Psychol., Vol. IV. Copenhagen: Munksgaard, 1962. [To be reprinted January, 1964, in Bennis, W. G., *et al.,* eds., *Interpersonal Dynamics.* Essays and Readings on Interpersonal Actions. Homewood, Ill.: The Dorsey Press.] Also available from *The Psychedelic Review* as a special offprint, together with Huxley, A., Visionary Experience.

MacLean, J. R., MacDonald, D. C., Byrne, U. P., and Hubbard, A. M., The use of LSD-25 in the treatment of alcoholism and other psychiatric problems. *Quart. J. Stud. Alcohol,* 1961, *22,* 34-45.

Savage, C., Terrill, J., and Jackson, D. D., LSD, transcendence and the new beginning. *J. Nerv. Mental Disease,* 1962, *135,* 425-439.

Sherwood, J. N., Stolaroff, M. J., and Harman, W. W., The psychedelic experience — a new concept in psychotherapy. *J. Neuropsychiatry,* 1962, *4,* 69-80.

Unger, S. M., Mescaline, LSD, psilocybin, and personality change: A review. *Psychiatry,* 1963, *26,* 111-125.

Van Dusen, W., LSD and the enlightenment of Zen. *Psychologia* (Kyoto), 1961, *4,* 11-16.

Watts, A. W., *The Joyous Cosmology.* Foreword by Leary, T., and Alpert, R. N. Y.: Pantheon, 1962.

FROM
PSYCHEDELIC
REVIEW
NUMBER THREE

Notes on the Present Status of Ololiuhqui and the Other Hallucinogens of Mexico *

R. GORDON WASSON

Picietl, peyotl, teonanacatl, and ololiuhqui—these were the four great divinatory plants of Mexico at the time of the Conquest. We give the names in Nahuatl, the *lingua franca* of that time, spoken as a mother tongue by the Aztecs and many other peoples. By 'divinatory' we mean plants that served in Middle American cultures as keys to knowledge withheld from men in their normal minds, the keys to Extra-sensory Perception, the Mediators (as the Indians believed) between men and their gods. These plants were hallucinogens, psychotropic agents, psychotomimetics, if we must use the nonce words of contemporary science.

Among the remote monolingual peoples of Mexico these plants continue to this day playing their divine role. Whenever the Indian family is troubled by a grave problem, it is likely to turn to one or the other of these plants and consult it according to the usage prevailing in the region. There were other drugs, certainly, that belong to the same class, and of these more will be said later. But if we may rely on the number and quality of the witnesses, the importance that they attribute to these plants, and the strangely moving episodes that they tell us of the Indians' utter faith in and defense of them—then these four were preëminent.

The civilization of Europe had known nothing like these novel drugs of Mexico, at least not in recorded history. Similar miraculous

*This article is reprinted, with slight corrections, from *Botanical Museum Leaflets,* Harvard University, Vol. 20, No. 6, Nov. 22, 1963, pp. 161-212.

powers were attributed, in a way, to the Elements in the Mass; and the Catholic Church in Mexico was quick to perceive this, to it, alarming parallel. But belief in the divinity of the Sacrament called for an act of faith, whereas the Mexican plants spoke for themselves. In a number of situations the record is clear: the friars conceded the miracles wrought by these agents[1] but attributed them to the machinations of the Evil One. Root and branch, the Church strove to extirpate what is called this superstition, this idolatry of the miracle-working plants. The Church was unsuccessful; just how unsuccessful can be seen from the fact that these plants are taken today, throughout the Indian country, in ceremonials invoking the very name of the Virgin Mary, of the Saints (especially St. Peter and St. Paul), of Our Lord. The accessories to the rite are sold in every market place, at a special stall, often in the shadow of the parish church. The miracle-working plants pass from hand to hand by private arrangement; they are never exposed like ordinary garden produce. The rite takes place in midnight vigils, sometimes accompanied by stirring age-old chants in the vernacular. The Indians attending these rites may include prominent lay officials of the church; rumor hath it that in certain places the priest is the leading *curandero*. Let it not be forgotten that the primary use of the sacred plants was and continues to be religious—and by the same token medicinal. Religion and medicine have not yet been separated out in many of the Indian communities.

Picietl — Nicotiana rustica L.

The bright green powder of *picietl* leaves is familiar all over the Indian country in Mexico. The *curandero* rubs it on the skin, over the forearms, temples, stomach, legs. It is this that constitutes a *limpia* or ritual cleansing. Formerly, when mixed with one part of lime to ten of *picietl,* it was made into a wad that the Indian inserted between teeth and gums and sucked, much as the Quechua sucks coca, to give him strength. The friars inveighed against *picietl* with a vehemence that is proof of its importance in the native culture. It is still indispensable in the religious life of the Indians. Is it possible that *picietl* has pharmacological properties not yet discovered by science? May there be surprises for us in this plant?

Picietl is *Nicotiana rustica* L., a sister species to our ordinary tobacco, *Nicotiana Tabacum* L. They both grow in Mexico. In Nahuatl together they are *yetl,* the former alone was *picietl* (now in the vernacular *pisiete*), the latter alone was *quauhyetl.* Tobacco was already widely diffused throughout the Americas at the time of the Conquest. The Spaniards found it in the Antilles, the Portuguese in Brazil, the English in Virginia. Along with the plant the Spaniards took the name 'tobacco' from the Taíno people of Hispaniola and Cuba. Long since dead and gone, this Arawakan tribe bequeathed to the world a legacy of important words that gives us an engaging image of a blameless people: 'canoe', 'hammock', 'tobacco', 'maize', and 'potato', not to speak of a sixth, 'barbecue', that is in vogue today. And so the Taínos, cultivating their maize and sweet potatoes, smoking tobacco in their hammocks, paddling their canoes to the neighboring barbecue, were destined to be exterminated by the ferocious Caribs and the Europeans![2]

The use of tobacco spread throughout the world with epidemic speed. European explorers penetrating to lands far distant in Africa and Asia sometimes found that tobacco had reached there before them. Even the Church did nothing to combat it—outside of Mexico, that is. The Frence *abbé* with his snuff box is a familiar figure in Europe's cultural history.

Peyotl — Lophophora Williamsii (Lem.) Coult.

The history of *peyotl*, known to science as *Lophophora Williamsii* (Lem.) Coulter, has been utterly different but equally spectacular. A cactus,[3] it is by that fact exclusively a New World plant, native to the arid regions of northern Mexico—to Coahuila, Zacatecas, San Luis Potosí, and Querétaro. Presumably the plant in colonial times grew only in the north, but its use extended south as far as the state of Oaxaca.[4] Today the Indians of central and southern Mexico seem to know it no longer. But the Indians of the north still consume it in their religious ceremonies, and it is extending its range, inching its way northward from tribe to tribe in the Plains area until it has now finally reached Canada. In the same spirit of blind misunderstanding that actuated the Church in colonial Mexico, there are elements in the North American community that would invoke the police and courts to stop a practice that gives spiritual solace to our surviving Indian population.

On a different cultural plane, *peyotl* made its bow in the great world in 1888, when the toxicologist Louis Lewin of Berlin published the first paper attempting to classify it botanically and describing its sensational qualities. He was followed by Dr. S. Weir Mitchell (1896) and Havelock Ellis (1897), men who commanded wide attention in the English-speaking world.[5] These papers served to

165

alert the scientific and learned world to a new order of vegetable product, and opened the sluice-gates to an astonishing flow of discussion and experimentation. Though a booster dose was hardly needed, Aldous Huxley gave the theme a new dimension when he published his *The Doors of Perception* in 1954 and *Heaven and Hell* in 1955.[6]

The bibliography on *peyotl* is enormous: one North American anthropologist, Weston La Barre, has devoted an important part of his professional life to keeping up with it and chronicling current developments.[7] The question presents itself seriously whether the output of articles can be laid solely to the scientific interest of a strange drug, or whether supplementing this there is a subjective effect that compels those who have eaten the plant to embark upon a mission to make known what they have experienced.

Peyotl (which has commonly been eroded to 'peyote') is a Nahuatl word. Alonso de Molina in his *Vocabulario* (1571) gives its meaning as *capullo de seda, o de gusano,* 'silk cocoon or caterpillar's cocoon,' which fits well the small woolly cactus that is its source. This is probably the explanation. Others[8] cite a number of similar words in Nahuatl that invoke splendor or illumination. May these words not be secondary, having been born of the splendor of the visions that *peyotl* gives? For reasons that seem to have sprung from popular confusion, the English-speaking population of the Southwest came to call the dried *peyotl* 'mescal buttons.' Lewin, Mitchell, and Ellis, by their use of the term, fixed this grievous misnomer in the English language. Later, when the active agent came to be isolated, the chemists called the alkaloid 'mescaline', thus compounding the mistake. 'Mescal' comes from the Spanish of Mexico *mezcal,* derived in its turn from Nahuatl *mexcalli,* the name for the agave, *maguey,* or century plant from which pulque is made, which, when distilled, yields *mezcal. Mezcal* has nothing to do with 'mescal buttons' or 'mescaline'. This confusion is the lexicographers' nightmare, as can be seen in many English-language dictionaries where erroneous citations are given under the respective meanings of the word.

On the other hand there is an important *mejicanismo* that has largely escaped the lexicographers: *piule,* a generic name in Mexico for the hallucinogens. J. J. Santamaría traces it to Zapotec, in my opinion on insufficient grounds. I have heard it applied to hallucinogenic mushrooms among the Zapotec-speakers of the Sierra Costera, at San Augustín Loxicha: *piule de barda, piule de cherís,* these being distinct species of such mushrooms, or simply *piule.*[9] Does it not stem from *peyotl,* thus : *péyotl/péyutl* → *peyúle* → *piule?* As Dr. Aguirre Beltrán has shown us, in early colonial times *peyotl* was in use in Oaxaca. The present-day currency of the word among some monolingual Zapotecs might come down from that period.

Teonanacatl — 'God's flesh'

At least twenty-five of our early sources, many of them among our most important, speak of *teonanacatl,* 'God's flesh',[10] the sacred mushrooms of Middle America. Bernardino de Sahagún refers to them repeatedly and at some length. He gives in Nahuatl the text of his native informants. Of the Nahuatl poems preserved for us, one mentions them, and probably others refer to them metaphorically. There are miniatures of them in two of the early codices. We in the 20th Century would have expected the European in colonial Mexico to try them out, to satisfy his curiosity as to their properties. There is no record of any such experiment. The Spaniards (if we may judge by their words) at first rejected them with horror and loathing as an abomination, and in the ensuing centuries simply ignored them.

Such was this neglect that in 1915 William E. Safford, a North American economic botanist of established reputation, found it possible to read a major paper before a learned society, afterwards published in a respectable learned journal, denying that there had ever been sacred mushrooms in Mexico.[11] Virtually no one challenged him. In a world indifferent to such matters, torn by warfare, his arguments won by default. Only a single thin voice was raised in persistent protest, the voice of Dr. Blas Pablo Reko, a Mexican citizen born in Austria of Slavic family background, a tireless and enthusiastic field worker but one given to fanciful theories and so not taken seriously.[12] He kept insisting not only that the mushrooms had existed but that the cult survived in places off the beaten track in Oaxaca.

Twenty years went by until, one day in 1936, Ing. Roberto J. Weitlaner got his hands on some of the sacred mushrooms in Huautla de Jiménez. He sent them to Reko, who forwarded them to Harvard, where they arrived in such a state that they could not be identified. On the record Ing. Weitlaner was the first white man in modern times to have seen the *teonanacatl.* Two years later, on July 16, 1938, his daughter Irmgard, with the young anthropologist who was destined to become her husband, Jean Bassett Johnson, together with two others, Bernard Bevan and Louise Lacaud, attended a mushroom rite in Huautla, in the home of José Dorantes. Johnson later gave

167

a full account of the event.[13] So far as the sources go, they were the first white persons to attend such a ceremony.

One month later, in mid-August, the Harvard botanist Richard Evans Schultes, also in Huautla, received from native informants specimens of three species that they said were of the sacred class. He took them back to Cambridge. His field notes describe with unmistakable precision the species that was to be defined in 1956 by Roger Heim as *Psilocybe caerulescens* Murr. var. *mazatecorum* Heim.[14] Dr. David Linder, Harvard mycologist, confirmed another as *Panaeolus campanulatus* L. var. *sphinctrinus* (Fr.) Bresad. Some time later the third species was identified at Harvard by Dr. Rolf Singer as *Stropharia cubensis* Earle,[15] but he did not disclose his discovery, not even to Schultes, until many years later when it was too late to serve a purpose.

Then the Second World War supervened. Johnson was killed in North Africa in 1942. Reko died in 1953. Schultes' activities were diverted to other geographical regions. The outside world had been on the brink of discovering the Mexican mushrooms, but the war blanketed everything and the mushrooms slipped back into the well of the forgotten.

Meanwhile the matter was being approached from an altogether different angle in New York, by the Wassons, husband and wife, who had spent more than two decades gathering data on the role of mushrooms in primitive societies in Eurasia. This theme in anthropology, which we called *ethnomycology,* had never before been explored in the West. Eurasia embraced so many cultures and so much history and literature that we had resolved early in our inquiries to stop with Eurasia and leave Africa and the Americas to others. Our Eurasian studies had led us to formulate a bold surmise: *viz.,* that mushrooms had played a religious role in the lives of our remote ancestors, a role far more important than the world had supposed. We were still preoccupied with this idea when in September 1952, suddenly, we learned that a mushroom cult had been reported in 16th Century Mexico. On receipt of this, to us, sensational news, we resolved to embark upon a quest for surviving traces of that cult. At the time we knew nothing, absolutely nothing, about the cultures of Middle America. What awaited us in Mexico turned out to exceed our most sanguine anticipations, in the intellectual adventure of discovering for ourselves the rich Indian cultures of Middle America and in our rediscovery of the rite of the sacred mushroom.

In the beginning we discovered Ing. Roberto J. Weitlaner. Without minimizing what we owe to others, I rejoice that this occasion presents itself when I may properly define my debt to him.* He led us by the hand on our first excursion on muleback into the Indian country, to Huautla de Jiménez; on my second trip to Mazatlán de los Mixes; then on my visits to San Agustín Loxicha in the Sierra Costera, and to the Mazahua country. For ten years I have had repeated recourse to him, to tap his immense knowledge of the Indians, their ways, their languages, their history. He has guided my steps in the libraries, unearthed apt quotations in the sources bearing on our theme, introduced me to others working in the field who could also pin down facts. His patience, good humor, and *joie de vivre,* in the Sierra and in Mexico City, are unfailing. But above all else I have tried to learn from him his secret of dealing with the Indians. The Indians are simply living by the conventions of an orally trans-mitted culture such as our own forebears lived by only a little while ago. When you visit their villages you make allowances for this time lag. You do not treat them kindly as inferiors or children. You do not treat them *as though* they were equals. The Indians are quick to see through such fronts. Ing. Weitlaner taught us to treat the Indians *as* equals—a secret simple yet elusive. As the poet said, truly 'this is the famous stone that turneth all to gold.'

The news of the Mexican sacred mushrooms burst upon the world in the spring of 1957 with the publication of our book, *Mush-rooms, Russia & History,* and our articles in the popular magazines.[16] Roger Heim, Membre de l'Institut, Director of the Muséum National d'Histoire Naturelle, visited the Indian country of Mexico three times in response to our invitation, seeking out the sacred mushrooms. He identified fourteen species belonging to three genera—*Psilocybe, Stropharia,* and *Conocybe*—besides a number of subspecies. Most of them were new to science, although they had been known to the Indians for centuries, probably millennia. Dr. Albert Hofmann in the Sandoz laboratories of Basel undertook the delicate task of isolating the active agents, defining their molecular structure, and finally synthesizing them. By 1958, a surprisingly short time, he had accomplished his work. Many investigators began to study the properties of *psilocybine* and *psilocine,* as Dr. Hofmann called the active agents, and their possible use. In a recent bibliography I have

---

*This paper was written in honor of Robert J. Weitlaner on the occasion of his 80th birthday and will be published in Spanish in the *Homenaje* edited under the auspices of a committee headed by Dr. Alfonso Caso in Mexico City.

listed some 200 papers on work with these mushrooms that have already appeared in the past five years, in learned and scientific journals;[17] not to speak of the hundreds of articles that have come out in a score of countries in the lay press. Here again there seem to be signs that those who have experienced the mushrooms feel a compulsion to impart to others the staggering effects of *teonanacatl*.

Pipiltzintzintli — Salvia divinorum Epling & Jávito

Though *teonanacatl* has been rediscovered and identified, there still remain other plants classed with it in the colonial sources as possessed of divine (or Satanic) attributes that defeat our efforts at interpretation. Both Sahagún and Juan de Cárdenas refer to a plant that they call respectively *poyomatli* or *poyomate*,[18] grouping it with other hallucinogens. Its identity is unknown. In his *Medicina y Magia* Dr. Aguirre Beltrán cites other references to this plant in the unpublished records of the Inquisition. He likewise supplies numerous references to a second plant that belongs in the divinatory group, a plant the name of which is variously spelled in his sources but that he thinks in the original Nahuatl should be *pipiltzintzintli*.[19] Its identity, too, is unknown. The plant grew in the area where *ololiuhqui* flourished; but whereas *ololiuhqui* is the seed of a morning glory, the seed of *pipiltzintzintli* is never mentioned. It is called an *hierba*, never an *hiedra* or *bejuco* like the morning glory. There was a *macho* and an *hembra*, or male and female varieties. It was cultivated.

All of these attributes fit the *hojas de la Pastora* that the Mazatecs generally use as a divinatory plant. In September 1962 we gathered specimens of the *hojas de la Pastora*, and they were found to be a species new to science: Epling and Játiva named it *Salvia divinorum*. [20] Among the Mazatecs I have seen only the leaves ground on the *metate*, strained, and made into an infusion. The colonial records speak of an infusion made from the roots, stems and flowers. But this is not incompatible with our information about *Salvia divinorum*: the Mazatecs may confine themselves to the leaves of a plant that has the divine virtue in all its parts. I suggest that tentatively we consider *pipiltzintzintli*, the divine plant of pre-Conquest Mexico, identical with the *Salvia divinorum* now invoked in their religious supplications by the Mazatecs.

Of divinatory plants in use today that could have been used in Middle America before the Conquest, we have had experience with two: *toloache*, presumably the seeds of *Datura meteloides* Dun., and *colorines*, the seeds of *Rhynchosia pyramidalis* (Lam.) Urb. Though

PLATE I

Flowering *Salvia divinorum* E. & J., 'hojas de la Pastora', held by
Irmgard Weitlaner Johnson. 1962.　　　*Photo by* WASSON

I know of no references to *colorines* in colonial sources, I think that they are present in the famous Tepantitla fresco where strings of seeds and mushrooms are falling from the hand of Tlaloc, and where some of the seeds are red and black, with the hilum distinctly placed in the red field.[21] On the slopes of Popacatepetl the sacred mushrooms are still taken with *colorines*. It is vital that the hilum be in the red field; if it is in the black patch, it is the toxic seed of *Abrus precatorius* L., also called *colorines* and much used for beads by the Veracruzanos.

Ololiuhqui — Rivea corymbosa (L.) Hall. fil.*

Note by R. E. Schultes:

*There have recently been suggestions that the correct name of ololiuhqui is *Turbina corymbosa* (L.) Raf.

These suggestions arise from two articles which have appeared in the past several years: Roberty, G.—"Genera Convolvulacearum" in Candollea 14 (1952) 11-60; Wilson, K. A.—"The genera of Convolvulaceae in the southeastern United States" in Journ. Arn. Arb. 41 (1960) 298-317.

Roberty separates *Ipomoea, Rivea* and *Turbina,* putting the three into different subfamilies. He keeps in Rivea only one species of India and Ceylon. In Turbina, he has three species: *T. corymbosa* (which he states occurs in tropical America, the Canary Islands and the Philippines) and two other species of Mexico.

Wilson, in a key to the genera of Convolvulaceae in the southeastern states, separates out Turbina as a genus distinct from Ipomoea. While Turbina is keyed out as a distinct genus, there is no technical consideration of it in the body of the paper which follows the key. One must assume, consequently, that Turbina (as conceived by Wilson) does not occur in southeastern United States. There is, furthermore, no reference to the binomial *Turbina corymbosa* as such. Wilson pointed out that: "Generic lines are difficult to draw in this family, and treatments vary with different authors depending upon the emphasis placed on the taxonomic characters used . . ."

The question of whether to use the binomial *Rivea corymbosa,* or to assign the concept to Ipomoea on the one hand or Turbina on the other is, in effect, one of personal evaluation, by botanists, of the importance of characters.

When I first discussed ololiuhqui in 1941 (Schultes, R. E.: "A contribution to our knowledge of *Rivea corymbosa,* the narcotic ololiuqui of the Aztecs"), I looked into the problem of the generic position of the concept. I decided that, if indeed one were justified in separating this concept from Ipomoea, it must be accommodated in Rivea. The outstanding Argentine specialist on the Convolvulaceae, the late Dr. Carlos O'Donell, who was spending a year at Harvard University at that time, worked with me closely in this study and was in complete agreement. I have studied this problem again in connection with Wasson's recent work and see no reason to change my opinion. Furthermore, it is clear that such an authority as the late Professor E. D. Merrill referred this concept to Rivea, placing Turbina in synonymy under Rivea and *T. corymbosa* in synonymy under *R. corymbosa*.

In view of the fact that such authorities as O'Donell and Merrill elected to use *Rivea corymbosa;* that Wilson acknowledges that "the entire family is in need of intensive study and . . . all characters must be thoroughly re-evaluated"; that Roberty's article is hardly conservative and actually adds little to our basic knowledge of the family; and that the ethnobotanical and chemical literature has accepted *Rivea corymbosa*—in view of all these circumstances perhaps we might well continue to use the best known name until a really comprehensive study by a recognized specialist indicates that it is wrong.

Rivea corymbosa *(L.) Hallier fil.* in Engler Bot. Jahrb. 8 (1893) 157.

Convolvulus corymbosus Linnaeus Syst. Nat. Ed. 10, 2 (1759) 923.
Ipomoea corymbosa (L.) Roth Nov. 11. Sp. Ind. Orient. (1821) 109.
Turbina corymbosa (L.) Rafinesque Fl. Tellur. 4 (1838) 81.

The least known in the outside world of our quartet of major Mexican divinatory agents is *ololiuhqui;*[‡] yet it is perhaps the best known and most widely used among the Indians of that country. In the race for world attention *ololiuhqui* has been a slow starter. Beyond the confines of the Sierra Madre few except specialists have heard of it, and the bibliography on it is short. But its properties are as sensational as those of *teonanacatl* and *peyotl*. Its identity was settled in 1941. The enigma of its chemistry was resolved in 1960 when, on August 18 of that year, Dr. Albert Hofmann read his paper in Australia before an audience of scientists, many of whom

---

[‡]Although the spelling *ololiuqui* has gained wide acceptance and is now the commonest orthography, linguistic evidence indicates that this Nahuatl word is correctly written *ololiuhqui*.

were plainly incredulous, so astonishing were his findings.[22]

Ololiuhqui in Nahuatl is the name of the seeds, not of the plant that yields the seeds. The word means 'round thing', and the seeds are small, brown, and oval. The plant itself is a climber, called appropriately *coaxihuitl,* 'snake-plant', in Nahuatl, and *hiedra* or *bejuco* by the Spanish writers. It is a morning glory, and it grows easily and abundantly in the mountains of southern Mexico. Unlike *teonanacatl,* it bears seed over months, and the seed can be kept indefinitely and carried far and wide to regions where the plant itself does not grow. In Spanish it is commonly known as *semilla de la Virgen,* and in the various Indian languages there are names for it that should be carefully assembled by teams of linguists and then studied for their meanings and associations. In Oaxaca, only among the Trique of Copala have I found no familiarity with it.

Past experience has shown that for a divinatory plant to enlist the attention of the outside world two steps are usually necessary. First, it should be correctly and securely identified. Second, its chemistry should be convincingly worked out. Richard Evans Schultes settled the identity of *ololiuhqui* in the definitive paper published in 1941.[23] It is the seed of a species of *Convolvulaceae*: *Rivea corymbosa* (L.) Hall. fil. Schultes was not the first to link *ololiuhqui* with this family, but for decades there had been disputes over its identity, and since Schultes published his paper there has been none. The starting point for any student of the subject is Schultes's paper.

It is not my intention here to tell over again the story told by Schultes. I will only supplement what he had to say with this observation. In the writers of the colonial period *ololiuhqui* receives frequent mention, especially in the *Tratado* of Hernando Ruíz de Alarcón. Throughout these references there runs a note of sombre poignancy as we see two cultures in a duel to death—on the one hand, the fanaticism of sincere Churchmen, hotly pursuing with the support of the harsh secular arm what they considered a superstition and an idolatry; on the other, the tenacity and wiles of the Indians defending their cherished *ololiuhqui.* The Indians appear to have won out. Today in almost all the villages of Oaxaca one finds the seeds still serving the natives as an ever present help in time of trouble.

The Present Status of Ololiuhqui and Hallucinogens of Mexico

Tlitliltzen — Ipomoea violacea L.*

Since the appearance of the Schultes paper in 1941, and apart from the chemical findings of Dr. Hofmann, there has been only one important contribution to our knowledge of the morning glory seeds. In 1960 Don Tomás MacDougall published his discovery that in various parts of Oaxaca, especially in the Zapotec area, another seed is used exactly as *ololiuhqui* is.[24] This is the seed of a second morning glory, *Ipomoea violacea* L. In Zapotec *ololiuhqui* is known currently as *badoh;* the second seed is *badoh negro* or *badungás,* the full Zapotec equivalent of *badoh negro.* The black seeds are long and somewhat angular. In Nahuatl they could hardly be called *ololiuhqui,* since this terms means the 'round things' or 'pellets'.

The Nahua must have known them: what then did they call them? We believe the answer is to be found in Pedro Ponce's *Breve Relación de los Dioses y Ritos de la Gentilidad,* Par. 46, where he speaks of *ololiuhqui, peyote,* and *tlitliltzin,* all with the same magic properties. The third, possibly a hapax in the corpus of surviving classic Nahuatl documentation, is clearly not *ololiuhqui,* since both are mentioned in the same sentence as distinct products. The word comes from the Nahuatl root meaning 'black', with a reverential suffix. May we not assume that this was the name current in classic Nahuatl for the black seeds that Don Tomás found in wide use among the Zapotecs in the 1950's? Apparently there is a further reference to *badoh negro* in the records of the Inquisition: a Negro slave who was also a *curandero* used the term *ololiuhqui del moreno,* which Dr. Aguirre Beltrán thinks was his way of saying 'black *ololiuhqui'.* But since this Negro was obviously a stranger both to Nahuatl and to Spanish, little can be deduced from his terminology.[25]

According to Don Tomás, in San Bartolo Yautepec, a village of the Sierra Costera, only the black seed is used, but in many villages

---

Note by R. E. Schultes:

*Taxonomically, the genus Ipomoea is extremely difficult. The binomial *Ipomoea tricolor* has already crept into the limited literature that has grown up in connection with this second kind of ololiuqui. Inasmuch as some confusion may result in the use of two names—*Ipomoea tricolor* and *I. violacea*—we should point out that, after a study of plant material and the taxonomic history of these binomials, I am in agreement with the American specialist in the Convolvulaceae, H. D. House (House, H. D.: "The North American species of the genus Ipomoea" in Ann. N.Y. Acad. Sci. 18 [1908] 259), that both names actually refer to one polymorphic species. In this case, then, the older name is *Ipomoea violacea* L. Sp. Pl. (1753) 161, which should be used in preference to its synonym *I. tricolor* Cav. Ic. Pl. Rar. 3 (1794) 5, t. 208.

both kinds are known. The black is widely regarded as the more potent. In some places the black seed is called *macho*, 'male', and the men take it; the *Rivea* seed, known as *hembra*, 'female', is for the women. The dose is often seven or a multiple thereof— seven, or 14, or 21; or the seeds are measured in the cup of the hand; or, as one informant in the Sierra Mazateca told me, one takes a beer-cap full of *Rivea* seed.

Capsule and seed of *Ipomoea violacea*, enlarged two and one half times.

In recent years a number of experimenters have taken the *Rivea* seeds with no effects, and this has led one of them to suggest that the reputation of ololiuhqui is due wholly to auto-suggestion.[26] These negative results may be explained by inadequate preparation. The Indians grind the seeds on the *metate* (grinding stone) until they are reduced to flour. Then the flour is soaked in cold water, and after a short time the liquor is passed through a cloth strainer and drunk. If taken whole, the seeds give no result, or even if they are cracked. They must be ground to flour and then the flour soaked briefly in water. Perhaps those who took the seeds without results did not grind them, or did not grind them fine enough, and did not soak the resulting flour. The chemistry of the seeds seems not to vary from region to region, and seeds grown in the Antilles and in Europe are as potent as those grown in Oaxaca. I have taken the black seeds twice in my home in New York, and their potency is undeniable.

PLATE II

Photo by WASSON

Ipomoea violacea

THE PSYCHEDELIC READER

Don Tomás MacDougall and his colleague Francisco Ortega of Tehuantepec, both old and excellent friends of Ing. Weitlaner, have given us permission to use their notes and photographs for this article. We publish for the first time a map showing the villages in Oaxaca where they have found the *Ipomoea* seeds in use, a group of seven Zapotec villages visited by Don Tomás, and also six villages in the Chatino country visited at my express request by 'Chico' Ortega in 1962, since we had a suspicion that the black seed was used in that linguistic area.[27] The area of diffusion is certainly far wider than these villages, but this is a start.

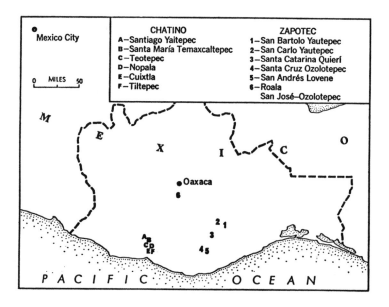

The black seeds are called variously in the Zapotec country: *badoh negro* seems to be the prevalent name. But in the Zapotec dialect spoken in San Bartolo Yautepec they are called *la'aja shnash*, 'seed of the Virgin'. In this town Francisco Jiménez ('Chico Bartolo') took a series of photographs in the course of a routine vigil. A relative of his, Paula Jiménez, is a *curandera*, and she officiated, and also dictated an account of the steps taken in the rite. We give a paraphrase of what she said.

PLATE III

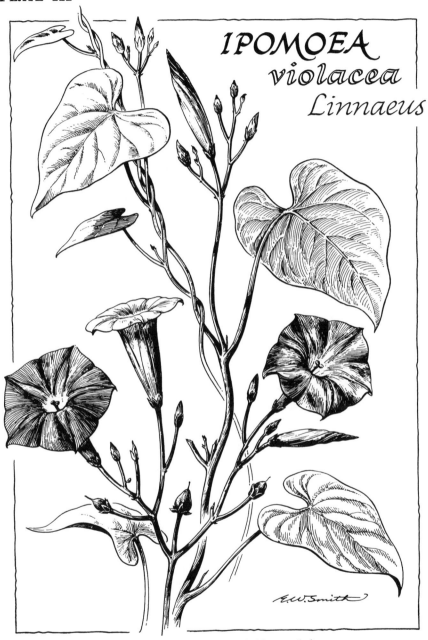

IPOMOEA
violacea
Linnaeus

Drawn approximately one-half natural size.
Drawn by ELMER W. SMITH

First, the person who is to take the seeds must solemnly commit himself to take them, and to go out and cut the branches with the seed. There must also be a vow to the Virgin in favor of the sick person, so that the seed will take effect with him. If there is no such vow, there will be no effect. The sick person must seek out a child of seven or eight years, a little girl if the patient is a man, a little boy if the patient is a woman. The child should be freshly bathed and in clean clothes, all fresh and clean. The seed is then measured out, the amount that fills the cup of the hand, or about a thimbleful. The time should be Friday, but at night, about eight or nine o'clock, and there must be no noise, no noise at all. As for grinding the seed, in the beginning you say , 'In the name of God and of the Virgencita, be gracious and grant the remedy, and tell us, Virgencita, what is wrong with the patient. Our hopes are in thee.' To strain the ground seed, you should use a clean cloth—a new cloth, if possible. When giving the drink to the patient, you must say three Pater Nosters and three Ave Marias. A child must carry the bowl in his hands, along with a censer. After having drunk the liquor, the patient lies down. The bowl with the censer is placed underneath, at the head of the bed. The child must remain with the other person, waiting to take care of the patient and to hear what he will say. If there is improvement, then the patient does not get up; he remains in bed. If there is no improvement, the patient gets up and lies down again in front of the altar. He stays there a while, and then rises and goes to bed again, and he should not talk until the next day. And so everything is revealed. You are told whether the trouble is an act of malice or whether it is illness.

The photographs illustrate the *curandera's* account of a ceremony invoking the divine power of the morning glory seeds. A feature of this recital is the child who serves the beverage. He (or she) is ritually cleansed, a symbol of purity. I encountered this practice for the first time in 1960, in the Mixteca, in the Valley of Juxtla-huaca, when Robert Ravicz and I were looking for survivals of the mushroom cult. The mushrooms were to be gathered by a virgin, they were ground on the *metate* by a virgin.[28] In 1962, in Ayautla and also in San José Tenango, in the Sierra Mazateca, again a maiden ground the leaves of the *Salvia divinorum*. Here then is a general pattern, whether in the Sierra Mazateca, or among the Mixtecs of the Valley of Juxtlahuaca, or among the Zapotecs of San Bartolo Yautepec, for the preparation of the divinatory agent, either the seeds of the morning glory or the mushrooms or the *hojas de la Pastora*. (Had we been warned in advance to look for this, perhaps we should have discovered the same custom in other regions visited in

PLATE IV

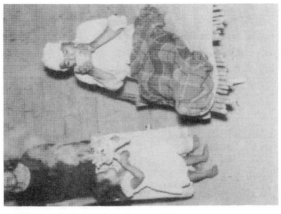

(Left) Paula Jiménez, *curandera* of San Bartolo Yautepec, making infusion of *Ipomoea violacea* seeds. 1959. (Center) Child serving the infusion to patient, with incense burner. (Right) Patient taking infusion of *I. violacea* seeds, to be enlightened as to the cause and cure of his malady.

Photos by CHICO BARTOLO

years previous to 1960.) Suddenly it dawns on us that a deep-seated harmony exists between the role of the child in preparing the divine agent and the names circulating throughout the Nahuatl area for the sacred mushrooms themselves: we have found them called *los niños,* 'the children', and *los hombrecitos y las mujercitas,* 'the little men and the little women', and *los señoritos,* 'the lordlings'. Marina Rosas, *curandera* of San Pedro Nexapa, on the slopes of Popocatepetl, called the sacred mushrooms in Nahuatl *apipiltzin,* 'the noble princes of the waters', a singularly appropriate name, in which the prefix *'a'* conveys the sense of 'water'. And here we revert to the miraculous plant that we think is the *Salvia divinorum,* called (as we believe) in Nahuatl *pipiltzintzintli,* in the records of the Inquisition dating from 1700. This is obviously related to the name for the sacred mushrooms used by Marina Rosas. Dr. Aguirre Beltrán translates it as 'the most noble Prince' and relates it to *Piltzintli,* the young god of the tender corn. In the accounts of the visions that the Indians see after they consume the sacred food—whether seeds or mushrooms or plant— there frequently figure *hombrecitos,* 'little men', *mujercitas,* 'little women', *duendes,* 'supernatural dwarfs'. Beginning with our maiden at her *metate,* here is a fascinating complex of associations that calls for further study and elaboration. For example, are these Noble Children related perchance to the Holy Child of Atocha, which gained an astonishing place in the hearts of the Indians of Middle America? Did they seize on this Catholic image and make it a charismatic icon because it expressed for them, in the new Christian religion, a theme that was already familiar to them in their own supernatural beliefs?

The tradition of the *doncella* at the *metate* is of venerable age. Jacinto de la Serna, writing his *Manual para Ministros* toward the middle of the 17th Century, said in his Chap. XV:3 about *ololiuhqui* and *peyotl*:

> como para algunas medicinas es menester molerlo, dicen que para que haga éste effecto à de ser molido *por mano de doncella.*

Nor is this citation unique. An Indian afflicted in his nether limbs was told to take *pipiltzintzintli:*[29]

> que la había de beber *molida por una doncella,* desleída en agua tibia, en ayunas, habiendo confesado y comulgado antes de tomarla y ayunado viernes y sábado y el día siguiente beberlo en el nombre de la Santísima Trinidad y de la Virgen de Guadalupe y de San Cayetano . . . y que el aposento había de estar muy abrigado, sin luz, ni aire,

PLATE V

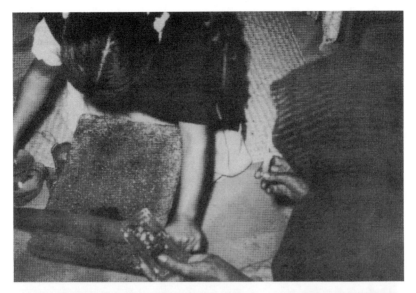

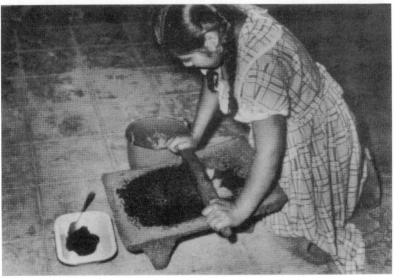

(Top) Young girl grinding sacred mushrooms (*Psilocybe mexicana* Heim) in Juxtlahuaca, Oaxaca, in Mixteca). 1960. (Bottom) Young girl grinding *Salvia divinorum* leaves, Ayautla, Sierra Mazateca. Sept. 1962.

Photos by WASSON

ni ruido, y que no se había de dormir, sino estar en silencio aguar-
dando a ver dichas figuras (un viejecito vestido de blanco y unos
muchachos pequeñitos vestidos del mesmo color) que ellas lo untarían y
desengañarían si tenía remedio su mal o no.

What an extraordinary recapitulation of the salient features of
the divinatory ritual as practiced in Middle America! There is the
interweaving of Christian elements and pagan. There is the maiden
grinding the divine element, and the preparation of the suppliant, con-
fessing and communicating before he consults the Mediator. There
is the sheltered spot—protected from sound and light. There is the
consultation on an empty stomach. There is the clear intimation as
to what one sees: a little old man clothed in white and little boys
garbed in the same. Finally there is the august pronouncement
whether the affliction of the suppliant can or cannot be remedied. All
these features are always present, regardless of the divinatory plant
that is consulted.

Perhaps there is testimony far older than the colonial records of
the Inquisition. In the collection of Hans Namuth of New York is a
'mushroom stone' of extraordinary features.[30] The cap of the mushroom carries the grooved ring that, according to Stephan F. de Borhegyi, is the hallmark of the early pre-Classic period, perhaps 1000
B.C. The stone comes from the Highlands of Guatemala. Out of
the stipe there leans forward a strong, eager, sensitive face, bending
over an inclined plane. It was not until we had seen the *doncella*
leaning over a *metate* and grinding the sacred mushrooms in Juxtla-
huaca in 1960, that the explanation of the Namuth artifact came to
us. The inclined plane in front of the leaning human figure must be
a *metate*. It follows that the face must be that of a woman. Dr.
Borhegyi and I went to see the artifact once more: it was a woman!
A young woman, for her breasts were only budding, a *doncella*. How
exciting it is to make such a discovery as this: a theme that we find in
the contemporary Mixteca, and in the Sierra Mazateca, and in the
Zapotec country, is precisely the same as we find recorded in Jacinto
de la Serna and in the records of the Santo Oficio. Again it is precisely the same (if our interpretation of the silent witness in the
New York studio of Mr. Namuth be correct) as in a stone carving
that dates back perhaps 2,500 years!

PLATE VI

Two views of mushroom stone in Namuth collection; early pre-classic, B.C. 1000-500. The figure emerging from stipe is believed to be that of a young woman before *metate* or grinding stone. Note her breasts.

Photos by HANS NAMUTH

THE PSYCHEDELIC READER

NOTES

Abbreviations:

AGN : Archivo General de la Nación, ramo Inquisición.

AB : Gonzalo Aguirre Beltrán : Medicina y Magia, 1955, México.
[Later edition, Instituto Nacional Indigenista, 1963.]
(A thoughtful monograph with numerous quotations from
AGN, indispensable for every student of its subject.)

1. *Vide, e.g.,* AGN, vol. 340, folios 354-359.

2. The Caribs were also called Canibs or Calibs. From 'Canib' the English-speaking world derived 'cannibal', which it prefers to 'anthropophage'. Shakespeare in his *Tempest* took his foul monster Caliban from the 'Calibs'.

3. There is a well known sentence in Sahagún, Bk. X, Chap. XXIX, 2, that is usually read as follows: 'Hay otra hierba como tunas de tierra que se llama peyotl . . .' According to Professor Charles E. Dibble, the Florentine Codex, folios 129v-130r, reads thus: 'Ay otra yerva, como turmas de tierra, que se llama peyotl . . .' *Turmas* is a Spanish word of ancient lineage and obviously makes sense. *Vide* Joan Corominas: *Diccionario Critico Etimológico de la Lengua Castellana,* entry *turmas.*

4. AB, Chap. 7, Area Cultural y Foco de Difusión.

5. a) Lewis Lewin: Über Anhalonium Lewinii', Arch. für experim. Path. und Pharma., 24:401: 1888. This article also appeared in translation in the same year in the *Therapeutic Gazette,* London. In these initial articles there was a misunderstanding about which species of cactus *peyotl* was.

   b) Havelock Ellis: 'A Note on Mescal Intoxication.' *The Lancet,* No. 3849, June 5, 1897.

   c) S. Weir Mitchell: 'Note upon the Effects of Anhalonium lewinii.' *Brit. Med. Journal,* Dec. 5, 1896.

   After their initial papers these three authors continued writing on the subject in books and articles. Lewin in his 1888 paper did not report on human experiences with *peyotl*: the first such report appeared in *The Therapeutic Gazette,* on Sept. 16, 1895: 'Anhalonium Lewinii (Mescal Buttons). A study of the drug, with especial reference to its physiological action upon man, with report of experiments', by D. W. Prentiss and Francis P. Morgan.

6. Now published as one volume by Harper, in paperback (Colophon series) and hardcover.

7. *Vide* Weston La Barre: 'Twenty years of peyote studies', *Current Anthropology,* Vol. 1, No. 1, Jan. 1960. To be included in a second reprinting of La Barre's *The Peyote Cult* (originally Yale Univ. Publications, No. 19) by Shoe String Press, Hamden, Conn., August, 1964, with an added chapter bringing the research up to date.

8. AB, Chap. 7, Etimología.

The Present Status of Ololiuhqui and Hallucinogens of Mexico

9. *Vide* V. P. Wasson and R. G. Wasson: *Mushrooms, Russia and History,* Pantheon Books, N.Y., 1957, pp. 311, 313, and 315.

10. 'Teo' means 'god' in Nahuatl; no Nahuatl word is more richly documented than this. The resemblance to the Latin and Greek word for 'god' is one of those fortuitous convergences of sound and meaning that occur in language studies. Given the multiplicity of languages in the world and the limited number of sounds that the human voice can utter, they are inevitable. 'Nacatl' means 'flesh', and 'nanacatl' is used for mushroom, a plural form of the word for 'flesh'. This interpretation of the word was accepted from the beginning: three early colonial sources take it for granted. No modern Nahuatl scholar disputes it.

11. 'Identification of the Teonanacatl, or "Sacred Mushroom" of the Aztecs, with the narcotic cactus, *Lophophora,* and an account of its ceremonial use in ancient and modern times', an address delivered May 4, 1915, before the Botanical Society of Washington. Published as an 'An Aztec Narcotic (Lophophora Williamsii)' in *Journal of Heredity,* Vol. 6, July 1915.

12. For Reko references, *vide* my bibliography on the hallucinogenic mushrooms published in the Botanical Museum Leaflets, Harvard Univ., Sept. 7, 1962, Vol. 20, No. 2, Entries 144-147. Second edition, with corrections and addenda, March 10, 1963, No. 2a.

13. 'The Elements of Mazatec Witchcraft', Gothenburg Ethnographical Museum. *Ethnographical Studies 9,* 1939, pp. 119-149. Also 'Some Notes on the Mazatec'. Lecture before Sociedad Mexicana de Antropología, Mexico, Aug. 4, 1938, published by Editorial Cultura, 1939. In both papers Johnson speaks of the Mazatec practice of consuming an infusion of a plant known as *hierba María* for divination purposes. This is surely the plant that we have called *hojas de María,* 'leaves of the Virgin Mary', and that has lately been named *Salvia divinorum* Epling & Játiva: we suppose it is the *pipiltzintzintli* of Colonial Nahuatl. Incidentally Ing. Weitlaner discovered a Mazatec informant in the Chinantla who gave him the most extensive testimony about this plant that we had had until it was identified in 1962. See 'Curaciones Mazatecas', AINAH, Vol. IV, No. 32, 1949-50.

14. *Vide* Harvard Botanical Museum Leaflets, Feb. 21, 1939, Vol. 7, No. 3, p. 38 ftnt.

15. *Vide* Roger Heim and R. Gordon Wasson: *Les Champignons hallucinogènes du Mexique,* Archives du Muséum National d'Histoire Naturelle, Series 7, Vol. VI, p. 184.

16. *Vide* above, Note 8. Also 'Seeking the Magic Mushroom', *Life,* May 13, 1957; International Edition, June 10; 'En Busca de los Hongos Mágicos', *Life en Espanol,* June 3. Also 'I Ate the Sacred Mushroom', by Valentina P. Wasson, *This Week,* May 19, 1957.

17. *Vide* Harvard Botanical Museum Leaflets, Sept. 7, 1962, Vol. 20, No. 2: also second edition, with corrections and addenda, March 10, 1963, No. 2a.

187

THE PSYCHEDELIC READER

18. Sahagún: X:24:27. Juan de Cárdenas: De los problemas y secretos maravillosos de las Indias, Mexico, 1591, folio 243v. Also AB: Chap. 5, Note 9, and Chap. 7, Note 97.

19. AB: Chap. 5, *Pipiltzintzintli.*

20. Harvard Botanical Museum Leaflets, Dec. 28, 1962. Vol. 20, No. 3. Carl Epling and Carlos D. Játiva-M.: 'A New Species of Salvia from Mexico.'

21. V. P. Wasson and R. Gordon Wasson: *Mushrooms, Russia and History.* pp. 324-6; also Plate LIV. Also Roger Heim and R. Gordon Wasson, *Les Champignons Hallucinogènes du Mexique,* Chap. III, Fig. 15 bis.

22. 'The Psychotropic Active Principles of *Ololiuqui,* an Ancient Aztec Narcotic', lecture delivered at the IUPAC Symposium on 'The Chemistry of Natural Products', in Melbourne, August 18, 1960.

23. 'A Contribution to our Knowledge of *Rivea corymbosa,* the narcotic ololiuqui of the Aztecs', published by Botanical Museum of Harvard University, Cambridge, Mass., 1941.

24. Thomas MacDougall: *'Ipomoea tricolor:* A Hallucinogenic Plant of the Zapotecs', published in Boletín del Centro de Investigaciones Antropológicas de México, No. 6, March 1, 1960.

25. AB: Chap. 6, El Complejo del Ololiuhqui, Para 7. The author did not know of the use of *Ipomoea* seeds when he published his book; in fact, he associated ololiuhqui with the *Solanaceae* rather than the *Convolvulaceae.* He explained the blackness of the seeds as an attribute caused by age.

26. For example, V. J. Kinross-Wright: 'Research on Ololiuqui: The Aztec Drug.' *Neuro-Psychopharmacology.* Vol. 1, Proc. 1st Intern. Congr. of Neuro-Pharmacology, Rome, Sept. 1958, pp. 453-56. Also 'Das Mexikanische Rauschgift Ololiuqui,' by Blas Pablo Reko. *El México Antiguo,* Vol. III, Nos. 3/4, Dec. 1934, pp. 1-7; especially p. 6. But for a powerful reaction see Humphry Osmond: 'Ololiuqui: the Ancient Aztec Narcotic,' published in *Jour. of Mental Science,* Vol. 101, No. 424, July 1955.

27. *Vide* R. Gordon Wasson: 'The hallucinogenic fungi of Mexico: An inquiry into the origins of the religious idea among primitive peoples.' Harvard Botanical Museum Leaflets, Vol. 19, No. 7, Feb. 1961, pp. 152-3, ftnt., last sentence.
    Chico's visit to the Chatino country served a dual purpose. In *Beyond Telepathy* (Doubleday, N.Y., 1962) Andrija Puharich on p. 20 had written, 'The author was also informed by certain *brujos* among the Chatino Indians (living in Southern Oaxaca) that they used the *Amanita muscaria* for hallucinogenic purposes. The proper dose is one-half of a mushroom.' If true, this would be sensational. It is not true. *A. muscaria* is the hallucinogenic mushroom of the Siberian tribesmen in their rites. It is not used in Mexico.
    When we first began visiting the Indian country of southern Mexico, we were expecting to find that the hallucinogenic mushroom there was *A.*

188

muscaria. For ten years we combed the various regions and we have invariably found that it played no role in the life of the Indians, though of course it is of common occurrence in the woods. We had visited the Chatino country, where we were accompanied by Bill Upson of the Instituto Lingüistico de Verano, who speaks Chatino. Later he likewise helped Puharich, but he informs us that no *brujo* in his presence testified to the use of a mushroom answering to the description of *A. muscaria.* After the Puharich statement had appeared, I gave Bill a photograph in color of *A. muscaria,* and he returned to Juquila and Yaitepec. An informant named Benigno recognized the mushroom at once and identified the stage of development that it had reached, as would be expected of a countryman intimately familiar with his environment. He said the people in his area do not take that kind of mushroom. Chico Ortega is a Zapotec Indian of mature years, keen intelligence, high sense of responsibility, and vast experience throughout the villages of the State of Oaxaca. In the summer of 1962 I sent him, with the color photo, to sound out Chatino villagers as to the use they made of it. Discreetly, he went from village to village. The results were uniformly and unanimously negative.

Puharich in *The Magic Mushroom* as well as in his most recent book is unduly impressed with the occurrence of *A. muscaria.* Wherever the species of trees occur with which it lives in mycorrhizal relationship, it is common. It is one of the commonest of fungi in North America and Eurasia. Puharich quotes at length as an authority Victor Reko, a notorious *farceur,* not to be confused with his cousin, Blas Pablo Reko.

Puharich does not identify the spot where he met his *brujos,* though it seems probable that he did not get beyond the mestizo town of Juquila. He does not explain how he put his question to them, how he explained over a double linguistic barrier what *A. Muscaria* looked like. He does not explain what precautions he took to avoid a leading question that would almost certainly produce his desired answer.

28. *Vide* Robert Ravicz: 'La Mixteca en el Estudio Comparativo del Hongo Alucinante.' AINAH, Vol. XIII, 1960 (1961), pp. 73-92; see pp. 79, 80, 86.

29. AB: 'La Familia de los Solanos,' ftnt. 45.

30. It is important to note that the nine miniature mushroom stones found at Kaminaljuyu, Guatemala, and reported by Borhegyi, 1961, figure 1, were found in a sealed cache together with nine miniature legless *metates* accompanied by *manos.* The fact that the *metates* were found together in association with the mushroom stones indicates the possibility that they were used together in ceremonials, probably for crushing or grinding mushrooms or ololiuhqui seeds.
    (Stephan F. de Borhegyi: 'Miniature Mushroom Stones from Guatemala', *Amer. Antiquity,* Vol. 26, No. 4, pp. 498-504, April 1961.)

The Religious Experience:

Its Production and Interpretation *

TIMOTHY LEARY

THREE YEARS AGO, on a sunny afternoon in the garden of a Cuernavaca villa, I ate seven of the so-called "sacred mushrooms" which had been given to me by a scientist from the University of Mexico. During the next five hours, I was whirled through an experience which could be described in many extravagant metaphors but which was above all and without question the deepest religious experience of my life.

Statements about personal reactions, however passionate, are always relative to the speaker's history and may have little general significance. Next come the questions "Why?" and "So what?"

There are many predisposing factors—intellectual, emotional, spiritual, social—which cause one person to be ready for a dramatic mind-opening experience and which lead another to shrink back from new levels of awareness. The discovery that the human brain possesses an infinity of potentialities and can operate at unexpected space-time dimensions left me feeling exhilarated, awed, and quite convinced that I had awakened from a long ontological sleep.

A profound transcendent experience should leave in its wake a changed man and a changed life. Since my illumination of August, 1960, I have devoted most of my energies to try to understand the revelatory potentialities of the human nervous system and to make these insights available to others.

I have repeated this biochemical and (to me) sacramental ritual over fifty times personally and, almost every time, I have been awed

[*Lecture delivered at a meeting of Lutheran psychologists and other interested professionals, sponsored by the Board of Theological Education, Lutheran Church in America, in conjunction with the 71st Annual Convention of the American Psychological Association, Philadelphia, Bellevue Stratford Hotel, August 30, 1963.]

by religious revelations as shattering as the first experience. During this period I have been lucky enough to collaborate in this work with more than 50 scientists and scholars who joined our various research projects. We have arranged transcendent experiences for over one thousand persons from all walks of life, including 69 full-time religious professionals, about half of whom profess the Christian or Jewish faith and about half of whom belong to Eastern religions.

Included in this roster are two college deans, a divinity college president, three university chaplains, an executive of a religious foundation, a prominent religious editor, and several distinguished religious philosophers. In our research files and in certain denominational offices there is building up a large and quite remarkable collection of reports which will be published when the political atmosphere becomes more tolerant. At this point it is conservative to state that over 75 percent of these subjects report intense mystico-religious responses, and considerably more than half claim that they have had the deepest spiritual experience of their life.[3]

The interest generated by this research led to the formation of an informal group of ministers, theologians and religious psychologists who have been meeting once a month (summers excepted) for over two years, with an average of 20 persons in attendance. In addition to arranging for spiritually oriented psychedelic sessions and discussing prepared papers, this group provided the supervisory manpower for the dramatic "Good Friday" study, and was the original planning nucleus of the organization which assumed sponsorship of our research in consciousness-expansion: IF-IF (the International Federation for Internal Freedom). The generating impulse and the original leadership of IFIF came from a seminar in religious experience, and this fact may be related to the alarm which IFIF aroused in some secular and psychiatric circles.

THE "GOOD FRIDAY" STUDY, which has been sensationalized recently in the press as "The Miracle of Marsh Chapel", deserves further elaboration not only as an example of a serious, controlled experiment, involving over 30 courageous volunteers, but also as a systematic demonstration of the religious aspects of the psychedelic revelatory experience. This study was the Ph.D.-dissertation research of a graduate student in the philosophy of religion at Harvard University, who is, incidentally, both an M.D. and a Bachelor of Divinity. This investigator set out to determine whether the transcendent experience reported during psychedelic sessions was similar to the mystical experience reported by saints and famous religious mystics.

The subjects in this study were 20 divinity students selected from a group of volunteers. The subjects were divided into five groups of four persons, and each group met before the session for orientation and preparation. To each group were assigned two guides with considerable psychedelic experience. The ten guides were professors and advanced graduate students from Boston-area colleges.

The experiment took place in a small, private chapel, beginning about one hour before noon on Good Friday. The Dean of the Chapel, who was to conduct a three-hour devotional service upstairs in the main hall of the church, visited the subjects a few minutes before the start of the service at noon, and gave a brief inspirational talk.

Two of the subjects in each group and one of the two guides were given a moderately stiff dosage (i.e., 30 mg) of psilocybin, the chemical synthesis of the active ingredient in the "sacred mushroom" of Mexico. The remaining two subjects and the second guide received a placebo which produced noticeable somatic side effects, but which was not psychedelic. The study was triple-blind: neither the subjects, guides, nor experimenter knew who received psilocybin.

Because the dissertation describing this study has not yet been published,[1] any detailed discussion of the results would be premature and unfair to the investigator. I can say, however, that the results clearly support the hypothesis that, with adequate preparation and in an environment which is supportive and religiously meaningful, subjects report mystical experiences significantly more than placebo controls.

Our studies, naturalistic and experimental, thus demonstrate that if the expectation, preparation, and setting are spiritual, an intense mystical or revelatory experience can be expected in from 40 to 90 percent of subjects ingesting psychedelic drugs. These results *may be* attributed to the bias of our research group, which has taken the "far-out" and rather dangerous position that there are experiential-spiritual as well as secular-behavioral potentialities of the nervous system. While we share and follow the epistemology of scientific psychology (objective records), our basic ontological assumptions are closer to Jung than to Freud, closer to the mystics than to the theologians, closer to Einstein and Bohr than to Newton.

193

In order to check on this bias, let us cast a comparative glance at the work of other research groups in this field who begin from more conventional ontological bases.

Oscar Janiger, a psychiatrist, and William McGlothlin, a psychologist, have reported the reactions of 194 psychedelic subjects. Seventy-three of these took LSD as part of a psychotherapy program, and 121 were volunteers. The religious "set" would not be expected to dominate the expectations of these subjects. The results, which are abstracted from a paper published in *The Psychedelic Review*,[2] are as follows:

ITEM	PERCENT Janiger-McGlothlin (non-religious setting) N = 194
Increased interest in morals, ethics . . . :	35
Increased interest in other universal concepts (meaning of life) :	48
Change in sense of values	48
LSD should be used for	
becoming aware of oneself:	75
getting new meaning to life:	58
getting people to understand each other:	42
An experience of lasting benefit:	58

Two other studies, one by Ditman *et al.*, another by Savage *et al.*, used the same questionnaire, allowing for inter-experiment comparison. Both Ditman and Savage are psychiatrists, but the clinical environment of the latter's study is definitely more religious (subjects are shown religious articles during the session, etc.). Summarizing the religious items of their questionnaires:

ITEM	PERCENT	
	Ditman (supportive) environment) N = 74	Savage (supportive environment & some religious stimuli) N = 96
Feel it [LSD] was the greatest thing that ever happened to me:	49	85
A religious experience . . . :	32	83
A greater awareness of God or a Higher Power, or an Ultimate Reality:	40	90

Here, then, we have five scientific studies by qualified investigators—the four naturalistic studies by Leary *et al.*,[3] Savage *et al.*,[4]

Ditman *el al.*,[5] and Janiger-McGlothlin,[6] and the triple-blind study in the Harvard dissertation mentioned earlier—yielding data which indicate that (1) if the setting is supportive but not spiritual, between 40 to 75 percent of psychedelic subjects will report intense and life-changing religious experiences; and that (2) if the set and setting are supportive and spiritual, then from 40 to 90 percent of the experiences will be revelatory and mystico-religious.

It is hard to see how these results can be disregarded by those who are concerned with spiritual growth and religious development. These data are even more interesting because the experiments took place during an historical era when mysticism, individual religious ecstasy (as opposed to religious religious behavior), was highly suspect, and when the classic, direct, non-verbal means of revelation and consciousness-expansion such as meditation, yoga, fasting, monastic withdrawal and sacramental foods and drugs were surrounded by an aura of fear, clandestine secrecy, active social sanction, and even imprisonment.[7] The 69 professional workers in religious vocations who partook of psychedelic substances (noted earlier), were responsible, respected, thoughtful, and moral individuals who were grimly aware of the controversial nature of the procedure and aware that their reputations and their jobs might be undermined (and, as a matter of fact, have been and are today being threatened for some of them). *Still* the results read: 75% spiritual revelation. It may well be that the most intense religious experience, like the finest metal, requires fire, the heat of external bureaucratic opposition, to produce the keenest edge. When the day comes—as it surely will—that sacramental biochemicals like LSD will be as routinely and tamely used as organ music and incense to assist in the attainment of religious experience, it may well be that the ego-shattering effect of the drug will be diminished. Such may be one aspect of the paradoxical nature of religious experience.

◆ ◆ ◆

THE RELIGIOUS EXPERIENCE. You are undoubtedly wondering about the meaning of this phrase which has been used so freely in the preceding paragraphs. May I offer a definition?

The religious experience is the ecstatic, incontrovertibly certain, subjective discovery of answers to four basic spiritual questions. There can be, of course, absolute subjective certainty in regard to secular questions: "Is this the girl I love? Is Fidel Castro a wicked man? Are the Yankees the best baseball team?" But issues which do not involve the four basic questions belong to secular games, and

195

such convictions and faiths, however deeply held, can be distinguished from the religious. Liturgical practices, rituals, dogmas, theological speculations, can be and too often are secular, i.e., completely divorced from the spiritual experience.

What are these four basic spiritual questions? There is the Ultimate-Power question, the Life question, the Human-Destiny question, and the Ego question.

1. The Ultimate-Power Question:
What is the Ultimate Power or Basic Energy which moves the universe, creates life? What is the Cosmic Plan?

2. The Life Question:
What is life, where did it start, where is it going?

3. The Human-Destiny Question:
What is man, whence did he come, and where is he going?

4. The Ego Question:
What am I? What is my place in the plan?

While one may disagree with the wording, I think most thoughtful people—philosophers or not—can agree on something like this list of basic issues. Do not most of the great religious statements—Eastern or monotheistic—speak directly to these four questions?

Now one important fact about these questions is that they are continually being answered and re-answered, not only by all the religions of the world but also by the data of the natural sciences. Read these questions again from the standpoint of the goals of (1) astronomy-physics, (2) biochemistry, (3) genetics, paleontology, and evolutionary theory, (4) neurology.

We are all aware of the unhappy fact that both science and religion are too often diverted towards secular game goals. Various pressures demand that laboratory and church forget these basic questions and instead provide distractions, illusory protection, narcotic comfort. Most of us dread confrontation with the answers to these basic questions, whether these answers come from science or religion. But if "pure" science and religion address themselves to the same basic questions, what is the distinction between the two disciplines? Science is the systematic attempt to record and measure the energy process and the sequence of energy transformations we call life. The goal is to answer the basic questions in terms of objective, observed, public data. Religion is the systematic attempt to provide answers *to the same questions* subjectively, in terms of direct, incontrovertible, personal experience.

Science is a social system which evolves roles, rules, rituals, values, language, space-time locations to further the quest for these goals—these answers. Religion is a social system which has evolved its roles, rules, rituals, values, language, space-time locations to further the pursuit of the same goals—the revelatory experience. A science which fails to address itself to these spiritual goals, which accepts other purposes (however popular), becomes secular, political, and tends to oppose new data. A religion which fails to provide direct experiential answers to these spiritual questions becomes secular, political, and tends to oppose the individual revelatory confrontation. R. C. Zaehner,[8] whose formalism is not always matched by his tolerance, has remarked that "experience, when divorced from revelation, often leads to absurd and wholly irrational excesses." Like any statement of polarity the opposite is equally true: revelation, when divorced from experience, often leads to absurd and wholly rational excesses. Those of us who have been researching the area of consciousness have been able to collect considerable sociological data about the tendency of the rational mind to spin out its own interpretations. But I shall have more to say about the political situation in a later section of this paper.

◆ ◆ ◆

At this point I should like to present my main thesis. I am going to advance the hypothesis that *those aspects of the psychedelic experience which subjects report to be ineffable and ecstatically religious involve a direct awareness of the processes which physicists and biochemists and neurologists measure.*

We are treading here on very tricky ground. When we read the reports of LSD subjects, we are doubly limited. First, *they* can only speak in the vocabulary they know, and for the most part they do not possess the lexicon and training of energy scientists. Second, *we researchers* only find what we are prepared to look for, and too often we think in crude psychological-jargon concepts: moods, emotions, value judgments, diagnostic categories.

In recent months we have re-examined our data and have begun to interview subjects from the perspective of this present hypothesis. The results are interesting. To spell them out in brief detail I am going to review some of the current scientific answers to these four basic questions and then compare them with reports from psychedelic subjects.

197

(1) The Ultimate-Power Question:

A. *The scientific answers* to this question change constantly—Newtonian laws, quantum indeterminacy, atomic structure, nuclear structure. Today the *basic energy* is located within the nucleus. Inside the atom,

> a transparent sphere of emptiness, thinly populated with electrons, the substance of the atom has shrunk to a core of unbelievable smallness: enlarged 1000 million times, an atom would be about the size of a football, but its nucleus would still be hardly visible—a mere speck of dust at the center. Yet that nucleus radiates a powerful electric field which holds and controls the electrons around it.[9]

Incredible power and complexity operating at speeds and spatial dimensions which our conceptual minds cannot register. Infinitely small, yet pulsating outward through enormous networks of electrical forces—atom, molecule, cell, planet, star: all forms dancing to the nuclear tune.

The *cosmic design* is this network of energy whirling through space-time. More than 15,000 million years ago the oldest known stars began to form. Whirling disks of gas molecules (driven of course by that tiny, spinning, nuclear force)—condensing clouds—further condensations—the tangled web of spinning magnetic fields clustering into stellar forms, and each stellar cluster hooked up in a magnetic dance with its planetary cluster and with every other star in the galaxy and each galaxy whirling in synchronized relationship to the other galaxies.

One thousand million galaxies. From 100 million to 100,000 million stars in a galaxy—that is to say, 100,000 million planetary systems per galaxy and each planetary system slowly wheeling through the stellar cycle that allows for a brief time the possibility of life as we know it.

Five thousand million years ago, a slow-spinning dwarf star we call the sun is the center of a field of swirling planetary material. The planet earth is created. In five thousand million years the sun's supply of hydrogen will be burned up, the planets will be engulfed by a final solar explosion. Then the ashen remnants of our planetary system will spin silently through the dark infinity of space. And then is the dance over? Hardly. Our tiny solar light, which is one of one hundred thousand million suns in our galaxy, will scarcely be missed. And our galaxy is one of a thousand million galaxies spinning out and up at rates which exceed the speed of light—each galaxy eventually burning up, to be replaced by new galaxies to preserve the dance equilibrium.

Here in the always changing data of nuclear physics and astronomy is the current scientific answer to the first basic question—material enough indeed for an awesome cosmology.

B. *Psychedelic reports* often contain phrases which seem to describe similar phenomena, subjectively experienced.

(a)   I passed in and out of a state several times where I was so relaxed that I felt open to a total flow, over and around and through my body (more than my body) . . . . All objects were dripping, streaming, with white-hot light or electricity which flowed in the air. It was as though we were watching the world, just having come into being, cool off, its substance and form still molten and barely beginning to harden.

(b)   Body being destroyed after it became so heavy as to be unbearable. Mind wandering, ambulating throughout an ecstatically-lit indescribable landscape. How can there be so much light—layers and layers of light, light upon light, all is illumination.

(c)   I became more and more conscious of vibrations—of the vibrations in my body, the harp-strings giving forth their individual tones. Gradually I felt myself becoming one with the Cosmic Vibration. . . . In this dimension there were no forms, no deities or personalities—just bliss.

(d)   The dominant impression was that of entering into the very marrow of existence . . . . It was as if each of the billion atoms of experience which under normal circumstances are summarized and averaged into crude, indiscriminate wholesale impressions was now being seen and savored for itself. The other clear sense was that of cosmic relativity. Perhaps all experience never gets summarized in any inclusive overview. Perhaps all there is, is this everlasting congeries of an infinite number of discrete points of view, each summarizing the whole from its perspective.

(e)   I could see the whole history and evolution along which man has come. I was moving into the future and saw the old cycle of peace and war, good times and bad times, starting to repeat, and I said, "The same old thing again, oh God! It has changed though, it is different," and I thought of the rise of man from animal to spiritual being. But I was still moving into the future and I saw the whole planet destroyed and all history, evolution, and human efforts being wiped out in this one ultimate destructive act of God.

199

Subjects speak of participating in and merging with pure (i.e., content-free) energy, white light; of witnessing the breakdown of macroscopic objects into vibratory patterns, visual nets, the collapse of external structure into wave patterns, the awareness that everything is a dance of particles, sensing the smallness and fragility of our system, visions of the void, of world-ending explosions, of the cyclical nature of creation and dissolution, etc. Now I need not apologize for the flimsy inadequacy of these words. We just don't have a better experiential vocabulary. If God were to permit you a brief voyage into the Divine Process, let you whirl for a second into the atomic nucleus or spin you out on a light-year trip through the galaxies, how on earth would you describe what you saw, when you got back, breathless, to your office? This metaphor may sound farfetched and irrelevant, but just ask someone who has taken LSD in a supportive setting.

(2) The Life Question:

A. *The Scientific Answer*:

Our planetary system began over five billon years ago and has around five billion years to go. Life as we know it dates back to about one billion years. In other words, the earth spun for about 80 percent of its existence without life. The crust slowly cooled and was eroded by incessant water flow. "Fertile mineral mud was deposited . . . now giving . . . for the first time . . . the possibility of harboring life." Thunderbolts in the mud produce amino acids, the basic building blocks of life. Then begins the ceaseless production of protein molecules, incalculable in number, forever combining into new forms. The variety of proteins "exceeds all the drops of water in all the oceans of the world." Then protoplasm. Cell. Within the cell, incredible beauty and order.

> When we consider the teeming activity of a modern city it is difficult to realize that in the cells of our bodies infinitely more complicated processes are at work—ceaseless manufacture, acquisition of food, storage, communication and administration . . . . All this takes place in superb harmony, with the cooperation of all the participants of a living system, regulated down to the smallest detail.[9]

Life is the striving cycle of repetitious, reproductive energy transformations. Moving, twisting, devouring, changing, the unit of life is the cell. And the blueprint is the genetic code, the two nucleic acids—the long, intertwined, duplicating chains of DNA and the controlling regulation of RNA—"which determine the structure of the living substance."

And where is it going? Exactly like the old Hindu myths of cyclical rotation, the astrophysicists tell us that life is a temporary sequence which occurs at a brief midpoint in the planetary cycle. Terrestrial life began around four billion years A.B. ("after the beginning" of our solar cycle) and will run for another two billion years or so. At that time the solar furnace will burn so hot that the minor planets (including Earth) will boil, bubble and burn out. In other planetary systems the time spans are different, but the cycle is probably the same.

There comes an intermediate stage in the temperature history of a planet which can nourish living forms, and then life merges into the final unifying fire. Data here, indeed, for an awesome cosmology.

B. *The psychedelic correlates* of these biological concepts sound like this: confrontation with and participation in cellular flow; visions of microscopic processes; strange, undulating, multi-colored, tissue patterns; being a one-celled organism floating down arterial waterways; being part of the fantastic artistry of internal factories; recoiling with fear at the incessant push, struggle, drive of the biological machinery, clicking, clicking, endlessly, endlessly—at every moment engulfing you. For example:

(a)   My eyes closed, the impressions became more intense. The colors were brilliant blues, purples, and greens with dashes of red and streaks of yellow-orange. There were no easily identifiable objects, only convolutions, prisms, and continuous movement.

(b)   My heart a lizard twitching lithely in my pocket, awaiting the wave again, my flesh sweating as it crawled over my bones, the mountains curved around my heart, the surf crashing against my mucoused lungs, coughing into heart beats, pulsing death to scare me. Futile body. Awaiting the undertow escaping under the wave which crashed so coughingly over my heart, blue lighted into YES. An undertow going UP . . . . The universe has an axis which is not perpendicular, and round it flock the living colors, pulsing eternal involutions.

(c)   I then gradually became aware of movement, a rocking type of movement, like on a roller-coaster, yet I did not move my body at all . . . . With an overwhelming acceleration I was turning around and around, swirling, then shuttling back and forth, like a piece of potassium on water, hissing, sparkling, full of life and fire.

201

THE PSYCHEDELIC READER

(3) The Human-Destiny Question:

A. *The Scientific Answer*:

The flame of life which moves every living form, including the cell cluster you call your*self*, began, we are told, as a tiny single-celled spark in the lower pre-Cambrian mud; then passed over in steady transformations to more complex forms. We like to speak of higher forms, but let's not ignore or patronize the single-cell game. It's still quite thriving, thank you. Next, your ancestral fire glowed in seaweed, algae, flagellate, sponge, coral (about one billion years ago); then fish, fern, scorpion, milliped (about 600 million years ago). Every cell in your body traces back (about 450 million years ago) to the same light-life flickering in amphibian (and what a fateful and questionable decision to leave the sea—should we have done it?). Then forms, multiplying in endless diversity—reptile, insect, bird—until, one million years ago, comes the aureole glory of Australopithecus.*

The torch of life next passes on to the hand-axe culture (around 600,000 years ago) to Pithecanthropus (can you remember watching for the charge of Southern elephants and the sabre-tooth tiger?); then blazing brightly in the radiance of our great-grandfather Neanderthal man (a mere 70,000 years ago), suddenly flaring up in that cerebral explosion that doubled the cortex of our grandfather Cromagnon man (44,000 to 10,000 years ago), and then radiating into the full flame of recent man, our older Stone Age, Neolithic brothers, our Bronze and Iron Age selves.

What next? The race, far from being culminated, has just begun:

The development of Pre-hominines Australopithecus . . . to the first emergence of the . . . Cromagnons lasted about . . . fifteen thousand human life-spans . . . . In this relatively short period in world history the hominid type submitted to a positively hurricane change of form; indeed he may be looked upon as one of the animal groups whose potentialities of unfolding with the greatest intensity have been realized. It must, however, by no means be expected that this natural flood of development will dry up with *Homo sapiens recens.* Man will be unable to remain man as we know him now, a modern sapiens type. He will in the courses of the next hundreds of millennia presumably change considerably physiologically and physically.[10]

---

*The fossils of the newly discovered "Homo Habilis" from East Africa are estimated to be 1,750,000 years old. (*N. Y. Times,* March 18, April 3 & 4, 1964. Another estimate traces human origins back about 15 million years!—*N. Y. Times,* April 12, 1964.)

B. *The Psychedelic Correlate*:

What does all that evolutionary business have to do with you or me or LSD or the religious experience? It might, it just might, have a lot to do with very current events. Many, and I am just bold enough to say most, LSD subjects say they experience early forms of racial or sub-human species evolution during their sessions. Now the easiest interpretation is the psychiatric: "Oh yes, hallucinations. Everyone knows that LSD makes you crazy, and your delusions can take any psychotic form." But wait; not so fast. Is it entirely inconceivable that our cortical cells, or the machinery inside the cellular nucleus, "remembers" back along the unbroken chain of electrical transformations that connects every one of us back to that original thunderbolt in the pre-Cambrian mud? Impossible, you say? Read a genetics text. Read and reflect about the DNA chain of complex protein molecules that took you as a uni-celled organism at the moment of your conception and planned every stage of your natural development. Half of that genetic blueprint was handed to you intact by your mother, and half from your father, and then slammed together in that incredible welding process we call conception.

"You", your ego, your good-old American-social-self, have been trained to remember certain crucial secular game landmarks: your senior prom, your wedding day. But is it not possible that others of your ten billion brain cells "remember" other critical survival crossroads like conception, intra-uterine events, birth? Events for which our language has few or no descriptive terms? Every cell in your body is the current-carrier of an energy torch which traces back through millions of generation-transformations. Remember that genetic code?

You must recognize by now the difficulty of my task. I am trying to expand your consciousness, break through your macroscopic, secular set, "turn you on", give you a faint feeling of a psychedelic moment, trying to relate two sets of processes for which we have no words—speed-of-light energy-transformation processes and the transcendent vision.

I'm going to call for help. I could appeal to quotes from Gamow the cosmologist, or Eiseley the anthropologist, or Hoyle the astronomer, or Teilhard du Chardin the theological biologist, or Aldous Huxley the great visionary prophet of our times, or Julian Huxley whose pharmacological predictions sound like science-fiction. I could call upon a hundred articulate scientists who talk in dazed poetry about the spiritual implications of their work. Instead, I am going to read a passage by the German anthropologist Egon Freiherr von Eickstedt. The topic is the spiritual attitude of Australopithecus. The point is that this description of the world-view of a tiny monkey-man who lived a million years ago could be a quote from any one of a hundred LSD reports I've read in the last three years. Von Eickstedt's research leads him to say that,

> In the way of experience there is dominant, throughout, a kaleidoscopic interrelated world. Feeling and perception are hardly separated in the world of visions; space and time are just floating environmental qualities . . . Thus the border between I and not-I is only at the border of one's own and actually experienced, perceptible world . . . But this by no means denotes merely bestial brutality and coarseness which is so erroneously and often ascribed to the beginnings of humanity. Quite the reverse. The thymality within his own circle means just the opposite, tenderness, goodness and cheerfulness, and allows with complete justification the presumption of a picture of intimate family life and the specific teaching of the children, also need of ornament, dance and much happiness. Thus the extremes of feeling swing with the mood between fear and love, and the dread of the unknowable . . .[11]

We have in our files an LSD report from a world-renowned theologian with astonishing parallels to this quotation.

> The best way I can describe the experience as a whole is to liken it it to an emotional-reflective-visual kaleidoscope . . . . Experiences involving these three components kept dissolving continuously from one pattern into another. Emotionally the patterns ranged from serene contentment and mild euphoria to apprehension which boarded on, but never quite slipped into, alarm. But overwhelmingly they involved (a) astonishment at the absolutely incredible immensity, complexity, intensity and extravagance of being, existence, the cosmos, call it what you will. Ontological shock, I suppose. (b) The most acute sense of the poignancy, fragility, preciousness, and significance of all life and history. The latter was accompanied by a powerful sense of the responsibility of all for all . . . . Intense affection for my family . . . . Importance and rightness of behaving decently and responsibly.

(4) The Ego Question:

A. *The Scientific Answer*:

The question "Who am I?" can be answered at many levels. Psychologists can describe and explain your psychogenesis and personal evolution. Sociologists and anthropologists can explain the structure of the tribal games which govern your development. Biologists can describe your unique physical structure. But the essence of you and "you-ness" is your consciousness. You are not a psychological or social or bodily robot. No external description comes close. What cannot be measured, replaced, understood by any objective method is your consciousness. And where is this located? In your nervous system. The secular-game engineers can entertain you with their analyses of your macroscopic characteristics, but the biochemical neurologist is the man to listen to. He is the person who can locate "you" in the five-billion-year sequence by describing the capacities of your cortex. Your consciousness is a biochemical electrical process.

The human brain, we are told,

> is composed of about 10 billion nerve cells, any one of which may connect with as many as 25,000 other nerve cells. The number of interconnections which this adds up to would stagger even an astronomer— and astronomers are used to dealing with astronomical numbers. The number is far greater than all the atoms in the universe . . . . This is why physiologists remain unimpressed with computers. A computer sophisticated enough to handle this number of interconnections would have to be big enough to cover the earth.[12]

Into this matrix floods "about 100 million sensations a second from . . . [the] various senses." And somewhere in that ten-billion-cell galaxy is a tiny solar system of connected neurons which is aware of your social self. Your "ego" is to your cortex what the planet Earth is to our galaxy with its 100,000 million suns.

B. *The psychedelic answer* to the "I" question is the crux of the LSD experience. Most of the affect swirls around this issue. As Erik Erikson reminds us, it's hard enough to settle on a simple tribal role definition of "Who am I?" Imagine the dilemma of the LSD subject whose cortex is suddenly turned on to a much higher voltage, who suddenly discovers his brain spinning at the speed of light, flooded by those 100 million sensations a second. Most of the awe and reverent wonder stems from this confrontation with an unsuspected range of consciousness, the tremendous acceleration of images, the shattering insight into the narrowness of the learned as opposed to the potentiality of awareness, the humbling sense of where one's ego is in relationship to the total energy field.

(a) I was delighted to see that my skin was dissolving in tiny particles and floating away. I felt as though my outer shell was disintegrating, and the 'essence' of me was being liberated to join the 'essence' of everything else about me.

(b) Two related feelings were present. One was a tremendous freedom to experience, to be I. It became very important to distinguish between

205

'I' and 'Me', the latter being an object defined by patterns and structures and responsibilities—all of which had vanished—and the former being the subject experiencing and feeling. My normal life seemed to be all Me, all demands and responsibilities, a crushing burden which destroyed the pleasure and freedom of being 'I'. Later in the evening the question of how to fit back into my normal life without becoming a slave of its patterns and demands became paramount. The other related feeling was one of isolation. The struggle to preserve my identity went on in loneliness; the 'I' cannot be shared or buttressed. The 'Me', structured as it is, can be shared, and is in fact what we mean when we talk about "myself", but once it is thus objectified it is no longer *I*, it has become the known rather than the knower. And LSD seemed to strip away the structure and to leave the knowing process naked—hence the enormous sense of isolation: there was no Me to be communicated.

c)   All this time, for about 2-3 hours, although there was thinking, talking going on, my mind was being used, yet there was no ego . . . . I could with total dispassion examine various relationships that 'I' had with parents, friends, parts of 'myself', etc. People who walked into the room were accepted with the same serene equanimity that I felt about accepting my own mental products; they were really walking around in my mind.

d)   I was entering into another dimension of existence. 'I' was not. Everything was totally dissolved into a flow of matter continuously moving. No time, no space. A feeling of color, but indescribable. Feeling of movement mainly. Awareness that I, the others, are only collections of clusters of molecules, which are all part of the same stream.

For the small percentage of unprepared subjects who take LSD in careless or manipulative settings and experience terror and paranoid panic, their misery invariably centers around the struggle to reimpose ego control on the whirling energy flow in them and around them. Theirs is the exhausting and sad task of attempting to slow down and limit the electrical pulse of the ten-billion-cell cerebral computer. Thorazine, alcohol and narcotics help apply the brakes. So, I fear, do words.

WHEN WE READ about the current findings of the energy sciences such as those I have just reviewed, how can our reaction be other than reverent awe at the grandeur of these observations, at the staggering complexity of the design, the speed, the scope? Ecstatic humility before such Power and Intelligence.   Indeed, what a small, secular concept—intelligence—to describe that Infinitude of

Harmonious Complexity! How impoverished our vocabulary and how narrow our imagination!

Of course, the findings of the pure sciences *do not* produce the religious reaction we should expect. We are satiated with secular statistics, dazed into robot dullness by the enormity of facts which we are not educated to comprehend. Although the findings of physics, genetics, paleontology and neurology have tremendous relevance to our life, they are of less interest than a fall in the stock market or the status of the pennant race.

The message is dimly grasped hypothetically, rationally, but never experienced, felt, known. But there can be that staggering, intellectual-game ecstasy which comes when you begin to sense the complexity of the Plan. To pull back the veil and see for a second a fragment of the energy dance, the life power. How can you appreciate the Divine unless you comprehend the smallest part of the fantastic design? To experience (it's always for a moment) the answers to the four basic spiritual questions is to me the peak of the religious-scientific quest.

But how can our ill-prepared nervous systems grasp the message? Certainly the average man cannot master the conceptual, mathematical bead game of the physics graduate student. Must his experiential contact with the Divine Process come in watered-down symbols, sermons, hymns, robot rituals, religious calendar art, moral-behavior sanctions eventually secular in their aim? Fortunately the Great Plan has produced a happy answer and has endowed every human being with the equipment to comprehend, to know, to experience directly, incontrovertibly. It's there in that network of ten billion cells, the number of whose interconnections "is far greater than all the atoms in the universe."

If you can, for the moment, throw off the grip of your learned mind, your tribal concepts, and experience the message contained in the ten-billion-tube computer which you carry behind your forehead, you would know the awe-full truth. Our research suggests that even the uneducated layman can experience directly what is slowly deduced by scientists—for example physicists, whose heavy, conceptual minds lumber along at three concepts a second, attempting to fathom the speed-of-light processes which their beautiful machines record and which their beautiful symbols portray.

But the brakes can be released. Our recent studies support the hypothesis that psychedelic foods and drugs, ingested by prepared subjects in a serious, sacred, supportive atmosphere, can put the subject in perceptual touch with other levels of energy exchanges. Remember the data—the Good Friday study, the Savage study, the 69 religious professionals. Forty to ninety percent telling us they experienced "a greater awareness of God, or a Higher Power, or an Ultimate Reality."

But to what do these LSD subjects refer when they report spiritual reactions? Do they obtain specific illuminations into the four basic questions, or are their responses simply awe and wonder at the experienced novelty? Even if the latter were the cause, could it not support the religious application of the psychedelic substances and simply underline the need for more sophisticated religious language coordinated with the scientific data? But there is some evidence, phenomenological but yet haunting, that the spiritual insights accompanying the psychedelic experience might be subjective accounts of the objective findings of astronomy, physics, biochemistry, and neurology.

Now the neurological and pharmacological explanations of an LSD vision are still far from being understood. We know almost nothing about the physiology of consciousness and the body-cortex interaction. We cannot assert that LSD subjects are directly experiencing what particle physicists and biochemists measure, but the evidence about the detailed complexity of the genetic code and the astonishing design of intra-cellular communication should caution us against labeling experiences outside of our current tribal cliches as "psychotic" or abnormal. For three thousand years our greatest prophets and philosophers have been telling us to look within, and today our scientific data are supporting that advice with a humiliating finality. The limits of introspective awareness may well be sub-microscopic, cellular, molecular and even nuclear. We only see, after all, what we are trained and predisposed to see. One of our current research projects involves teaching subjects to recognize internal physical processes much as we train a beginning biology student to recognize events viewed through his microscope.

No matter how parsimonious our explanations, we must accept the fact that LSD subjects do claim to experience revelations into the basic questions and do attribute life-change to their visions.

We are, of course, at the very beginning of our research into these implications. A new experiential language and perhaps even new metaphors for the Great Plan will develop. We have been working on this project for the past two years, writing manuals which train subjects to recognize energy processes, teaching subjects to communicate via a machine we call the experiential typewriter, and with movies of microbiological processes. And we have continued to pose the question to religious and philosophic groups as I am doing tonight. What do you think? Are these biochemical visions religious?

Before you answer, remember that God (however you define the Higher Power) produced that wonderful molecule, that extraordinarily powerful organic substance we call LSD, just as surely as "He" created the rose, or the sun, or the complex cluster of molecules you insist on calling your "self".

Among the many harassing complications of our research into religious experience has been the fact that few people, even some theological professionals, have much conception of what a religious experience really is. Few have any idea how the Divine Process presents Itself. If asked, they tend to become embarrassed, intellectual, evasive. The adored cartoonists of the Renaissance portray the Ultimate Power as a Dove, or a Flaming Bush, or as a man— venerable, with a white beard, or on a Cross, or as a Baby, or a Sage seated in the Full Lotus Position. Are these not incarnations, temporary housings, of the Great Energy Process?

Last fall a minister and his wife, as part of a courageous and dedicated pursuit of illumination, took a psychedelic biochemical called dimethyltryptamine. This wondrous alkaloid (which closely approximates serotonin, the natural "lubricant" of our higher nervous system) produces the most intense psychedelic effect of any sacramental food or drug. In 25 minutes (about the duration of the average sermon), you are whirled through the energy dance, the cosmic process, at the highest psychedelic speed. The 25 minutes are sensed as lasting for a second and for a billion-year Kalpa. After the session, the minister complained that the experience, although shattering and revelatory, was disappointing because it was "content-free"—so physical, so unfamiliar, so scientific, like being beamed through microscopic panoramas, like being oscillated through cellular functions at radar acceleration. Well, what do you expect? If God were to take you on a visit through His "workshop", do you think you'd walk or go by bus? Do you really think it would be a stroll through a celestial Madame Tussaud waxworks? Dear friends, the *Divine Product* is evident in every macroscopic form, in every secular event. The Divine Product we can see. But the *Divine Process* operates in time dimensions which are far beyond our routine, secular, space-time limits. Wave vibrations, energy dance, cellular transactions. Our science describes this logically. Our brains may be capable of dealing with these processes experientially.

So here we are. The Great Process has placed in our hands a key to this direct visionary world. Is it hard for us to accept that the key might be an organic molecule and not a new myth or a new word?

◆ ◆ ◆

And where do we go? There are in the United States today several hundred thousand persons who have experienced what I have attempted to describe to you tonight—a psychedelic, religious revelation. There are, I would estimate, several million equally thoughtful people who have heard the joyous tidings and who are waiting patiently but determinedly for their psychedelic moment to come.

There is, of course, the expected opposition. The classic conflict of the religious drama—always changing, always the same. The doctrine (which was originally someone's experience) now threatened by the *new* experience. This time the administrators have assigned the inquisitorial role to the psychiatrists, whose proprietary claims to a revealed understanding of the mind and whose antagonism to consciousness-expansion are well known to you.

The clamor over psychedelic drugs is now reaching full crescendo. You have heard rumors and you have read the press assaults and the slick-magazine attacks-by-innuendo. As sophisticated adults you have perhaps begun to wonder: why the hysterical outcry? As scientists you are beginning to ask: where is the evidence? As educated men with an eye for history, you are, I trust, beginning to suspect that we've been through this many times before.

In the current hassle over psychedelic plants and drugs, you are witnessing a good-old-fashioned, traditional, religious controversy. On the one side the psychedelic visionaries, somewhat uncertain about the validity of their revelations, embarrassedly speaking in new tongues (there never is, you know, the satisfaction of a sound, right academic language for the new vision of the Divine), harassed by the knowledge of their own human frailty, surrounded by the inevitable legion of eccentric would-be followers looking for a new panacea, always in grave doubt about their own motivation— (hero? martyr? crank? crackpot?)—always on the verge of losing their material achievements—(job, reputation, long-suffering wife, conventional friends, parental approval); always under the fire of the power-holders. And on the other side: the establishment (the administrators, the police, the fund-granting foundations, the job-givers) pronouncing their familiar lines in the drama: "Danger! Madness! Unsound! Intellectual corruption of youth! Irreparable damage! Cultism!" The issue of chemical expansion of consciousness is hard upon us. During the next months, every avenue of propaganda is going to barrage you with the arguments. You can hardly escape it. You are going to be pressed for a position. Internal Freedom is becoming a major religious and civil-rights controversy.

How can you decide? How can you judge? Well, it's really quite simple. Whenever you hear anyone sounding off on internal freedom and consciousness-expanding foods and drugs—whether pro or con—check out these questions:

(1) Is your advisor talking from direct experience, or simply repeating cliches? Theologians and intellectuals often deprecate "experience" in favor of fact and concept. This classic debate is falsely labeled. Most often it becomes a case of "experience" versus "inexperience".

(2) Do his words spring from a spiritual or from a mundane point of view? Is he motivated by a dedicated quest for answers to basic questions, or is he protecting his own social-psychological position, his own game investment?

(3) How would his argument sound if it were heard in a different culture (for example, in an African jungle hut, a ghat on the Ganges, or on another planet inhabited by a form of life superior to ours); or in a different time (for example in Periclean Athens, or in a Tibetan monastery, or in a bull-session led by any one of the great religious leaders—founders—messiahs); or how would it sound to other species of life on our planet today—to the dolphins, to the consciousness of a redwood tree? In other words, try to break out of your usual tribal game-set and listen with the ears of another one of God's creatures.

(4) How would the debate sound to you if you were fatally diseased with a week to live, and thus less committed to mundane issues? Our research group receives many requests a week for consciousness-expanding experiences, and some of these come from terminal patients.[13]

(5) Is the point of view one which opens up or closes down? Are you being urged to explore, experience, gamble out of spiritual faith, join someone who shares your cosmic ignorance on a collaborative voyage of discovery? Or are you being pressured to close off, protect your gains, play it safe, accept the authoritative voice of someone who knows best?

(6) When we speak, we say little about the subject-matter and disclose mainly the state of our own mind. Does your psychedelic advisor use terms which are positive, pro-life, spiritual, inspiring, opening, based on faith in the future, faith in your potential, or does he betray a mind obsessed by danger, material concern, by imaginary terrors, administrative caution or essential distrust in your potential. Dear friends, there is nothing in life to fear, no spiritual game can be lost. The choice is not double-bind but double-win.[14]

(7) If he is against what he calls "artifical methods of illumination", ask him what constitutes the natural. Words? Rituals? Tribal customs? Alkaloids? Psychedelic vegetables?

(8) If he is against biochemical assistance, where does he draw the line? Does he use nicotine? alcohol? penicillin? vitamins? conventional sacramental substances?

(9) If your advisor is against LSD, what is he for? If he forbids you the psychedelic key to revelation, what does he offer you instead?

◆ ◆ ◆

SUMMARY

The outline of this paper can be summarized as follows:

(1) Evidence is cited that, depending on the set and setting, from 40 to 90 percent of psychedelic subjects report intense religious experiences.

(2) The religious experience was defined as the ecstatic, incontrovertibly certain, subjective discovery of answers to four basic questions which concern ultimate power and design, life, man and self. It was pointed out that science attempts to provide objective, external answers to these same questions.

(3) We considered the hypothesis that the human being might be able to become directly aware of energy exchanges and biological processes for which we now have no language and no perceptual training. Psychedelic foods and drugs were suggested as one key to these neurological potentials, and subjective reports from LSD sessions were compared with current findings from the energy sciences.

(4) The current controversy over the politics of the nervous system (which involves secular-external versus spiritual-internal commitments) were reviewed, and a checklist for the intelligent voter was presented.

REFERENCES

[1] Walter N. Pahnke, *Drugs and Mysticism: An Analysis of the Relationship between Psychedelic Drugs and the Mystical Consciousness.* A thesis presented to the Committee on Higher Degrees in History and Philosophy of Religion, in partial fulfillment of the requirements for the degree of Doctor of Philosophy, Harvard University, Cambridge, Mass., June, 1963.

[2] "The Subjective After-Effects of Psychedelic Experiences: A Summary of Four Recent Questionnaire Studies." *The Psychedelic Review,* Vol. I, No. 1 (June 1963), 18-26.

[3] Leary, T., Litwin, G. H., and Metzner, R., "Reactions to Psilocybin Administered in a Supportive Environment." *J. Nervous & Mental Disease,* Vol. 137, No. 6, (December 1963), 561-573.

[4] Savage, C., Harman, W. W., Fadiman, Jr., and Savage, E., "A Follow-up Note on the Psychedelic Experience." [Paper delivered at a meeting of the American Psychiatric Association, St. Louis, Mo., May, 1963.]

[5] Ditman, K. S., Haymon, M., and Whittlesey, J. R. B., "Nature and Frequency of Claims Following LSD." *J. Nervous & Mental Disease,* Vol. 134 (1962), 346-352.

[6] McGlothlin, W. H., *Long-Lasting Effects of LSD on Certain Attitudes in Normals: An Experimental Proposal.* [Privately printed, The Rand Corporation, Santa Monica, California, June 1962. Pp. 56.] Cf. McGlothlin, W. H., Cohen, S., & McGlothlin, M.S., *Short-Term Effects of LSD on Anxiety, Attitudes, and Performance. Ibid.,* June 1963. Pp. 15.

[7] A continuing present-day instance is the case of members of the Native American Church, a duly constituted and recognized religious denomination numbering almost a quarter of a million adherents. A good popular account of their situation is presented in "Peyote," by A. Stump, in *Saga,* Vol. 26, No. 3 (June 1963), 46-49, 81-83. Cf. the Supreme Court's decision, *Oliver v. Udall,* 306 F2d 819 (1962). The most recently proposed legislation against peyote is seen in the *Congressional Record* (House) for Dec. 13, 1963. W. La Barre's famous book, *The Peyote Cult,* will be reprinted in an enlarged edition in August, 1964, by the Shoe String Press (Hamden, Conn.) and will bring the entire discussion up to date. For a good general statement in another area of research, see "The Hallucinogenic Drugs," by Barron, Jarvik, and Bunnell. *Sci. Amer.,* Vol. 210, No. 4 (April 1964), 29-37.

[8] Zaehner, R. C., *At Sundry Times.* An Essay in the Comparison of Religions. London: Faber & Faber, 1958, p. 57.

[9] Woltereck, H., *What Science Knows About Life.* N.Y.: Association Press, 1963.

[10] Schenk, G., *The History of Man.* Phila., N. Y.: Chilton Co., 1961, pp. 56-57.

[11] *Ibid.,* p. 238.

[12] Campbell, R., "The Circuits of the Senses," in a series on "The Human Body" (Part IV). *Life,* Vol. 54, No. 27 (June 27, 1963), 64-76b.

[13] The medical press has recently reported on the analgesic use of LSD with terminal cancer patients. Cf. *Medical World News,* Aug. 30, 1963, *Medical Tribune,* April 8, 1963, and *J. Amer. Med. Assoc.,* Jan. 4, 1964.

[14] Levitsky, A.—personal communication.

FROM
PSYCHEDELIC
REVIEW
NUMBER FOUR

Psychedelics and the Law

A Prelude in Question Marks

ROY C. BATES

Im Innern ist ein Universum auch.
Goethe

. . . & every Word & every Character
Was Human according to the Expansion or Contraction,
the Translucence or
Opakeness of Nervous fibres : such was the variation of
Time & Space
Which vary according as the Organs of Perception vary.
William Blake, *Jerusalem*

No individual can keep these Laws, for they are death
To every energy of man and forbid the springs of life.
William Blake, *The Devil's Party
and the Part of Angels* (Jesus
answering Los from the fire.)

When Kaga no Chiyo, the poetess who lived toward the end of the Tokugawa regime, wrote her famous haiku (*Asagao ya* !) in humble homage to the morning-glory, she had no premonition that the seeds of this twining plant might contain a hallucinogenic substance and alarm legislators, governmental agencies, and law enforcement officers. Yet on August 1, 1963, Senator Vance Hartke, Democrat of Indiana, urged the Senate Commerce Committee to investigate whether the sale of morning-glory seeds should not be controlled to prevent harm to public health. Dr. Abram Hoffer, director of psychiatric research for the Province of Saskatchewan, Canada, contends that repeated or heavy ingestion of the seeds may cause ergot poisoning and thus gangrene. Following his lead, biochemists on the staff of the Food and Drug Administration are doing analyses. It is safe to presume that the police watch certain areas in Boston, New York, and San Francisco where young people, chiefly students, are suspected of buying the seeds "for kicks".

Whether or not Chiyo's plant, descendant of *Ipomoea nil* which grows in the Eastern Hemisphere, in fact shares the psychopharmacological qualities of *Rivea corymbosa*, or ololiuqui, a hallucinogenic morning-glory whose active components have been identified as similar

217

to LSD, is of some interest in view of the international traffic in drugs. An affirmative answer would place the seeds of the Japanese morning-glory in the same category as ololiuqui and possibly other psychedelics.

At present, a definition of psychedelics, acceptable to the majority of qualified experts, does not exist. No one has attempted a denotational or enumerative description of these substances; the class of psychedelics, though theoretically finite, has been explored only to a small extent and often with controversial results. There seems to be agreement about the "recognition" of LSD, mescaline and derivatives such as TMA, psilocybin (the chief active ingredient of the magic or sacred mushroom of Mexico) as well as psilocin, dimethyltryptamine (DMT), Ditran (or JB 329), Sernyl (or phencyclidine), DET, peyote buttons and morning-glory seeds. In the "doubtful" category are other substances and compounds, such as harmine, harmaline, adrenolutin, adrenochrome, carbon dioxide, nitrous oxide. And the oldest of all consciousness-altering drugs, marihuana (hashish), is in the process of revaluation.

Nor has anyone offered a valid structural definition, which presupposes that the elements and relations constituting a psychedelic are known in full. Until that day, a number of criteria, tentatively selected and in part hypothetical rather than factual, must serve. The newly coined term "psychedelic" — "mind-manifesting" — itself remains vague and ambiguous.

Uncertainties are inherent in any novel experimentation. They are dramatically intensified when a venture of the intellect assumes the extraordinary forms of personal adventure and when research becomes a search for transcendental values. The adventurers are also members of a well-ordered society governed in minute detail by written state and federal constitutions, legal precedents, statutes, ordinances, rules and regulations. Thus it hardly comes as a surprise that almost everyone involved in psychedelics is grasping, like the proverbial drowning man, at a — law.

Radical innovations in the pursuit of ideas or the manufacture of products, perspectives never before seen by a judge, compel the lawyer to deviate from his usual method and dig deeper and wider into cross-disciplinary studies that will enable him to think in terms of laws *to be made* and clear the ground on which new laws can be built. He is confronted with such a task when entering the little-travelled land of psychedelics which has not as yet been surveyed by legal trigonometry. Any move may lead to a pitfall. This is also true for the steps taken by officialdom. Their informative or warning instructions, though issued in good faith and a humane spirit, have not so far been tested in the high courts. Are they "according to law"?

Pragmatically speaking, law is a system of principles, doctrines, and precepts of social control, the basis of a prediction of what an institutional power — the government, a court, an administrative agency, a district attorney, a policeman ("the Law"!) — will do in a given situation. The factors that enter into the prediction are innumerable and by no means embodied in the messages and threats of the system alone. Decision-making does not operate in the rarefied sphere of deductive logic. It is influenced by political, ethical, sociological, economic, and a host of other considerations; by the latitude of words and phrases seldom precise enough to exclude divergent meanings; by idiosyncrasies and frequently unconscious moods of the moment; by the variant vistas of the facts themselves which are to be subsumed under the rules. These vistas change with the biases prevailing in each of the cultural orbits of mankind. We know, for example, that the East looks at phenomena such as observed in the study of psychedelics quite differently from the West; its law, whatever it may be, is not ours. Without world law as a basis, prediction must rest on sources of national laws, one by one, as well as relevant international treaties and agreements. Federal law frames the standards within which the states may constitutionally enact food and drug laws of their own.

Legal prediction sinks to the level of stock-market or horse-race forecasts where existing law is relied upon to deal with newly created types of human enterprise, and its chance of being right becomes infinitesimal where a scheme that breaks with all tradition in purpose, outlook, and method is put to the test and spawns unheard-of situations and relationships. Here the problem of the unprovided case presents itself, so embarrassingly that officials tend to close their eyes before it. They are apt to maintain that the existing law covers the "novel imposition"; that the law is complete and self-contained because of the rational web of its rules; and that the rule to apply in any particular case, however outlandish in aspects, can be deduced from known principles or found by analogy with precedents and the wider or stricter interpretation of terms. In short, they hold that tomorrow is today and today is yesterday. Unfortunately, the doctrine of logical completeness of the law, which flourished unassailed until about the turn of the century, still dominates the American scene of justice and is not without followers in Europe. Everywhere, though, the legal *avant-garde* recognizes "gaps" due to technological progress and cultural mutation, and bridges them with timber from the behavioral and other sciences or vaults over them, as it were, with a pole of humane values derived from natural law.

The existence of such gaps in the international arena is generally acknowledged. Everyone concedes, for instance, that outer space is legally as empty as it is to naive realism.

Not a mere gap, but a legal wasteland, is left by the "Copernican revolution" fomented by applying physical substances, psychedelics, to a goal-directed inquiry into the inner space of private experiences. Scientific means and methods are being turned from objective phenomena, coolly observed, tested, and evaluated, to experiments with individuals which not only engage the experimenter himself as a person but are aimed at discovering new dimensions of consciousness and making them fruitful for society and, perhaps, the metabiological or psychometabolic development of the human species. The wasteland is a call to battle. On this battle-ground the laws of psychedelics will be clarified, if not decided with finality. It will be a global war, and a long one, fought with patient endurance by those who will not yield to any authority until they have exhausted all ways of persuasion, review, appeal, revision on the local, state, national, and international level, and have created a climate of opinion in which "each individual is entitled to effective legal protection of fundamental and inalienable human rights without distinction of race, religion, or belief."*

The main issue is not drug law but individual human rights. Some of the secondary problems can be solved from precedents. Some are smoothed away by canons of ethics and other standards of various professions. To indicate the range of legal research needed it might be helpful to list the players who appear on the stage of psychedelics and illuminate a few selected scenes of potential conflict and confusion.

Physician (psychiatrist, medical practitioner), treating a patient. Pharmacologist experimenting with a new drug. Psychologist. Psychoanalyst. Psychotherapist. Biochemist. Philosopher. Theologian.

Declaration of General Principles For a World Rule of Law. Adopted at the First World Conference on World Peace Through the Rule of Law. Athens, Greece, July 6, 1963.

Artist. Volunteers : Everyman; groups (free, captive, regimented), such as alcoholics, and drug addicts, prisoners in jail, members of the armed forces, e.g., astronauts, hospitalized mental patients. Enter the Statesman, Law-giver, Judge, Governmental Administrator, Attorney, Law Enforcement Officer. The plot thickens around purchase, sale, storage, and distribution of psychedelics; personal qualifications and licensing; age and sex of participants; safety measures; place and time; negligence (what constitutes negligence?); release from liability; penal law; bill of rights. Chorus : diverse makers of public opinion. The authorities always refer to drug legislation as the *sedes materiae* in their dealings with psychedelics. For the sake of argument let us concede that drug law governs psychedelics *if* they are drugs. *Are psychedelics drugs?* The question is not rhetorical, the answer far from clear-cut. To illustrate the need for legal inquiry I move to analyze pertinent provisions of American drug laws, in preference to foreign ones which might serve as well, because of the discrepancy between the concern for psychedelic research in this country and the official resistance to permitting the researcher to carry it on. The Federal Food, Drug, and Cosmetic Act, as amended last in 1962, is the main source from which the restrictive policy against the use of psychedelics emanates and therefore of paramount importance for our subject. The Act, intended to prohibit the movement of impure or misbranded food, drugs, etc., in inter-state commerce, has been incorporated in many state laws. Tangential to our inquiry are the Harrison Narcotic Act, the Narcotic Drug Import and Export Act, and the Marihuana Tax Act — laws whose inclusion in the Internal Revenue Code indicates a budgetary motive beyond public health and welfare — as well as various other federal, state, and local laws for the control of narcotics.

The Act distinguishes between food and drugs and defines drugs by categories. Articles are "drugs" per se if listed as such in an official compendium or intended for specified purposes; they are "new drugs" according to certain criteria and qualifications.

"The term 'food' means : (1) articles used for food or drink for man or other animals, (2) chewing gum, and (3) articles used for components of any such article. The term 'drug,' without qualifier, means : (1) articles recognized in the official United States Pharmacopoeia, official Homoeopathic Pharmacopoeia of the United States, or official National Formulary, or any supplement to any of them; and (2) articles intended for use in the diagnosis, cure, mitigation, treatment, or prevention of disease in man or other animals; and (3) articles (other than food) intended to affect the structure or any function of the body of man or other animals; and (4) articles intended for use as a component of any articles specified in clause (1), (2), or (3). . . . The term 'new drug' means : (1) any drug, the composition of which is such that such drug is not generally recognized among experts qualified by scientific training and experience to evaluate the safety and effectiveness of drugs, as safe and effective for use under the conditions prescribed, recommended, or suggested in the labeling thereof, except that such a drug not so recognized shall not be deemed to be a 'new drug' if at any time prior to the enactment of this Act it was subject to the Food and Drugs Act of June 30, 1906, as amended, and if at such time its labeling contained the same representations concerning the conditions of its use; or (2) any drug the composition of which is such that such drug, as a result of investigations to determine its safety and effectiveness for use under such conditions, has become so recognized, but which has not, otherwise than in such investigations, been used to a material extent or for a material time under such conditions."

In Alice's legal wonderland, where chewing gum is food, scientific usage counts as little as Webster's definitions. It is irrelevant that specialists in science call psychedelics, whatever their origin, birthday, or job, "drugs" (and on occasion, somehow timidly, "psychedelic substances"). The official compendia fail to mention psilocybin, mescaline, LSD and, it would seem, any psychedelics, which, therefore, are not drugs per se under the Act though a very few must be so regarded under consitutionally dubious narcotic laws. *I submit that psychedelics are drugs only if and when used for therapeutic purposes, as medicine, and otherwise not!*

Our burden of persuasion is limited to clause (3) of the "drug" definition, for we admit that clause (2) applies to psychedelics instrumental in medical therapy. Since they alter so-called mental processes, such as perceiving, imagining, thinking, evaluating, they "affect" a "function in the body of man," and they are "intended" to do so. Read out of context, clause (3) would not snatch psychedelics in non-medical use from the jaws of the Act. But it is a rule of statutory construction that even plain and seemingly clear words must yield to the impact of provisions adjoining in print as well as others and must, moreover, be interpreted in the light of the statute as a whole, the legislative policy expressed in it, related laws, and precedents. There can hardly be a doubt that clause (3) is but an extension of clauses (1) and (2); they all are linked by "and" and form an inseparable unit suffused with one principle of demarcation : purpose of use. The *raison d'être* of the compendia to which clause (1) refers is the practice of medicine; their keynote is the reliability of pharmacological substances prescribed by physicians. To be admitted to the United States Pharmacopoeia the product must conform to legal specifications of purity and be of recognized therapeutic value. Similar curative properties are required for listing in the two other official books.

That it is the medical purpose which transforms — one is tempted to say, transubstantiates — a substance into a "drug" is comprehensively spelled out in clause (2), which is needed to catch up with the volume of medicines not yet listed in the compendia. Clause (3) owes its existence to the same effort to make our world safe for medical therapy. It was not deemed sufficient to include unlisted "articles intended for use in the diagnosis, cure, mitigation, treatment, or prevention of disease" in the term "drug" — clause (2) — without clarifying, in clause (3), that this term also applies *if* the articles *used in the diagnosis, and so forth, of disease,* are "intended to affect the structure or any function of the body of man or other animals."

We are bound to conclude that clause (3) is inapplicable to psychedelics employed for non-medical purposes. Not being "drugs" they cannot be "new drugs" either.

The courts, from Maine to California, from Washington to Florida, hold without exception that any vegetable, animal or mineral substance is a potential drug, but an actual one only if the substance is used in the composition of medicine and its use bears a reasonable relation to the policy underlying the Act, i.e., the furtherance of public health, safety, and welfare. By this test, cigarettes which contained combustible tartaric acid and allegedly reduced weight while preventing respiratory diseases, were considered drugs; in one amusing case — whiskey! As a rule, alcoholic beverages and cigarettes share with non-medical psychedelics the negative feature of not being drugs, so the secondary question about the reasonable relation of the three groups to public health does not arise although it may be worth pondering in connection with the law of psychedelics for therapy.

As media in the treatment of a patient and therefore "drugs" governed by the Act, psychedelics fall under the recently amended provisions for "new drugs". They were never subject to the Food and

223

Drug Act of June 30, 1906, as amended; they are not generally recognized among qualified experts as both safe and effective; they have not been used to a material extent and for a material time in medical practice. It follows that they are controlled by the 1962 amendment, which imposes severe restraints on the drug industry — its primary target — on physicians, clinical investigators, and other experts. Just as the sulfanilamide disaster in the fall of 1937 quickened the passage (1938) of the Act itself, so the frenzied furor raised by thalidomide is echoed in the amendment, and the emotional after-effects of this scare induced the authorities to wield their regulatory powers with redoubled caution.

Of particular interest for the law of psychedelics-as-medicine are the meaning of "effective" in the definition of "new drugs" and the franchise that may be granted to research. Before a "new drug" can be approved for marketing, the manufacturer must show that it will have the effect it purports or is represented to have under the conditions of use prescribed, recommended, or suggested in the labeling or proposed labeling thereof. The evidence of effectiveness must be "substantial," that is, gathered by scientifically trained and experienced specialists, qualified to evaluate the effectiveness of the drug involved, in adequate and well-controlled basal *and clinical* investigations. If in the light of new evidence the drug does not measure up to standards, it will be ordered off the market. A short grace period for manufacturers of new drugs marketed prior to the 1962 amendment does not concern psychedelics, not yet, if ever, regular items of prescriptions. Psychiatrists may never be able to treat mental cases with LSD, etc., unless the discretion entrusted to the authorities in dealing with experimental drugs is most liberally exercised and research widely promoted. The law generally authorizes the Department of Health, Education and Welfare to exempt new drugs from certain encumbrances and allow their distribution for research on conditions related to the public health. It specifically authorizes the Secretary of the Department to prevent the testing of new drugs on human patients if detailed safety conditions are not met. It explicitly directs the Secretary to issue regulations conditioning the exemption of experimental drugs. A certification must be obtained by the drug manufacturers from the scientific investigators, stating that the latter will inform patients to whom the drug is to be administered, or their representatives, of the experimental nature of the drug and secure their consent except where the investigator deems this not feasible or, in his professional judgment, contra-indicated. Among other things, as a precondition for testing safety and effectiveness on human patients, the regulations may require : submission of reports of preclinical tests, including animal tests, adequate to justify the proposed clinical testing; obtainment, by the sponsor, of signed agreements from investigators that work will be done under their personal supervision and drugs used will not be supplied to others; keeping of records and making of reports for the benefit of scientists in the employ of the Federal Drug Administration who are called to evaluate the safety and effectiveness of the new drug when an application is filed. Be it noted in passing that the research provisions refer to human "patients", and not to human beings at large. This clinches our argument : the nonmedical use of psychedelics is not governed by the Act.

In a Zen monastery, perhaps, the contention that psychedelics are both drugs and no-drugs might lead to a "mondo", if not a spontaneous combustion of satori. In this country, the even more paradoxical fact that the authorities fail to notice the paradox and regulate beyond the pale of their jurisdiction can only lead to a day, a month, a year, a decade in court. Who are the complainants? All who have a stake (material, ideal, or personal) in these substances. Whether they know it or not, the drug manufacturer, the psychiatrist, the scientist and scholar, the theologian, the seeker after happiness . . . are indispensable parties and must join to reach a sound determination of the controversy. The Act provides for judicial review over the denial or withdrawal of a new drug from the district court to the United States courts of appeals. Apart from this special provision, administrative orders and regulations, though sometimes shielded against attack, are generally subject to a judge's supervision buoyed up by the federal Administrative Procedure Act of 1946 and corresponding state laws. "Discretion" does not mean arbitrariness, however well-intended, and the court will draw the boundary lines. Eventually, the statute itself, or portions thereof, may be found unconstitutional by the Supreme Court of the United States and set aside.

This may suffice to illustrate — not to examine in depth — at least one of the secondary moot points. The primary problem is human rights, and it ought to be seen under the perspective of mankind. Regrettably, here again we must confine ourselves to a few glimpses at the legal home front.

Psychedelics manifest and affect the "mind". Mind, then, is the object of psychedelic investigation but it is not a clear word. The French have no equivalent. Neither *esprit* nor *intelligence* fit the term, and *mémoire,* the nearest rendering of "mind," alludes to a psychological theory without indication that consciousness has a seat or subject, while *âme* implies a religious or metaphysical belief of which "mind" is free. German parallels French in this regard : *Geist, Seele, Gedächtnis, Bewusstsein* — never mind. . . . The courts, always anxious to explain difficult words by familiar ones — *definitio semper periculosa sed necessaria* — have wrestled with "mind," too. In U.S. v. Boylen, D.C. Or. 41 F. Supp. 724, 725 it "appeared" to the judge that "the word 'mind' is synonymous with the 'memory' as used in Blackstone and other ancient authorities." Similarly, in re Forman's Will, N.Y., 54 Barb. 274, 286, equates mind with memory. "The use of the word 'mind' and 'memory' as convertible terms is not so unphilosophical as might at first seem, for without memory a person would be the mere recipient of a succession of present sensations like the lowest type of animal life." A working definition of the term, be it ever so metaphorical, is basic for the law of psychedelics and will evolve at the proper time. It will not resemble any of the existing legal shards inscribed "sound and normal," "unsound and insane," "disposing and testamentary," but may borrow from topographies such as Dante's or Freud's, adding one or more dimensions. Meanwhile, before there can be a "meeting of minds" about "mind," we are to rely on the non-conceptual knowing that permits us to say *"sub specie aeternitatis"* or *"human rights"* and mean it. Where concepts fail, concerns may still prevail.

The amendments of the Federal Constitution do not contain a Universal Declaration of Human Rights, but they emphasize individual freedom — the lever that may dislodge the administrative weight on psychedelics. It has been done, ephemerally and sideways, on July 26, 1960, at 3 p.m. when the Honorable Yale McFate pronounced his decision in the case of the State of Arizona v. Mary Attakai. The defendant, a member of the Navajo Indian Tribe, was charged with the illegal possession of peyote, a crime under an Arizona statute. She admitted the possession but pleaded not guilty on the ground that the prayers, rites, and ceremonies of the Native American Church, to which she belonged, centered on the cult and use of peyote and that, therefore, the statute deprived her of the freedom of religious worship guaranteed by the Fourteenth Amendment of the Federal Constitution, and the Arizona Constitution as well. The court found that under the circumstances the statute was unconstitutional, dismissed the complaint, and released the defendant. In the opinion of the court, the peyote plant, believed to be of divine origin, bears a similar relation to the largely illiterate Indians as does the Holy Bible to the white man. "It is conceived of as a sacrament, a means of communion with the Spirit of the Almighty." Nor does the practice of the church — first incorporated under the law of Oklahoma, October 10, 1918 — threaten the peace and safety of the public, for the hallucinogenic phenomena produced by peyote, the court averred, leave all the mental faculties unimpaired, and "there are no harmful aftereffects. . . . Peyote is not a narcotic. It is not habit-forming." The judge thought it "significant that many states which formerly outlawed the use of peyote have abolished or amended their laws to permit its use for religious purposes."

Once again we draw attention to the crucial role the purpose of use plays in the law of psychedelics. One group of experimenters has been denigrated in the press as "cultists," and undeniably the scientific study of religion through LSD, etc., is embraced and supported by many more devotees of the spiritual life, among them artists and writers, and theologians from divinity schools or at large, than by medical men, some of whom, ignorant of their own legal advantages in collaboration, strive to pre-empt the entire field. It may seem far-fetched but would be altogether in accord with the Constitution to organize this group as a church, with the prospect of privilege. There is another Navajo-peyote case on the books; it was decided on July 26, 1962, by the United States District Court of Appeals, District of Columbia Circuit, in favor of the appellee, Stewart Udall, individually and as Secretary of the Interior. The appellants, eight residents of the Navajo Indian Reservation, sued for a judgment to declare a section of the Code of Indian Tribal Offenses — "Peyote Violations" — "null and void, invalidly authorized and unconstitutional." In the construction of the court, the Navajo Tribe itself adopted, in 1959, the ban on peyote as tribal law, denouncing its use as not connected with the Navajo religious practice and foreign to the Navajo traditional way of life. The complaint was dismissed on evidence *in abstracto*, by a series of syllogisms. What moved the tribe to "adopt" and point the dagger of a criminal offense against themselves, only to be sorry about it shortly after, is a puzzle for an anthropologist to unravel. As to their traditional religious practices, William Blake (b. 1757) is a witness. "I then asked Ezekiel why he eat dung, & lay so long on his right & left side? he answer'd, 'the desire of raising other men into a perception of the infinite; this the North American tribes practice.' " (*The Marriage of Heaven and Hell*). Judge McFate said of peyote : "It is actually unpleasant to take, having a very bitter taste."

Included in the circle of freedoms which may give constitutional protection to psychedelic enterprise are not only those named and famous, in particular, the freedoms of religion, of speech, and of assembly, but innominate ones, such as the right of the individual to acquire, expand, and spread knowledge, and the "inalienable" right to the pursuit of happiness. This utterly anti-puritanic right, though enunciated in the Declaration of Independence, is the fixed star relative to which the constitutional luminaries are to move in a society of free men and women. Their courses foretell a constellation adjusted to the dynamism and the potential of psychedelics to realize a right inalienable and absolute. Then an equipoise will be attained between the desiderata of science, the rational requirements of public health and safety, and the yearnings of the human heart. Surely, a body politic that allows a machine to kill, year by year, tens of thousands of people and maim or injure over a million; allows liquors to intoxicate and cigarettes to hurt the whole nation — cannot with reason forbid or sharply curtail far less, if at all, harmful and far less common psychedelic experiments and experiences and thus retard medical progress, block discoveries and potential insights, and dry up a source of joy and enchantment.

Freedoms, it is understood, have a pathology of their own. They can be revelled in unwisely; that's a private affair. They can be abused to the detriment of public safety; then the law must be on hand to curb them. But they ought not to be legislated away as if adults were children of an overanxious mother. Sir William Blackstone's paradox holds true : "The public good is in nothing more essentially interested than in the protection of every individual's private rights." To assume such a right is to assume a risk. And — *volenti non fit injuria*. The maxim, codified in a California statute and analyzed by the judicature of the states, is important for the law of psychedelics, especially in regard to group sessions and group therapy where an enthusiast or coryphaeus, proclaiming that there is no danger at all, may confound the "free" volition of the participants. "Volenti" is not "scienti." While no legal wrong is done to him who, knowing and comprehending the risk, voluntarily exposes himself, without being negligent in so doing, the mere knowledge of the possible danger does not preclude him from the recovery of damages for injuries sustained. Even if he himself has no action whatsoever, the investigator or person administering a psychedelic could be liable to an outsider, e.g., when the patient or subject, still under the influence of the psychedelic, runs his car over a third party or damages his property. We mention this only to exemplify the fact that many legal problems will persist after the freedoms have been implemented.

It may seem too sanguine to expect a sweeping victory due to one of the sudden spurts which in the record of cultures appear with the abruptness of biological mutation. We can look forward, though, to a gradual change in freeing the study and the enjoyment of psychedelics. To be sure, there are troughs and crests in the policy of the Supreme Court in protecting the individual and his pursuits, even as against the state, but for a hundred years no trough ever declined to the low level of the preceding one, each crest surmounted the last. By its own momentum, acceleration of the progressive trend is inevitable.

Nowadays, with the concepts of "world law" and "mankind" emerging from a shrunken globe, the legal destiny of psychedelics will further depend on how they are assessed in foreign lands. The major part of law vital to the people grows, except under a dictatorship, from the bottom up, not from the top down. It roots in public opinion and collapses if no longer supported by it; the repeal of the Prohibition Amendment is a striking example. Public opinion denotes a cross-sectional mass judgment based on private attitudes. Therefore, in the last analysis, the private attitudes toward psychedelics abroad, which create public opinion, which in turn creates foreign law, are likely to radiate into American attitudes, American public opinion, and American law.

Brief notes on psychedelics abroad.

They meet with no governmental interference in the various parts of the world where untold millions of people chew or smoke cannabis as freely as we drink alcoholic beverages. The same appears to be true for a number of South American countries. West-German law permits the marketing of any pharmaceutical specialty if it has been registered by the Federal Department of Health; a report on the nature and extent of the pharmacological and clinical trials and an evaluation of observed side-effects must be filed. Before granting the sale of new drugs, Canada demands a statement that their safety has been established by tests. In the United Kingdom, on the basis of a skimpy statute, as many as fifteen different organizations may examine a new drug and prevent marketing. Each canton of Switzerland has its own pharmaceutical legislation; an intercantonal office has controlled "medicaments" since 1954. Italian drug law is up for a probably thorough-going revision. Until 1941, drugs were not regulated in France; since 1959, the Ministry of Public Health issues or denies a sales permit according to safety, stability, conditions of use, and contraindications; the newness of the drug is immaterial.

A legal framework into which psychedelics can be smoothly fitted does not exist. Inner-space law today is in the stage of underdevelopment which outer-space law was in A.D. 1903 when the Brothers Wright launched their airplane at Kittyhawk or, perhaps, when the Brothers Montgolfier ascended in the first air balloon, a hundred years earlier. Until it has matured, scholars in search of external on behalf of internal freedom will feel frustrated. They may believe themselves to be fugitives from injustice but in truth are victims of legal confusion engendered by the reversal of the scientific object, from the universe without to the universe within. Until psychedelics have found *their* place in law, a good many concrete questions will not be answerable with confidence.

[Editor's Note: Since this article went to press, an extremely important decision has been handed down by the California Supreme Court. The following description is quoted from the *San Francisco Chronicle,* August 25, 1964: ". . . in a 6-to-1 decision, the court ruled that American Indians using the hallucinatory drug peyote in their religious rites are not in violation of the State's narcotic laws. The landmark decision, written by Justice Mathew O. Tobriner, said use of the non-habit forming drug in 'honest rites' is protected by the First Amendment which guarantees freedom of religious beliefs. . . . Justice Tobriner wrote that 'law officers and courts should have no trouble distinguishing between church members who use peyote in good faith and those who take it just for the sensation it produces.' In a companion case, the court ruled that anyone arrested for possession of the drug must prove to a court that he falls within the religious exemption."]

The Treatment of Frigidity with LSD and Ritalin

THOMAS M. LING
and JOHN BUCKMAN

"Frigidity" is the inability to enjoy sexual love to its fullest capacity. It may vary in degree or in type.

The capacity of the human female to respond sexually depends upon a complex network of interdependent activators. These activator systems include the endocrinological, the somesthetic and the psychic.

In lower mammals, the endocrine system predominates, but in humans the somesthetic and the psychic are paramount, particularly the latter.

The recognized incidence of frigidity and its manifestations such as vaginismus, passivity, lack of vaginal orgasm and refusal to have intercourse, depends a good deal on the outlook of the gynaecologist. Thus Hamilton (1961) estimates that 40% of American women suffer from frigidity in some degree, while a London gynaecologist states approximately 30% of his private patients complain of sexual difficulties, a number of which are aggravated by the incompetence of their husbands. The incidence in hospital practice is apparently lower, which is attributed to the fact that owing to pressure of time, a detailed history covering emotional factors is usually impracticable.

The textbooks are not encouraging about treatment. Thus Curtis and Huftman (1950) write as follows :

> Female frigidity often presents an insolvable problem. Prudery, incompatibility, ill health and coital maladjustment are among the numerous factors involved. Common sense advice has been effective in some cases.

Young (1958) states :

> In many cases, there is no local lesion present at the vulva or in the pelvis to account for the symptoms. In such cases we can sometimes discover the history of a painful lesion from which the symptom has dated as a kind of neurosis. In other cases the condition is to be explained on the lines of a disturbed sex psychology.

MacLeod and Read (1955) write :

> Frigidity and most cases of dyspareunia are but further examples of

231

psychosomatic disorder. . . . A multitude of symptoms may unfold themselves, including neurasthenia, insomnia, loss of weight, and vaginal pain of wide distribution, in fact a state of chronic ill health. As few women will volunteer information on their sexual inadequacies, it should be the aim of the gynaecologist to ascertain whether such a state of affairs exists and if possible, correct it.

Judging by the above extracts from standard British and American text books, frigidity and its associated manifestations are diagnosed to a variable extent, while its alleviation is usually difficult and frequently impossible.

The Psychiatric Aspects of Frigidity

In psychiatry, sexual difficulties frequently form part of the total problem. Treatment is often as difficult for the psychiatrist as it is for the gynaecologist. O'Neill (1954) has written wisely on the subject.

Sexual maturity equates with emotional maturity, and frequently this has been arrested by early childhood experiences such as parental disharmony, sexual guilt absorbed by the small child from the parents or nurse, or a sexual assault in early life. These experiences are forgotten but continue indefinitely to influence the woman as wife and mother.

Their release from the unconscious by deep psychotherapy is very time-consuming and frequently unrewarding. On this account lysergic acid diethylamide (LSD-25), combined more recently with Ritalin, has been used as a part of a research program in this Hospital for the last five years in selected cases of neurosis for the speedy release of the unconscious material and alleviation of its associated sexual and other manifestations.

Action of Lysergic Acid Diethylamide (LSD-25)

LSD-25 was synthesized by Sandoz in 1938, is a synthetic amide of lysergic acid and belongs to the ergonovine group of alkaloids. After its ingestion, or injection in minute doses, it induces psychic states in which the subject, in a state of clear consciousness, becomes apparently aware of repressed memories of childhood and infancy and other unconscious material, including fantasy. The drug is administered to outpatients intra-muscularly, with the patient in bed in a quiet darkened single room. A session takes about four hours and leaves the patient fatigued.

The Treatment of Frigidity with LSD & Ritalin

When LSD is given alone, it frequently accentuates anxiety so that it is now combined with intravenous Ritalin (methylphenidate). The latter is a C.N.S. stimulant and acts particularly on the posterior hypothalamus. This combination enables the patient to recall forgotten material with less fear.

The patient develops the capacity of watching and understanding her own unconscious and the recovered childhood memories and fantasies. Often one of the most gratifying results of treatment is the progressive maturity that comes from self-understanding, and one is reminded of the inscription over the Delphic temple : "Know thyself."

Sessions are given every two weeks. Patients are seen regularly during treatment, and a varying amount of psychotherapy is given in all cases.

The selection of patients is important. Good intelligence, a real desire to be cured, absence of psychosis and being under fifty years of age are prerequisites.

The treatment is more effective with educated patients, as their active cooperation and appreciation of interrelated experiences are essential.

Sandison (1962), Bierer (1960), Martin (1957), Eisner & Cohen (1958), Robinson *et al.* (1963), and the authors of this article (1964) among others have described the clinical use of LSD in a wide variety of neurotic and psychosomatic conditions. Many of these cases include sexual difficulties among their multiple difficulties, while this article details the treatment of frigidity occurring as the patient's only problem. There were 1,122 references in the world literature as of January 1964, and this is the first contribution to its use in the treatment of frigidity.*

Details of Case

A married woman of thirty-three and the mother of two young children complained of lack of any sexual desire since marriage. She was fond of her husband, and their relationship during the daytime was harmonious. The husband was fully potent, successful in his profession, in love with his wife, and they were good parents.

Since girlhood, the patient had been frightened of sex and later

[* An extended popular account of psychoanalytic treatment of frigidity with LSD is seen in C. A. Newland, *My Self and I* (1962), reviewed in our previous issue.—*Ed.*]

233

had intercourse as a marital duty. Two years previously, she had been told by a consultant gynaecologist that she was physically normal. He was very sympathetic and suggested that she should learn to accept her disability. She was subsequently seen on a number of occasions by a psychiatrist without improvement.

The following is a summary of her experiences under LSD and Ritalin :

First Session. 50 µg (micrograms) LSD intramuscularly and 20 mg (milligrams) and 10 mg Ritalin intravenously.

My experiences were divided into four phases. I felt physical misery and depression. Then I felt frightened. Half of my mind desperately wanted to remember what had happened, and half would not allow it.

After the next injection of Ritalin, I pictured my father as a young man who rejected me. I felt disappointed, bitter and resentful. I could not understand why he did not love me. Then I seemed to travel backwards in time to a point where I had idolized him and felt possessive. My conscious mind prompted me that sex came into this and, at the same time, I knew it was because he was a man that this love was so important, but adult sexuality was not involved.

Following the last injection of Ritalin, I' felt a wonderful outpouring of love and a zest for life which I had never felt before. I felt that nothing would ever frighten or hurt me again. I thought "So you had a baby love affair with your father and you don't have to hide yourself away because he rejected you." The most important thing was to love and live life to the full, and the least important was to be afraid of anything. I felt that sex came somewhere halfway and was a healthy way of showing that you loved someone and were happy — like laughing. In this mood I felt that my erotic responses would be entirely different from those I had previously experienced, which were unsatisfying and guilt-ridden.

I felt that in sexual intercourse I had, unconsciously, been seeking that pinnacle of love that I had felt for my father and that, not having found it, I was left with a feeling of disgust.

I know that my father is totally incapable of showing affection. I have never seen him show affection to anyone, not even my children. Perhaps my rejection came when I felt that he did not show me any love at all.

Three weeks later she reported progress as follows :

The most obvious change in my feelings is in my reaction to sex. I now feel very differently about it, with varying enjoyment. I can now enjoy certain intimacies which previously I had indulged in with shame, and which afterwards I had preferred not to think about.

The other marked change in my feelings is the thought that I might become pregnant. I have always felt that to have another baby would be disastrous, but since the last treatment all the practical reasons have been swept aside by a purely emotional desire to have a small baby to care for again.

Second Session. 75 μg LSD, 20 mg Ritalin and 10 mg Ritalin.

After a short time, I felt that I was a tiny baby, suckling at the breast, and I felt the secure feelings that it gave me. I also remembered being held and cuddled by someone.

I would not let myself enjoy these memories for any length of time, as my mind kept telling me that it was not the experiencing of these infantile pleasures that would cure me, but that I must find out what it was that was so crushing, that had cast its shadow over my personality all my life.

After the last injection of Ritalin, I had a feeling of frustration and of being kept a prisoner. I desperately sought release from this tension, and I had the sensation of being physically held down and of something on top of me. I felt that this was an important experience, and the failure to recall it fully left me depressed.

A few days later, the patient reported progress :

I feel much more at ease over sex, but this is not yet right. Also I have got over my fear of spiders. Another change is that I am no longer afraid of being alone when my husband has to be away for the night. I feel much more tolerant towards the children and I feel more confident in dealing with them. My husband has noticed other changes which I have not, and says that I am much easier to live with.

Third Session. 75μg LSD, 20 mg, 10 mg, and 10 mg Ritalin.

I felt I wanted to remember my first awareness of sexuality and what happened. Then suddenly I remembered. I was a tiny baby about six months old, lying on my back with my legs in the air, with no clothes on and my father was looking at me. I was aware that he was male and I was female. He was looking at my private parts and I expected him to react in an approving way, but he did not. I cannot remember exactly what his reaction was. It was either indifference or disgust, but it was not what I expected and was a shattering blow to my self-esteem. I felt that here was the very essence of my femaleness, and the one male I most wanted to show approval, did not do so. I see now that this infantile rejection was the reason why I felt having a surgical induction with my first baby such a ghastly experience. It was much more than just embarrassment that I felt.

I felt that as a baby I tried more than once to gain my father's approval and failed. I felt that for some time I was competing with my mother for my father but in the end she won.

Looking at the session afterwards, it seems hardly credible that this incident could possibly have had such a shattering and lasting effect upon me. Being able to live through the experience and feel the way I felt at the time, makes me appreciate what a devasting experience it was, combined with my tremendous and useless competition with my mother. I feel enormously released.

It was decided to rest the patient after this session, and six weeks later both partners were seen again. The husband reported that the patient was a much happier person, a calmer mother, and was now sexually responsive on approximately every other occasion. The patient said she felt much more at peace with herself but still had considerable fear of her own sexuality. She felt she had not completed treatment.

Fourth Session. 75μg LSD, 20 mg, 20 mg, and 10 mg Ritalin.

At first I had the usual turmoil of unpleasant emotions, fear, guilt and a desire to run away and hide.

Later, when I had calmed down, I had a memory of tremendous sexual excitement. I felt that I was about six and that somebody had been "playing" with me sexually. I also seemed to be near water, perhaps a river.

Later the memory of this experience faded and after the last injection of Ritalin, I had a feeling of disgust, followed by a dream-like sequence of lavatories, drains and rushing water.

Three days later, the patient said she felt very tense, that her experience of the assault was incomplete and pleaded for another session as soon as possible. She felt fairly certain that it was her uncle who had assaulted her. She had always known that, as a child, she used to stay with her uncle and aunt who lived on the Thames.

Her summary of the session four days later was as follows :

Fifth Session. 80 μg LSD, 30 mg, 20 mg, and 10 mg Ritalin.

I have put off writing this report because I am very reluctant to put down on paper the incident which I have remembered, and am so ashamed of.

I remember mostly the emotions which went with this incident. I remember the feeling of sexual excitement, of knowing what was happening and the feelings of disgust afterwards, but I cannot remember the actual physical contact. After the last injection, I could remember being held down and the uncontrolled lustful look on my uncle's face absolutely vividly. It was as though it had happened yesterday.

I think we were on the bank of a river under trees and I had a feeling we were disturbed, but it was not clear. I also think that my uncle may have got me in this state of excitement more than once because I seem to remember two separate occasions, once when I was sitting on something high up and once when I was lying down.

I have still only experienced partial release from my tension and sexual difficulties, and still feel rather shocked and depressed.

At the next interview, she stated with embarrassment that she had remembered under treatment that her uncle had performed cunnilingus on her, a perversion of which she was totally unaware prior to the session. She agreed that the whole episode needed clarification with another session but was much less pressing than formerly, regarding immediate treatment. She felt the end of treatment was not far off now.

She stated that she had always known that there had been a violent quarrel between her father and her uncle about this time, and that she was never allowed to stay in her uncle's house again.

A further session was arranged in two weeks' time, of which the following is her summary :

Sixth Session. 80 µg LSD, 30 mg, 20 mg, and 10 mg Ritalin.

Under the drug I had the feeling that I was searching for an ideal, e.g., the first time I was sexually aroused, and the man who did it was a sort of god to me. Then things became blurred, but after the second injection of Ritalin I remembered with complete clarity that I had enjoyed my uncle playing with my privates. The enjoyment was brought to an abrupt end when he tried to rape me. I remember feeling a blow in the area of my vagina and a feeling of force, but he could not really enter me. There the memory ends. I cannot remember what the outcome of it all was.

I have felt much more tranquil after this last session than I did after the two various ones, and the physical effects have not been so severe as they were the time before.

Six weeks later the patient was seen again and reported as follows :

After the last treatment, I had my first intercourse with full orgasm internally, which was a completely new and wonderful experience. My sexual life is now completely different and I get a wonderful feeling out of it on most occasions. The marriage is now very much better, but I believe there is still room for improvement and for me to feel complete ecstasy on every occasion.

As she was improving steadily, it was agreed to leave further treatment in abeyance. Some patients may continue to improve and gain insight for weeks and occasionally months.

Six months later, the patient reported as follows :

Here are my latest views on my progress. My feelings towards sexual intercourse have undergone the greatest change. I can say with no reservations whatsoever that I have lost all my inhibitions regarding sex. I am completely free of all the feelings of distaste and guilt that I had, and am able to enjoy in a "down to earth" and healthy way.

In general I feel more confident and mature. I am now prepared to go more than half way to make friends with people. I am much happier about expressing my views.

I know my husband finds me much better company and I have a much more positive approach to him and life in general, and I have much more patience with the children.

I have scarcely given a thought to the incident with my uncle and when I have, I felt completely detached and unemotional about it.

During the interview, it transpired that she had had a full and completely satisfying vaginal orgasm on every occasion except once, when she felt particularly tired. She looked much happier and was now clearly at peace with herself and her surroundings.

Further treatment was considered unnecessary by psychiatrist and patient.

Conclusion

A case of complete frigidity without other neurotic features is reported which has been fully relieved after six sessions of LSD.

The patient re-experienced sexual excitement, rejection and guilt associated with her incestuous feelings and possible assault. She improved as a result of understanding that, early in her life, sex became associated with fear, violence and parental disapproval.

Her husband reports that the patient is a much happier and more relaxed person, and that their sexual life has been revolutionized so that the marriage is now outstandingly happy.

Apart from this case, the use of LSD and Ritalin, with appropriate psychotherapy, has cleared up frigidity occurring as part of a psychopathology in sixteen other selected cases. It appears more informative to report this one case in detail than to present a summary of all the other cases.

Summary

1. True frigidity is a common problem in gynaecology.
2. The specialities of gynaecology and psychiatry overlap in many syndromes. Psychological factors are solely responsible for true frigidity, which is a neurotic illness.
3. Other "symptom equivalents" often mask this "organ neurosis" since in the great majority of patients, there is some psychological cause for their physiologically expressed disturbances.

4. These cases are notoriously hard to treat by the traditional methods of gynaecology or psychiatry, since the causes are unconscious and deeply repressed.

5. Given good motivation, superior intelligence, a reasonably stable personality and a cooperative potent spouse, psychotherapy with LSD can help these cases by the recovery of early sexual fantasies or traumatic experiences responsible for the symptom formation.

6. Sixteen cases have been treated successfully in this way, and the facts of one such case are given in detail.

7. We would like to express our thanks to the Elmgrant Trust for their support and to Dr. J. Bierer for his cooperation and help.

8. We would like to thank Ciba Laboratories for kindly supplying the Ritalin.

REFERENCES

Bierer, J. (1960). *Proc. Roy. Soc. Med.*, Vol. 53, No. 11 (Nov. 1960), p. 95.

Curtis, A. H., and Huftman, J. W. (1950). *A Text Book of Gynaecology.* Phila. W. B. Saunders.

Eisner, B. G., and Cohen, S. (1958). "Psychotherapy with lysergic acid diethlamide." *J. Nerv. Mental Disease,* Vol. 127, No. 6 (Dec. 1958), pp. 528-539.

Hamilton, E. G. (1961). "Frigidity in the female." *Missouri Med.,* Vol. 58 (Oct. 1961), pp. 1040-51.

Ling, T. M. and Buckman, J. (1963). *Lysergic Acid (LSD 25) & Ritalin in the Treatment of Neurosis.* London: Lambarde Press.. (Distributed in U.S. by Medical Examination Pub. Co., Inc., Flushing 65, N.Y.)

Martin, A. J. (1957). "LSD treatment of chronic psychoneurotic patients under day-hospital conditions." *Intern. J. Soc. Psychiat.,* Vol. 3, pp. 188-195.

Macleod, D. H. and Read, C. D. (1955). *Gynaecology.* London: J. & A. Churchill, p. 723.

O'Neill, D. (1954). *Recent Developments in Psychosomatic Medicine.* London: Pitman & Son Ltd., p. 212.

Robinson, J., et al. (1963). "A controlled trial of abreaction with lysergic acid." *Brit. J. Psychiat.,* Vol. 109, No. 458, (Jan. 1963), pp. 46-53.

Sandison, R. A. (1962). "The role of the psycholytic agents in the therapeutic process." *Bull. Brit. Psychol. Soc.* (abstr.), No. 46, Jan. 1962.

Young, G. J. (1958). *A Text Book of Gynaecology.* London: Adam & Charles Black.

LSD and Psychotherapy:
A Bibliography of the English-Language Literature

SANFORD M. UNGER

(The first account of the use of LSD as an aid in psychotherapy was published by a pair of American investigators, Busch and Johnson, in 1950. Since that time, claims of clinical usefulness have appeared periodically, and from many countries besides the U.S. — from England and Canada, widely from South America, from Israel, from Germany, France, Italy, Holland, and Czechoslovakia. The bibliography that follows lists only English-language publications; readers interested in the foreign-language literature may consult the exhaustive *LSD : Annotated Bibliography* available from Sandoz Pharmaceuticals, Hanover, N.J.)

Bibliography

ABRAMSON, H. A. Lysergic acid diethylamide (LSD-25) : III. As an adjunct to psychotherapy with elimination of fear of homosexuality. *J. Psychol.*, 1955, *39*, 127-155.

ABRAMSON, H. A. Lysergic acid diethylamide (LSD-25) : XIX. As an adjunct to brief psychotherapy, with special reference to ego enhancement. *J. Psychol.*, 1956, *41*, 199-229.

ABRAMSON, H. A. Lysergic acid diethylamide (LSD-25) : XXII. Effect on transference. *J. Psychol.*, 1956, *42*, 51-98.

ABRAMSON, H. A. (Ed.). *The use of LSD in psychotherapy*. New York : Josiah Macy, Jr. Foundation Publications, 1960.

ABRAMSON, H. A. Lysergic acid diethylamide (LSD-25) : XXXII. Resolution of counter-identification conflict of father during oedipal phase of son. *J. Psychol.*, 1961, *51*, 33-87.

ANDERSON, E. W. M., & RAWNSLEY, K. Clinical studies of lysergic acid diethylamide. *Manchester Psychiat.*, 1954, *128*, 38-55.

ARENDSEN-HEIN, G. W. Treatment of the neurotic patient, resistant to the usual techniques of psychotherapy, with special reference to LSD. *Topic. Probl. Psychother.*, 1963, *4*, 50-57.

BALL, J. R., & ARMSTRONG, JEAN J. The use of LSD in the treatment of the sexual perversions. *Canad. Psychiat. Ass. J.,* 1961, *6,* 231-235.

BELDEN, E. & HITCHEN, R. The identification and treatment of an early deprivation syndrome in alcoholics by means of LSD-25. *Amer. J. Psychiat.,* 1963, *119,* 985-986.

BIERER, J., & BROWNE, I. W. An experiment with a psychiatric night hospital. *Proc. Roy. Soc. Med.,* 1960, *53,* 930-932.

BUSCH, A. K., & JOHNSON, W. C. LSD-25 as an aid in psychotherapy (preliminary report of a new drug). *Dis. Nerv. Syst.,* 1950, *11,* 241-243.

BUTTERWORTH, A. T. Some aspects of an office practice utilizing LSD-25. *Psychiat. Quart.,* 1962, *36,* 734-753.

CHANDLER, A. L., & HARTMAN, M. A. LSD-25 as a facilitating agent in psychotherapy, *AMA Arch. Gen. Psychiat.,* 1960, *2,* 286-299.

CHOLDEN, L. (Ed.). *Proceedings of the round table of lysergic acid diethylamide and mescaline in experimental psychiatry.* New York : Grune & Stratton, 1956.

CHWELOS, N., BLEWETT, D. B., SMITH, C. M., & HOFFER, A. Use of LSD-25 in the treatment of chronic alcoholism. *Quart. J. Stud. Alcohol,* 1959, *20,* 577-590.

COHEN, S. The therapeutic potential of LSD-25. In R. M. FEATHERSTONE & A. SIMON (Eds.). *A pharmacologic approach to the study of the mind.* Springfield, Ill. : Thomas, 1959.

COHEN, S. LSD : side effects and complications, *J. Nerv. Ment. Dis.,* 1960, *130,* 30-40.

COHEN, S. & DITMAN, K. S. Complications associated with lysergic acid diethylamide (LSD-25). *J. Am. Med. Ass.,* 1962, *181,* 161-162.

COHEN, S. & DITMAN, K. S. Prolonged adverse reactions to lysergic acid diethylamide, *Arch. Gen. Psychiat.,* 1963, *8,* 475-480.

COLE, J. O. & KATZ, M. M. The psychotomimetic drugs, an overview. *J. Am. Med. Ass.,* 1964, *187,* 758-765.

CROCKET, R., SANDISON, R., & WALK, A. (Eds.). *Hallucinogenic drugs and their psychotherapeutic use.* Springfield, Ill. : Thomas, 1963.

CUTNER, MARGOT. Analytic work with LSD-25. *Psychiat. Quart.,* 1959, *33,* 715-757.

DENBER, H. C. B., & RINKEL, M. (Eds.). Round Table : psychodynamic and therapeutic aspects of mescaline and lysergic acid diethylamide. *J. Nerv. Ment. Dis.,* 1957, *125,* 423-451.

LSD and Psychotherapy: A Bibliography

DITMAN, K. S., HAYMAN, M., & WHITTLESEY, J. R. B. Nature and frequency of claims following LSD. *J. Nerv. Ment. Dis.*, 1962, *134*, 346-352.

EISNER, BETTY G., & COHEN, S. Psychotherapy with lysergic acid diethylamide. *J. Nerv. Ment. Dis.*, 1958, *127*, 528-539.

FELD, M., GOODMAN, J. R., & GUIDO, J. A. Clinical and laboratory observations on LSD-25. *J. Nerv. Ment. Dis.*, 1958, *126*, 176-183.

FISHER, G. Some comments concerning dosage levels of psychedelic compounds for psychotherapeutic experiences. *Psychedelic Rev.*, 1963, *1*, 208-218.

FREDERKING, W. Intoxicant drugs (mescaline and lysergic acid diethylamide) in psychotherapy. *J. Nerv. Ment. Dis.*, 1955, *121*, 262-266.

Hallucinogenic drugs. *Lancet*, 1961, *1*, 444-445.

HARMAN, W. W. The issue of the consciousness-expanding drugs. *Main Currents in Modern Thought*, 1963, *20*, 5-14.

HOLLISTER, L. E., DEGAN, R. O., & SCHULTZ, S. D. An experimental approach to facilitation of psychotherapy by psychotomimetic drugs. *J. Ment. Sci.*, 1962, *108*, 99-101.

HOLZINGER, R. Analytic and integrative therapy with the help of LSD-25. *Psychologia*, 1962, *5*, 131-139.

JANIGER, O. The use of hallucinogenic agents in psychiatry. *The California Clinician*, 1959, *55*, 251-259.

JENSEN, S. E. A treatment program for alcoholics in a mental hospital. *Quart. J. Stud. Alcohol*, 1962, *23*, 243-251.

LEUNER, H., & HOLFELD, H. Psychotherapy under the influence of hallucinogens. *The Physician's Panorama*, 1964, *2*, 13-16.

LEWIS, D. J., & SLOANE, R. B. Therapy with lysergic acid diethylamide. *J. Clin. & Exper. Psychopath.*, 1958, *19*, 19-31.

LING, T. M., & BUCKMAN, J. The use of lysergic acid in individual psychotherapy. *Proc. Roy. Soc. Med.*, 1960, *53*, 927-929.

LING, T. M., & BUCKMAN, J. *Lysergic acid (LSD-25) and Ritalin in the treatment of neurosis.* London : Lambarde Press, 1963. (Distributed in the U.S. by Medical Examination Pub. Co., Inc., Flushing 65, N.Y., $5.00.)

MACLEAN, J. R., MACDONALD, D. C., BYRNE, U. P., & HUBBARD, A. M. The use of LSD-25 in the treatment of alcoholism and other psychiatric problems. *Quart. J. Stud. Alcohol*, 1961, *22*, 34-45.

MARTIN, A. JOYCE. LSD (lysergic acid diethylamide) treatment of chronic psychoneurotic patients under day-hospital conditions.

Internat. J. Soc. Psychiat., 1957, *3*, 188-195.

O'REILLY, P. O., & REICH, GENEVIEVE. Lysergic acid and the alcoholic. *Dis. Nerv. System*, 1962, *23*, 331-334.

OSMOND, H. A review of the clinical effects of psychotomimetic agents. *Ann. N. Y. Acad. Sci.*, 1957, *66*, 418-434.

ROBINSON, J., DAVIES, L., SACK, E., & MORRISSEY, J. A controlled trial of abreaction with LSD-25. *Brit. J. Psychiat.*, 1963, *109*, 46-53.

ROLO, A., KRINSKY, L. W., & GOLDFARB, L. LSD as an adjunct to psychotherapy with alcoholics. *J. Psychol.*, 1960, *50*, 85-104.

SANDISON, R. A. Psychological aspects of the LSD treatment of the neuroses. *J. Ment. Sci.*, 1954, *100*, 508-515.

SANDISON, R. A., SPENCER, A. M., & WHITELAW, J. D. A. The therapeutic value of lysergic acid diethylamide in mental illness. *J. Ment. Sci.*, 1954, *100*, 491-507.

SANDISON, R. A., & WHITELAW, J. D. A. Further studies in the therapeutic value of lysergic acid diethylamide in mental illness. *J. Ment. Sci.*, 1957, *103*, 332-343.

SAVAGE, C. Lysergic acid diethylamide (LSD-25). A clinical-psychological study. *Amer. J. Psychiat.*, 1952, *108*, 896-900.

SAVAGE, C., STOLAROFF, M., HARMAN, W., & FADIMAN, J. Caveat! The psychedelic experience. *J. Neuropsychiat.*, 1963, *4*, 4-5.

SAVAGE, C., HARMAN, W., SAVAGE, ETHEL, & FADIMAN, J. Therapeutic effects of the LSD experience. *Psychol. Rep.*, 1964, *14*, 111-120.

SCHMIEGE, G. R. The current status of LSD as a therapeutic tool : a summary of the clinical literature. *J. Med. Soc. of N. J.*, 1963, *60*, 203-207.

SCHOEN, S. LSD in psychotherapy. *Am. J. Psychother.*, 1964, *18*, 35-51.

SHELTON, J. LSD : notes on the psychotherapeutic use. *Mind : Psychiat. in Gen. Practice*, 1963, *1*, 339-342.

SHERWOOD, J. N., STOLAROFF, M. J., & HARMAN, W. W. The psychedelic experience — a new concept in psychotherapy. *J. Neuropsychiat.*, 1962, *3*, 370-375.

SMART, R. G. & STORM, T. The efficacy of LSD in the treatment of alcoholism. *Quart. J. Stud. Alcohol*, 1964, *25*, 333-338.

SMITH, C. M. A new adjunct to the treatment of alcoholism : the hallucinogenic drugs. *Quart. J. Stud. Alcohol*, 1958, *19*, 406-417.

SMITH, C. M. Some reflections on the possible therapeutic effects of the hallucinogens. *Quart. J. Stud. Alcohol*, 1959, *20*, 292-301.

Tenenbaum, B. Group therapy with LSD-25. *Dis. Nerv. Syst.*, 1961, *22*, 459-462.

Terrill, J., Savage, C., & Jackson, D. D. LSD, transcendence, and the new beginning. *J. Nerv. Ment. Dis.*, 1962, *135*, 425-439.

Unger, S. Mescaline, LSD, psilocybin, and personality change : a review. *Psychiatry*, 1963, *26*, 111-125.

Ward, J. L. The psychodrama of the LSD experience : some comments on the biological man. *Group Psychother.*, 1961, *14*, 121-128.

CONCLUDING NOTES

1. *Summary of claimed therapeutic effects.* Reported therapeutic effects have recently been summarized by Schmiege (1963) as follows :

"Those using LSD in multiple doses as an adjunct to psychotherapy feel that it is so useful because of its ability to do the following : (1) It helps the patient to remember and abreact both recent and childhood traumatic experiences. (2) It increases the transference reaction while enabling the patient to discuss it more easily. (3) It activates the patient's unconscious so as to bring forth fantastic and emotional phenomena which may be handled by the therapist as dreams. (4) It intensifies the patient's affectivity so that excessive intellectualization is less likely to occur. (5) It allows the patient to better see his customary defences and sometimes allows him to alter them. Because of these effects, therapists feel that psychotherapy progresses at a faster rate. . . . Those who administer lysergic acid in a single dose have as their goal, in the words of Sherwood, *et al.* (1962), an overwhelming reaction 'in which an individual comes to experience himself in a totally new way. . . .' Frequently, this is accompanied by a transcendental feeling of being united with the world. . . . Some spectacular, and almost unbelievable, results have been achieved by using one dose of the drug."

Exemplary descriptions of the use of LSD as an aid, adjunct, adjuvant, or facilitating agent in traditionally-conceived therapy are contained in Sandison and co-workers (1954), Abramson (1955), Eisner and Cohen (1958), and Chandler and Hartman (1960). Exemplary accounts of the recently-formulated "new concept" procedure — that is, with psychotherapy considered as preparation for a single, high-dosage, "psychedelic" session — are contained in Chwelos and co-workers (1959), MacLean and co-workers (1961), and Sherwood and co-workers (1962).

2. *Safety.* The issue of the safety (or danger) of LSD is quite complex. Leaving subtle questions aside — that is, speaking only "medically" — LSD appears quite safe. Two recent reviews concluded as follows : "LSD (or one of the other chemicals of this class) represents a potent and versatile tool requiring responsible handling and effective controls (as with electricity or automobiles). There are real hazards involved with casual or uninformed or maldirected usage of the psychedelic drugs. But any agent with the power to produce benefits has also the power to do harm. Safety is not a basic issue, but often is a camouflage for issues less easy or less comfortable to examine" (Harman, 1963).

" . . . warranted concern over the illicit abuse of these agents should not prevent the systematic study of their possible potential in the treatment of otherwise severely treatment-resistant psychiatric conditions" (Cole and Katz, 1964).

The incidence and occurrence of side effects and prolonged adverse reactions have been dealt with in the series of papers by Cohen (1960), Cohen and Ditman (1962), and Cohen and Ditman (1963). Their conclusion (1963) : "When properly employed, LSD is a relatively safe and important research tool." However, when *improperly* employed — that is, irresponsibly or unskillfully, or self-administered — the occurrence of LSD casualties is considered inevitable (opinion of the present author). It should be absolutely understood that safe and effective work with LSD (or other psychedelic agents) presupposes specialized training and experience.

3. *Miscellany.* There does exist a fair-sized clinical literature on psychedelic agents other than LSD. For early work with mescaline and the "Weir Mitchell treatment," see : Ross, T. A., *The common neuroses* (2d ed.) : London : Arnold, 1937. Mostly paralleling the uses of LSD, there has been considerable recent work with psilocybin (see *Psilocybin : Annotated Bibliography*, Sandoz Pharmaceuticals, Hanover, N.J.). Of special interest in the psilocybin literature, in view of the patient category (recidivist convicts) is an as yet unpublished paper : Leary, T., Metzner, R., Presnell, M., Weil, G., Schwitzgebel, R., & Kinne, Sara, "A change program for adult offenders using psilocybin," in press, *Psychother. : Theory, Res., Practice.* For a number of other incidental items, not included in the bibliography,

see : Bender, Lauretta, Goldschmidt, L., & Siva Sankar, D. V., "Treatment of autistic schizophrenic children with LSD-25 and UML-491," *Recent Advances Biol. Psychiat.*, 1962, *4*, 170-177 (which follows a chemo- rather than a psychotherapeutic model); and Kast, E., "The analgesic action of lysergic acid compared with dihydromorphinone and meperidine," *Bull. Drug Addiction and Narcotics*, 1963, Appendix 27, 3517-3529 (which recounts work with terminal cancer patients).

4. *Current legal situation.* Following the Thalidomide tragedy, Congress passed restrictive legislation governing the testing and research use in man of experimental or non-introduced drugs. Since the implementation of these regulations on June 7, 1963, the authorized distribution of psychedelic agents has been stringently controlled. They are legally available only to investigators functioning within federal or state agencies who have the formal approval of the agency, or to investigators carrying out research under grants from federal or state agencies. The intent has been to insure against misuse of these potent substances or unsafe research — which might be undertaken by well-meaning but unqualified investigators — by surrounding them with an adequate system of checks and balances. Cole and Katz (1964) have made a more detailed statement :

"Psychotomimetic agents are legally and scientifically 'investigational' drugs and can only be studied by experienced investigators under carefully controlled conditions. . . . None of these agents can legally be used, even on an investigational basis, except by investigators who have filed a formal research plan with the Food and Drug Administration through a sponsoring pharmaceutical company or by investigators who have themselves taken on both the role of sponsor and of investigator and have gone through the appropriate steps for providing the necessary information concerning the safety of the agents and their proposed research use in man with the Food and Drug Administration."

5. *Current status and prospects.* Not a single, methodologically-acceptable controlled study of the efficacy of LSD-assisted psychotherapy has yet been performed. The many claims of dramatic therapeutic changes in such highly treatment-resistant conditions as chronic alcoholism, severe chronic neurosis, and severe personality disorder must thus be regarded as *not proven* (for further discussion, see Cole and Katz, 1964). (In all fairness, it may be pointed out that method-

247

ologically-acceptable controlled studies of *other* psychotherapies, including psychoanalysis, hardly abound in the literature.)

One controlled study is presently in progress. Financed by a grant from the National Institute of Mental Health and proceeding under the auspices of the Department of Medical Research, Spring Grove State Hospital, Baltimore, Md. (Dr. Albert Kurland, Director), it is designed to assess both the short-term and possibly enduring therapeutic consequences in chronic, hospitalized alcoholics of "psychedelic therapy" — that is, two weeks of intensive psychotherapeutic preparation for one single, high-dosage, continuously-monitored LSD session (averaging ten hours in duration).

The only other installation in the United States at which extensive clinical research has been pursued in recent years is the International Foundation for Advanced Study, Menlo Park, California (Dr. Charles Savage, Medical Director). For accounts of this work, see : Sherwood and co-workers (1962), Savage and co-workers (1963, 1964), as well as the as yet unpublished papers : Savage, C., Hughes, Mary A., and Mogar, R., "The effectiveness of psychedelic (LSD) therapy — A preliminary report," in press, *Int. J. Soc. Psychiat.;* and Mogar, R., Fadiman, J., and Savage, C., "Personality changes associated with psychedelic (LSD) therapy," in press, *Psychother. : Theory, Res., Practice,* 1964.

INDEX

Abramson, H. A., 72, 241, 245
Abrus precatorius L., 172
Absolute, the, 146
Adams, Joe, 65-68
Adamson, Joy, 133, 148
Administrative Procedure Act,
    Federal, 225
Adonai, 32
Adrenochrome, 218
Adrenolutin, 218
Africa, 137, 165, 188, 211; East, 202n
Agapé, 35
Agni, 114
Agonistic principle, 42
Alarcón, Hernando Ruiz de, 174
Albarracín, 93, 96
Alcohol, 1, 3, 10, 28, 29, 110, 206
Alcoholism, LSD therapy of, 247-48
Alice's Adventures in Wonderland,
    83n, 222
Alienation, of psychotics, 70f, 83n. *See
    also* Communication; Normalization
Alkaloids, 98-99, 101, 106-07, 109, and
    passim. See also Mescaline
Allaesthetic characters, 131ff
Altenanthera Lehmanii, 95
Amanita muscaria, 26, 188-89n. *See also*
    Mushrooms
Amarillo, 79
Amazon valley, 90, 91ff, 102, 104, 107,
    109-10
America, Middle, 163-89 *passim. See also*
    Guatemala; Mexico; Oaxaca
America, North, 165, 168, 189n, 220, 231;
    culture of, 89; drug laws of, 221ff;
    narcotic plants in, 89-110. *See also*
    United States; Canada; individual
    names of states
America, South/Latin, 84n, 172, 229, 241,
    and *passim;* narcotic plants in, 89-110.
    See also Andes; Argentina; Bolivia;
    Brazil; Chile; Chinantla; Colombia;
    Ecuador; Peru; Venezuela
Anabaptists, 118
Analytic thought, 9
Andes, the, 90, 92, 93, 95, 97, 109, 110
Andrews, George, 59-61
Anhalonium, 101
Animals: behavior patterns of, 133ff;
    biological evolution of, 127-38;
    psychometabolism of, 131ff
Anthrophage, 186n
Antilles, 165, 176
Antinomianism, 83n
Apipiltzin, 182
Apocynac, 93
Appeasement attitude, 135

Argentina, 109, 173
Ariadne, 40
Ariocarpus, 101
Aristides, 31
Aristolochia, 93, 96
Aristotle, 10
Arizona, 97, 226-27
Art, Indian-Javanese, 42
Asagao ya!, 217
Asia, 165
Association for Humanistic Psychology,
    85n
Athens, Periclean, 211
Atmospheric setting for psychedelic
    experiments, 157-58
Atom, the, 198
Atomic Energy Commission, U.S., 2
Atropine, 98
Aubrey, 10
"Ausdruckswelt, Essays und Aphorismen,"
    39
Australopithecus, 202, 204
Austria, 167, 173
Autosuggestion, 176
Ayahuasca/caapi/yajé, 91-97
Ayautla, 180, 183

Bach, Johann Sebastian, 11, 122
Bacon, Francis, 2
Badoh/badoh negro/badugás (ololiuqui),
    34, 175, 178. *See also* Ololiuqui
Bahadurs, 42
Baldwin, Hanson, 84n
Banisteria/Banisteriopsis, 92ff
Banisterine, 96-97
Bark snuff, 107
Barnes, Harry Elmer, 84n
Barriga-Villalba, 94, 96
Barron, Jarvik, and Bunnell, 213n
Bartolo, Chico (Francisco Jiménez), 174-
    81, 188n; Paula, 178-81
Basel, 111, 169
Basque country, 25
Basydiomycetes, 105
Bates, Roy C., 217-30
Bateson, G., Jackson, D. D., Haley J., and
    Weakland, J. A., 71, 86
Bavarian health cults, 46
Bazelon, D. L., 67, 86
Bead Game, The (Magister Ludi), 111,
    121ff
Beats, the, 118
Behavior; animal, 133ff; genetic factors in,
    140; man's, in relation to environment,
    47-57
Bejuco, 170, 174
Beltrán, Aguirre, 167, 170, 175, 182

249